LESSONS FOR
EXTENDING
PLACE VALUE

GRADE 3

THE TEACHING ARITHMETIC SERIES

Lessons for First Grade
Lessons for Introducing Place Value, Grade 2
Lessons for Addition and Subtraction, Grades 2–3
Lessons for Extending Place Value, Grade 3
Lessons for Introducing Multiplication, Grade 3
Lessons for Introducing Division, Grades 3–4
Lessons for Extending Multiplication, Grades 4–5
Lessons for Extending Division, Grades 4–5
Lessons for Introducing Fractions, Grades 4–5
Lessons for Extending Fractions, Grade 5
Lessons for Multiplying and Dividing Fractions, Grades 5–6
Lessons for Decimals and Percents, Grades 5–6

Teaching ARITHMETIC

LESSONS FOR EXTENDING PLACE VALUE

▲▲▲▲▲

GRADE 3

MARYANN WICKETT
MARILYN BURNS

MATH SOLUTIONS PUBLICATIONS
SAUSALITO, CA

Math Solutions
One Harbor Drive, Suite 101
Sausalito, CA 94965
www.mathsolutions.com

Library of Congress Cataloging-in-Publication Data

Wickett, Maryann.
  Lessons for extending place value : grade 3 / Maryann Wickett.
    p. cm.
  Includes index.
  ISBN 0-941355-57-8 (acid-free paper)
  1. Arithmetic—Juvenile literature. 2. Decimal system—Juvenile
literature. I. Title.
  QA115.W644 2005
  372.7'2—dc22   2005003493

ISBN-13: 978-0-941355-57-5

Editor: Toby Gordon
Production: Melissa L. Inglis
Cover and interior design: Leslie Bauman
Composition: TechBooks

6 7 8 9 10 11 12 13 14 15   31   22 21 20 19 18 17 16 15 14 13

A Message from Marilyn Burns

We at Math Solutions Professional Development believe that teaching math well calls for increasing our understanding of the math we teach, seeking deeper insights into how children learn mathematics, and refining our lessons to best promote students' learning.

Math Solutions Publications shares classroom-tested lessons and teaching expertise from our faculty of Math Solutions Inservice instructors as well as from other respected math educators. Our publications are part of the nationwide effort we've made since 1984 that now includes

- more than five hundred face-to-face inservice programs each year for teachers and administrators in districts across the country;
- annually publishing professional development books, now totaling more than fifty titles and spanning the teaching of all math topics in kindergarten through grade 8;
- four series of videotapes for teachers, plus a videotape for parents, that show math lessons taught in actual classrooms;
- on-site visits to schools to help refine teaching strategies and assess student learning;
- free online support, including grade-level lessons, book reviews, inservice information, and district feedback, all in our quarterly *Math Solutions Online Newsletter*.

For information about all of the products and services we have available, please visit our website at *www.mathsolutions.com*. You can also contact us to discuss math professional development needs by calling (800) 868-9092 or by sending an email to *info@mathsolutions.com*.

We're always eager for your feedback and interested in learning about your particular needs. We look forward to hearing from you.

Math Solutions®
PUBLICATIONS

CONTENTS

ACKNOWLEDGMENTS

We wish to thank the following colleagues and their students for trying out these lessons in their classrooms and for providing valuable feedback, ideas, and support: Eunice Hendrix-Martin, Carrillo School, Carlsbad, California, San Marcos Unified School District, San Marcos, California, and Brenda Davis, Outley Elementary School, Alief Independent School District, Houston, Texas.

A special thanks to the 2003–2004 and 2004–2005 students of room 19, Carrillo School, Carlsbad, California, San Marcos Unified School District. Their patience, suggestions, and willingness to try new ideas have enriched this book for all of us.

INTRODUCTION

It was the second day of third grade and the magic of getting to know one another was very much in the air. To begin to build my understanding of how my students were thinking, I wrote the following problem on the board for the students to solve:

19 + 14 =
Show how you know using words, pictures, or numbers.

The children eagerly set to work to show me their skills. As they worked, I circulated through the class, carefully observing and stopping to ask or answer an occasional question. Several students were uncertain about what I meant by "Show how you know using words, pictures, or numbers." With a little encouragement and a few carefully chosen questions, the students were able to complete the task. We find the following questions helpful in clearing up confusion regarding this type of assignment: Can you draw a picture of the problem? What words would you use to explain how to do the problem to a friend who needed help? How could you use blocks to help you solve the problem? Can you draw a picture to show what you did with the blocks?

In my class of thirty-two students, almost one-third found the correct sum of 33. Of those, five correctly used the standard algorithm, while five others thought of 19 as 10 + 9 and 14 as 10 + 4, combined the tens and ones separately, and then added the partial sums. Another eight children arrived at the sum of 213, attempting to use the standard algorithm but failing to regroup. Five children arrived at the sum of 23; these children also tried to use the standard algorithm but again failed to correctly regroup from the ones to the tens. Three children arrived at the sum of 15. They used a strategy they called "touch math" and misapplied it, failing to understand that the value of each digit in each number is dependent on its place in the number, not merely on its face value.

$$19 + 14 = 15$$

The remaining six students made miscellaneous other errors.

I was concerned that less than one-third of my new students had found the correct sum, but I was more concerned about the types of errors they had made. Half the students—sixteen of them—had made errors indicating little or no understanding of place value! To understand the arithmetic of third grade and subsequent years, a student must have a firm understanding of our base ten place value number system. Included as part of this understanding is how to apply it accurately and efficiently to computation and how to use place value ideas to check that answers make sense and are reasonable.

What Does It Mean to Understand Place Value?

Here's what we've noticed over the years about students' understanding of place value at the beginning of their third-grade year:

▲ Most children can write the numbers up to 100 and even into the hundreds. However, some children still have difficulty accurately writing some numbers beyond 100, especially when zeros are involved. For example, instead of writing 103, children might write 1003 (writing as they think "one hundred" and then "three"), 130 (writing a 1 for one hundred and a 3 for three and then adding a 0 to make a three-digit number), or 13 (just writing a 1 for one hundred and a 3 for three).

▲ Given two two-digit numbers—sixty-three and thirty-six, for example—most children can identify which is greater and which is less. This is generally because they are familiar with our counting sequence and know that sixty-three comes after thirty-six. However, only some can explain that sixty-three is greater than thirty-six because it has six tens while thirty-six has only three tens.

▲ Most children can make drawings or use concrete materials such as base ten blocks or interlocking cubes to accurately represent two-digit numbers by using tens and ones.

▲ Some children are able to apply their knowledge of place value and efficiently and accurately compute two-digit addition and subtraction problems.

▲ Most children have not thought about the important notion that place value makes it possible to express all numbers with only the digits from zero to nine.

The following three components are important indicators of children's understanding of place value. These are not separate or sequential aspects of place value, but overlapping ideas that together contribute to children's overall understanding and ability to apply their knowledge to understand and solve increasingly complex problems.

1. The Relationship Between Numbers and Groups of Hundreds, Tens, and Ones—Children who have some understanding of the relationship between numbers and groups of hundreds, tens, and ones know that if they have one group of 100 objects, seven groups of 10 objects, and 4 extras, they have 174 objects altogether. Also, if they have 58 objects, they know they can make five groups of 10 objects with 8 extras.

2. The Significance of the Positions of Digits in Numbers—When children have learned the significance of the placement of digits in numbers, they can explain the meaning of each digit. For example, when asked about the 6 and 4 in 64, they know that the 4 stands for four individual units and the 6 stands for six groups of ten. In third grade this understanding should be extended to numbers in the hundreds and later into the thousands.

3. Solving Addition and Subtraction Problems—Children who understand place value can make use of the hundreds, tens, and ones structure of numbers to add and subtract, with and without regrouping. In traditional instructional programs, place value is taught before addition and subtraction as a prerequisite for learning to add and subtract with regrouping. Also, traditional programs see regrouping, carrying, and borrowing as an important aspect of mathematics instruction in the primary grades. However, this unit takes the approach that integrating place value with addition, subtraction, and even multiplication with regrouping helps children see the relationships among these ideas in a natural way. The lessons don't teach students the process of regrouping but present problems that can be solved by regrouping. The emphasis isn't on procedures but rather on problems to be solved. From children's solutions, teachers can assess their ability to make use of the place value structure of our number system when working with numbers.

The Goals of Place Value Instruction

The goal of these lessons is to help children develop an understanding of the ones, tens, and hundreds structure of our number system and the ability to use their understanding when thinking about and working with numbers. At the end of third grade, students should be able to

- ▲ count large numbers of objects in two or more ways;
- ▲ recognize that regardless of the groupings used to count a group of objects, the total number in that group remains unchanged;
- ▲ relate large quantities of objects to their numerical representations;
- ▲ explain that digits have different values depending on their positions in the numbers;
- ▲ understand that our place value system allows us to represent any number with just ten digits: 0, 1, 2, 3, 4, 5, 6, 7, 8, and 9;
- ▲ exchange ten ones for a ten, ten tens for a hundred, and ten hundreds for a thousand;
- ▲ compare and explain the relative size of numbers into the thousands;
- ▲ know that the same number can be represented with different but equivalent groupings; for example, forty-nine can be represented by 4 tens and 9 ones, or 3 tens and 19 ones, or 2 tens and 29 ones, or 1 ten and 39 ones, or 49 ones; and
- ▲ use place value ideas effectively to compute sums, differences, and products efficiently and accurately and be able to determine if an answer is reasonable.

Traditionally students have demonstrated their knowledge of place value by simply stating the number in a particular place. For example, a student might be asked how many hundreds are in 1,245. A response of two might be considered as evidence the student knows there are two groups of one hundred in that number. A response of two actually shows that the student knows where the hundreds place is, not that he understands that the 2 indicates two groups of one hundred. Developing the understanding of what a digit means and the idea that the value of a digit within a number is dependent on its location in that number is critical for success with regrouping in addition, subtraction, multiplication, and, later on, division.

The Structure of the Lessons

In order to help you with planning and teaching the lessons in this book, each is organized into the following sections:

Overview   To help you decide if the lesson is appropriate for your students, this is a nutshell description of the mathematical goals of the lesson and what the students will be doing.

Materials   This section lists the special materials needed along with quantities. Not included in the list are regular classroom supplies such as pencils and paper. Worksheets that need to be duplicated are included in the Blackline Masters section at the back of the book.

Time   The number of class periods needed is provided along with extra class periods needed for extensions. It is also indicated for some activities that they are meant to be repeated from time to time.

Teaching Directions   The directions are presented in a step-by-step lesson plan.

Teaching Notes   This section addresses the mathematics underlying the lesson and at times provides information about the prior experiences or knowledge students need.

The Lesson   This is a vignette that describes what actually occurred when the lesson was taught in one or more classes. While the vignette mirrors the plan described in the teaching directions, it elaborates with details that are valuable for preparing and teaching the lesson. Samples of student work are included.

Extensions   This section is included for some of the lessons and offers follow-up suggestions.

Questions and Discussion   Presented in a question-and-answer format, this section addresses issues that came up during the lesson and/or have been posed by other teachers.

While organized similarly, the lessons here vary in several ways. Some span one class period, others take longer, and some are suitable to repeat over and over, giving students a chance to revisit ideas and extend their learning. Some use manipulative materials, others ask students to draw pictures, and still others ask students to rely on reasoning mentally. And while some lessons seem to be more suited for beginning experiences, at times it's beneficial for more experienced students to engage with them as well. An activity that seems simple can reinforce students' understanding or give them a fresh way to look at a familiar concept. Also, a lesson that initially seems too difficult or advanced can be ideal for introducing students to thinking in a new way.

How to Use This Book

Teaching the lessons described in the fourteen chapters requires at least thirty-seven days of instruction, not including time for repeat experiences, as recommended for some lessons; extensions; or the ideas for assessment suggested at the end of the book. While it's possible to spend a continuous stretch of time on these lessons, we don't think that's the best decision. In our experience, children require time to absorb concepts, and we would rather spend a three- to four-week period of time and then wait two months or so before returning for another three-week period, or arrange for three chunks of time, each two or three weeks long or so, spaced throughout the year.

When students return to ideas after a break, they bring not only the learning they've done in other areas but also a fresh look that some distance can provide.

The first five lessons lay a foundation to support students' understanding of our base ten number system. These lessons build, beginning with an exploration of a 10-by-10 grid and culminating with the opportunity to count ten thousand tally marks. The other lessons are categorized according to their emphasis on a particular area of computation: addition and subtraction or multiplication and division. Most of these lessons involve more than one operation but tend to focus more on one than the others involved, and they are categorized accordingly. The chapters within these categories are sequenced in an order that reflects our experience after the lessons were taught in several classes. The assessments at the back of the book are closely linked with the place value ideas presented to students and can help you think about making assessment an integral part of your place value instruction.

Student participation is key to learning, and throughout the lessons in this book, students are expected to share their thinking. Students present their ideas in whole-class discussions, complete individual writing assignments, and talk in small groups, often preceded with a form of pair sharing called dyads. The use of dyads is based on the work of Dr. Julian Weisslass, a professor of education at the University of California at Santa Barbara. A dyad is an opportunity for all children to be listened to by another and for all children to listen. The following are the basic guidelines for using dyads:

1. Each person is given equal time to share and listen.
2. The listener does not interrupt the person who is talking. The listener also does not give advice, analyze, or break in with personal comments.
3. The listener does not share what the talker has said with anyone else. This confidentiality allows children to more fully explore their ideas without fear of being ridiculed or having their mistakes shared publicly.

It has been our experience that using these rules has given shy, less verbal children more opportunity to voice their ideas. In many cases, as these students gain confidence by sharing in a safe environment, they share more in class discussions, which often results in deeper thinking and understanding of the mathematics along with increased confidence. Using dyads frequently also helps keep more students engaged in the learning process.

Some children are more willing to share ideas than others. It's important, however, that all students learn to participate fully in our math classes. To facilitate this, we do the following:

▲ We make it a part of the classroom culture and our expectations that all students are capable and can think. They are expected to think and always do their best. Anything less is not acceptable.
▲ We support students by using our behavior as a model. We are constantly thinking about and exploring ideas with them. We do not expect them to believe that we know everything—we don't!
▲ To support students' thinking and development of strategies to use, we pose a question and then give students a few moments of quiet "think time," when all students are expected to focus their attention.
▲ After students have a few moments to form their own thoughts, we often use a form of pair sharing called dyads, as described earlier.

▲ Class discussions play a big role in our teaching. Before beginning a class discussion, we provide students the opportunity to think about the topic at hand, through think time, a written assignment, or a dyad. When students come to a class discussion prepared, the discussion is more lively and interesting and provides more opportunity for both the students and us to learn.

▲ In class discussions, students usually share strategies that they have used. We record each strategy, including the name of the student who shared the strategy, on the chalkboard or in some other highly visible place in the classroom, giving students a reference list of ideas.

As effective as these strategies are, occasionally a student will still get stuck. In this instance, it often helps to ask a question such as the following:

"How might you begin?"

"What do you think the problem is asking you to do?"

"What would happen if . . . ?"

"Can you draw a picture that represents the problem or find a pattern?"

"Can you think of a smaller, similar problem?"

Our role as teachers is to be supportive and encouraging of all students. Listening carefully with a curious attitude about what children have to say is one way. Writing their responses along with their names on the board or a chart during class discussion is another way. Responding to their thinking with probing questions is another way still. When teachers demonstrate these behaviors, students know that they and their thinking are being valued. Sometimes this means putting aside any preconceived ideas and expectations of hoped-for responses. Being listened to and respected is highly motivating and longer lasting than quick words of praise. Quick words of praise can limit children and actually cause them not to try new ideas for fear of loss of praise or of disappointing the teacher. The focus should be on children expressing their thinking and reasoning processes, not just giving correct answers.

Throughout the lessons, we ask children to work with a partner. There are many ways to assign partners. Some teachers have children change partners every day while others have their students keep the same partners throughout a unit of study. In some classrooms children choose their own partners while in others partners may be assigned randomly, by drawing names as an example, or the teacher may assign children to be partners. Some teachers simply have students work with the person sitting beside or across from them. There are a variety of ways to do this and what works best with one group of children may not be the best way for another group.

It's likely you will choose to use these lessons along with other instructional materials or learning activities. It's important, however, to be consistent so that in all lessons you encourage students to make sense of ideas, communicate about their reasoning both orally and in writing, and apply their learning to problem-solving situations.

CHAPTER ONE
PAIRS OF SQUARES ON A 10-BY-10 GRID

Overview

In this lesson, recommended for beginning instruction about place value with third graders, students explore the relationships between pairs of squares on a blank 10-by-10 grid. The lesson focuses students on several relationships—that it takes one step to count from a square to the square next to it and ten steps to count from a square to the square directly below it, for example. They also investigate the relationships between squares and those several rows directly above or below them and between squares and those nine or eleven steps away. Even though there are no numbers on the chart, the 10-by-10 grid provides students a visual structure for thinking about ones, tens, and multiples of ten, basic concepts embedded in our place value system.

Materials

▲ 10-by-10 grids, 1 per student (see Blackline Masters)
▲ transparency of 10-by-10 grid
▲ optional: 10-by-10 pocket wall chart with number cards turned to blank sides and 2 additional blank cards in a different color

Time

▲ one class period

Teaching Directions

1. Establish with the class that there are one hundred squares on a 10-by-10 grid. To do this, project a transparency of a 10-by-10 grid. Ask students how many squares are on the grid and have volunteers explain how they figured. Record students' strategies for figuring on the board.

1

2. To give all students a chance to figure, give each student a copy of a 10-by-10 grid. Ask students to use a previously shared strategy or any other strategy that makes sense to them to verify that there are one hundred squares on the grid. Then ask volunteers to share what they found out.

3. To introduce how to count steps from one square to another, on the overhead transparency of the grid, mark a dot in each of two squares that are side-by-side.

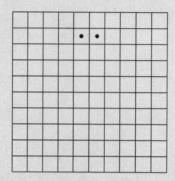

Ask students how many steps are needed to move from one of the marked squares to the other.

4. Erase the dots and repeat Step 3 with other side-by-side squares until students are comfortable and confident that it takes one step to move between squares that are side-by-side.

5. Again erase the dots and this time introduce how many steps it takes to go from a square to the one directly below it. Mark a dot in each of two squares, one directly above the other.

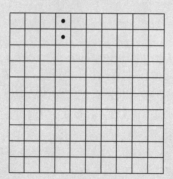

While moving your finger from left to right across the top row of the grid, ask: "If I count one step for each square as I move from the top square to the square underneath it, how many steps will I take?" Ask students to show you the number of steps using their fingers. Verify by counting to show that ten steps are needed.

6. Erase the dots and repeat Step 5 until you feel students understand. You can vary the routine by asking students to come to the overhead projector to count and verify.

7. To check for individual understanding, ask students to mark dots on their own 10-by-10 grids to show two squares that are ten steps apart. Circulate and check.

8. Next focus on squares that require a multiple of ten steps to get from one to another. On a clean transparency of the 10-by-10 grid, mark a square with a dot, then mark with a dot a second square two rows directly below the first. Ask: "How many steps will it take to move from the first square to the second?"

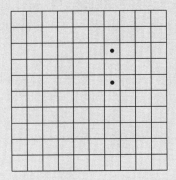

Call on students to answer and explain their reasoning.

9. Erase and repeat Step 8 for twenty steps. To vary the routine, ask a student to come up and mark two squares that are twenty steps apart. Then, to check for individual understanding, ask students to mark dots on their own 10-by-10 grids to show two squares that are twenty steps apart. Circulate and check.

10. Repeat Steps 8 and 9, this time marking with dots two squares that are thirty steps apart.

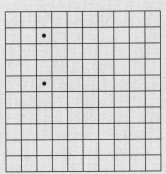

Repeat for sixty steps or for other multiples of ten until all children understand.

11. On a clean transparency of the 10-by-10 grid, mark dots in two squares that are eleven steps apart.

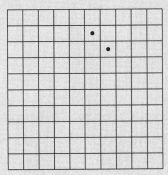

Ask students to figure the number of steps from the first marked square to the second. Ask students to share their strategies for figuring that eleven steps are needed.

12. Erase the dots and repeat for other pairs of squares that are eleven steps apart. Then, to check for individual understanding, ask students to mark dots on their own 10-by-10 grids to show two squares that are eleven steps apart. Circulate and check.

13. Draw the students' attention to the diagonal pattern on the grid of two squares that are eleven steps apart.

14. Repeat Steps 11–13 for pairs of squares that are nine steps apart.

Teaching Notes

The students in the following vignette were in their first week of third grade. Many of them had prior experience with 1–100 charts or 0–99 charts, but using a blank 10-by-10 grid offered those students with prior knowledge a new and fresh way to explore the structure of the grid while at the same time laying a foundation for those with little or no previous exposure.

In the lesson, students explore the number of steps it takes to move from one square to another. After establishing that it takes one step to move from a square to the square directly to its right, students discover that it takes ten steps to move from a square to the square directly below it, no matter the location of the starting square. While this seems obvious to us, it is not immediately obvious to children; however, the experience of counting to verify helps students build understanding of this relationship. Similarly, they discover that the number of steps when the second square is directly below the first but two or more rows down is a multiple of ten—twenty, thirty, forty, and so on. Finally, they discover how squares are positioned on the grid when they are eleven and nine steps apart.

Establishing these relationships on a grid without the interference of numbers is extremely useful for helping children become familiar with the structure of a 10-by-10 grid. When the students later explore similar relationships on a 1–100 chart (see Chapter 2), this learning helps them understand number patterns that relate to the structure of our place value system.

The Lesson

As the students settled, I used an overhead projector to project a transparency of a 10-by-10 grid. Without prompting from me, the students began talking among themselves, sharing ideas about how to figure the total number of squares in the grid. After a few moments, I asked for the students' attention.

I said to the class, "I heard many of you discussing how many small squares are in the grid. In a whisper voice, tell me the number of squares."

"One hundred!" many students quickly responded. Hands immediately shot into the air, indicating the students' eagerness to share their thinking.

"How did you figure?" I asked.

Jillian responded, "I think there are one hundred. If you count, each row has ten squares. You count by ten, ten times because there are ten rows. Ten, twenty, thirty, like that until you count ten rows, and that will be one hundred."

Abel shared next. "I think there are actually ninety-nine. In second grade we had charts that looked like that, except there were numbers instead of blank squares, and there were ninety-nine on it."

Jillian quickly responded. "I think I know what Abel is thinking. In second grade the chart we used had ten rows of ten like this one, and it started with zero and ended with ninety-nine. The zero took up a square."

Abel looked very confused for a moment and then brightened. "Oh, I think I get it," he said. "If I count the squares in the first row, there are ten if I start with one. But in the zero-to-ninety-nine chart, the first square is counted as zero, not one, so the first row has ten squares but only goes up to nine. I never thought of that before! But I'm still not sure there are one hundred squares."

I began a list on the board with Jillian's idea about how to figure the number of squares on the grid.

> *Jillian   Each row has 10; count by ten 10 times.*

Ben added, "I know that ten times ten is one hundred. There are ten rows of ten, that's ten times ten, so there must be one hundred squares."

Adama shared, "I just thought of this. I think there are probably one hundred squares, and I have a way you could check. There are two groups of five in each row; five plus five makes ten. You could count by fives and check to see if there are one hundred."

The students were quiet. I added Adama's and Ben's ideas to the list. The completed list looked as follows:

> *Jillian   Each row has 10; count by ten 10 times.*
> *Ben   10 × 10 = 100.*
> *Adama   Count by fives.*

As I handed each student a copy of the grid, I said, "Use the grid I'm giving you to figure the number of squares. You may use one of the strategies on the board or any other way that makes sense to you. You may ask your table group for help or ideas." Students studied the grid quietly for a few moments; then conversations began as they shared their thinking with one another. I circulated through the room quietly, answering questions, listening, and observing. Most children figured the number of squares in the first row by counting by ones, and then they counted by tens to confirm that there were one hundred squares on the grid. A few counted by ones, fives, or twos. One student counted by twenties. I called the class to order.

I asked, "How many squares?"

"One hundred!" the class responded together.

Kito was eager to share how thinking of the grid as a square helped him figure. "I know there are one hundred. But all I have to do is count just one row. It doesn't really matter which row because they are all the same. Even if I turn the grid sideways, they're all the same because it's a square!" Kito grinned, pleased with this insight. "I counted; there were ten in a row. All the rows are the same and there are the same number of rows as squares in a row, so that's ten, twenty, thirty, forty,

Pairs of Squares on a 10-by-10 Grid   5

fifty, sixty, seventy, eighty, ninety, one hundred."

Jael shared next how she counted. "I thought in the beginning that there were maybe twenty or thirty squares, or something like that." Several students giggled. It was early in the school year and we were in the process of building a safe learning community. I reminded the students that giggling was not an appropriate response to someone's idea. I further reminded the students that if they wished to respond, they needed to raise a hand and wait until their turn to share. I returned my attention to Jael. She continued, "I found out I was wrong. I counted the little squares and there were one hundred."

MOVING ON THE GRID

On the transparency I drew one dot in each of two squares that were side-by-side.

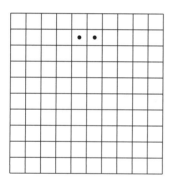

I pointed to the two squares with dots and asked, "How many steps would I have to take to move from this square to this one?"

"One," the students immediately responded. I erased the dots, marked two other adjacent squares, and asked the same question. I did this a few more times until the students' quick, confident, accurate responses convinced me this was easy for all of them.

Next, after erasing the dots, I marked one dot in each of two squares, one directly above the other:

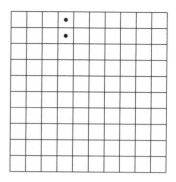

I said to the students as I moved my finger from left to right along the top row of squares on the overhead grid, "If I count one step for each square as I move from the square on top to the square underneath, how many steps will I take?"

Some students marked the same two squares on their grids and counted while others pointed and counted using the projected grid. No one had an instantaneous response. "Put your thumb up when you know," I said. After all thumbs were up, I asked the students to show me with their fingers the number of steps needed to move from the first dot to the dot immediately below it. Some students held up nine fingers, some ten, and a few held up ten fingers followed by one to indicate they thought eleven. This did not surprise me. I said, "I see nine, ten, and eleven. How can we check to be sure?"

"Count," several children responded. Children of this age sometimes make a counting error that results in eleven rather than ten. They count the first dotted square as one rather than taking a "step" and then counting that movement to the next square as one. With this thought in mind, I put my index finger on the first dotted square and said, "Here's where I have to begin. If my finger is on the dotted square, have I taken any steps yet?" The children shook their heads "no." Then I moved my finger from the dotted square to the right across the row to the next square. "That's one step or square," I said and continued moving my finger to the right across the row and counting. When I got to the end of the row, I explained, "Now it's time to move down a row to get to the second dotted square." I continued counting and the children joined in. We arrived at the second dotted square after ten steps. This careful, methodical approach provided many children with new insight and confidence and an idea they could try momentarily. Also, I was laying the foundation for important ideas we'd explore on another day using a 1–100 chart.

I erased the dots and again marked two different squares, one directly above the other. Again I asked the students how many steps they'd have to take to move from the top square to the one beneath it. This time hands popped up almost immediately. I paused a few extra moments to give all children time to respond. Again, I asked the children to hold up their fingers to indicate the number of steps needed. They all held up ten. I quickly verified their response by counting the steps as before. I repeated the process several more times until I was confident the children understood. Rather than counting the squares myself for these examples, I asked children to come to the overhead projector and count the squares.

To check for understanding in individual students, I asked the children to each mark on their grids two squares that were ten apart. The children quickly did this as I circulated, looking over shoulders to verify they understood. When all students had marked their papers, I asked for their attention again.

Tina was very excited about her discovery. She shared, "The only way you can mark two squares that are ten apart is to put one on top of the other. There's no other way to do it!"

There was a slight pause and then several students exclaimed "Oh yeah!" as they confirmed this on their own grids.

"Hey!" Roberto said. "It works going backwards, too! If you go from the bottom square to the one on top of it, it still takes

ten steps." He came to the overhead to prove his point.

MULTIPLES OF TEN STEPS

Next I projected a clean transparency of the grid. "How many steps will it take to move from this square," I asked as I marked a dot in a square, "to this square?" I drew a second dot in the square two rows directly below the first square:

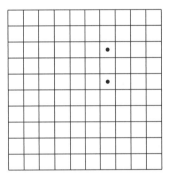

"Think quietly for a moment; then put your thumb up when you think you have an answer." A few children used their charts to count, but most simply put their thumbs up.

I called on Sam. He came to the overhead and pointed as he explained, "It has to be twenty because you count down one square, and that's ten, and then do it one more time to get to the second square, and that makes twenty. Ten plus ten more makes twenty." Several children nodded their agreement with Sam's thinking.

Olina shared, "I did it like Sam, but you could also count by ones. But counting by ones takes too long and it's easier to make a mistake and skip a square or count one twice or something like that." Olina came to the overhead and carefully counted by ones to verify that it took twenty steps to go between the two marked squares.

No one wanted to share other ideas. I asked, "Who would like to come to the overhead and mark two different squares that are twenty apart?" As I'd expected, the entire class was eager to do this. I called on Rachel. She came to the overhead and marked the chart as follows:

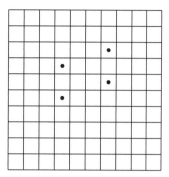

The students agreed that she'd marked two squares that were twenty steps apart. To check for understanding quickly, I had each student mark two squares that were twenty steps apart on his or her grid. I quickly checked over shoulders and found they were clear about this idea.

Once again, I projected a clean transparency of the grid. I made two new marks.

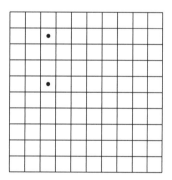

"How many steps to go from one of the marked squares to the other?" I asked. Students quickly raised their hands. I called on Jessie.

Jessie said, "It takes thirty steps. You can just count down by ten or if you want, it works the other way, too. You can start with the lower one and count up by tens and it takes thirty steps." The students indicated their agreement with Jessie's thinking by putting their thumbs up.

"What about this?" I asked as I marked two squares that were sixty apart.

"Sixty!" the students replied in unison.

ELEVEN STEPS AND NINE STEPS

"Give us a hard one!" James said.

James's request was a nice transition to what I had planned. I cleaned the transparency and marked two squares that were eleven steps apart.

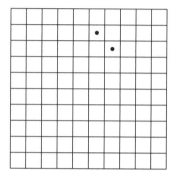

"How many steps to go from one of these squares to the other?" I asked. I gave the students time to think before calling on anyone.

Christopher shared first. "I counted by ones and got eleven."

Karena added, "You could count by ones, but you don't have to. You go down one square and that's a fast way of counting ten. Then you go over to the right one more square and that's eleven."

Vinay explained, "I know another way. I didn't do this, but it works. You could count down two squares; that's twenty. Then you have to go back until you get to the second square. It's twenty, nineteen, eighteen, seventeen, sixteen, fifteen, fourteen, thirteen, twelve, eleven."

Tobias speculated, "I bet any two squares on a diagonal like that will be eleven apart." If Tobias or another student hadn't come up with this conjecture, I would have asked the students to explore it. The students took a few moments to explore and confirm Tobias's idea on their grids.

Jillian said, "I think Tobias is right and I think something else! I think if you make diagonals going the other way, the squares will be nine apart." Jillian came to the overhead and demonstrated her idea. If Jillian hadn't made her observation, I would have taken the discussion in this direction.

"Why do you think that works?" I asked.

Jillian thought a moment and then explained, "It's logical, actually. You see, moving down one square is ten. Moving down one and over to the right is ten and one more, or eleven. Moving down one and over to the left is actually one less than ten, so that's nine."

"Can we try it?" Tanya asked. I nodded and had the students explore squares that were nine steps apart on their grids as we had done for the other numbers of steps.

EXTENSIONS

On other days, ask children to investigate how many steps there are between squares that are other numbers apart—nineteen, twenty-nine, twenty-one, or thirty-one squares, for example. Or mark dots on two squares and ask students how many steps it takes to go from the lower square back to the upper square. For some children, thinking about steps in reverse seems like a completely different problem.

Questions and Discussion

▲▲

▲ *What are alternatives to using an overhead projector?*

If you do not have an overhead projector available to you, you can use a commercially made 10-by-10 pocket wall chart. Reverse the number cards that typically come with these charts so that there are blank cards in the pockets; blank cards make it easier for the children to distinguish the squares. Make two blank cards in another color to use instead of marking dots. As another alternative, you can use a large sheet of butcher paper or poster board and draw a blank 10-by-10 grid. In either situation, you can use sticky notes to mark squares for discussion.

▲ *Why is using a chart without numbers beneficial to children with previous experience using 1–100 charts or 0–99 charts?*

Using a blank 10-by-10 grid engages students in using tens and ones without relying on or being distracted by numbers. It helps cement their understanding of the structure of the 10-by-10 grid, which can help them later when they think about numerical relationships involving tens and ones.

CHAPTER TWO
EXPLORING TENS AND ONES ON A 1–100 CHART

Overview

In this lesson, students add 1, 10, 11, and then other numbers to different numbers on the 1–100 chart. They look for patterns in the pairs of numbers that result, both numerically, by examining how the digits in the ones and tens places change from the first number to the second, and visually, examining the positions of pairs of numbers on the 1–100 chart. The lesson provides students experience with addition computation, gives them opportunities to think about using place value ideas when finding sums, improves their mental math skills, and builds their number sense. Also, the lesson helps them develop their understanding of regrouping. For additional challenges, students explore the effects on numbers of subtracting 1, 10, 9, and 11 and adding 12, 19, 20, and 21.

Materials

▲ chart paper, 2 sheets
▲ 10-by-10 pocket wall chart with number cards from 1 to 100
▲ 2 blank colored cards to fit in the pockets, $\frac{1}{2}$ inch taller so they can be seen when behind a number card
▲ 1–100 charts, 1 per student (see Blackline Masters)

Time

▲ three class periods

Teaching Directions

1. Before class, prepare a pocket wall chart by placing the number cards in sequential order and facedown.

10

2. Place one colored card on the pocket chart in the pocket holding the 4. Ask the students to show using their fingers what number card they think is hidden under the colored card. Together, count from the first space to verify what card is hidden, then turn the number card over to reveal the 4.

3. Place the second colored card directly below the first and one row down. Ask students to predict what number is hidden by the second colored card. Ask volunteers to share their predictions and why their predictions make sense. Reveal the hidden card to verify that 14 was the hidden number.

4. On chart paper, draw, label, and fill in a three-column T-chart, like this:

n	$n+10$	Total
4	$4+10$	14

5. Repeat Steps 2–4 for the numbers 3 and 13, 27 and 37, and 45 and 55 and, if you feel it's needed, for 19 and 29 and 84 and 94.

6. Tell the students you want to place a colored card in the pocket with the number card 63. Ask for explanations about how to figure out where to place the card. Then turn over the number card to verify that it's 63. Place the second colored card in the square directly below. After students guess the new hidden number, fill in the T-chart.

n	$n+10$	Total
4	$4+10$	14
3	$3+10$	13
27	$27+10$	37
45	$45+10$	55
19	$19+10$	29
84	$84+10$	94
63	$63+10$	73

7. Repeat Step 6 for the numbers 36 and 81 (and other numbers, if you feel it's necessary).

8. To move the students toward a generalization, write on the board:

When 10 is added to a number (n), *the number in the ones place* _____.

Exploring Tens and Ones on a 1-100 Chart   11

Refer to the T-chart and lead a class discussion about the effect on the number in the ones place when ten is added to it.

9. Repeat Step 8 by writing the following on the board:

When 10 is added to a number (n), *the number in the tens place* _____.

As in Step 8, lead a class discussion.

10. On Day 2, explore what happens when eleven is added to numbers. Turn all the number cards in the pocket wall chart facedown once again. Draw on chart paper a three-column T-chart as shown.

n	$n+11$	Total

11. Turn the number card 61 faceup. Ask students to predict which card is $n + 11$ if n is 61. Then verify by counting on eleven starting from 61 on the pocket chart. Record as shown on the T-chart.

n	$n+11$	Total
61	61+11	72

12. Repeat Step 11 for 35 and 46, 17 and 28, 88 and 99, 76 and 87, and 11 and 22. Direct students' attention to the diagonal pattern that emerges with these pairs of numbers.

13. Repeat Step 11 for the numbers 29 and 40. Discuss why this pair of numbers doesn't follow the same numerical pattern as the other pairs although it follows the same diagonal pattern on the chart. Ask students to suggest other pairs of numbers that behave in the same way as 29 and 40 (for example, 49 and 60 and 89 and 100).

14. Repeat Step 11 for the numbers 10 and 21. Discuss the numerical pattern and the pattern on the 1–100 chart.

15. On Day 3, introduce an independent exploration. Post the completed T-charts from Days 1 and 2.

n	$n+10$	Total
4	$4+10$	14
3	$3+10$	13
27	$27+10$	37
45	$45+10$	55
19	$19+10$	29
84	$84+10$	94
63	$63+10$	73
36	$36+10$	46
81	$81+10$	91

n	$n+11$	Total
61	$61+11$	72
35	$35+11$	46
17	$17+11$	28
88	$88+11$	99
76	$76+11$	87
11	$11+11$	22
29	$29+11$	40
49	$49+11$	60
89	$89+11$	100
10	$10+11$	21

When 10 is added to a number (n), the number in the ones place stays the same.

When 10 is added to a number (n), the number in the tens place goes up by 1.

Explain to the students they'll be working in pairs to explore one of the following:

$n+1$
$n+9$
$n+19$
$n+20$
$n+21$
$n-1$
$n-10$

Tell the students that they should record on their own papers for six or more pairs of numbers using a three-column T-chart. As students work, circulate through the class, observing, assisting, and asking and answering questions as appropriate.

16. Ask students who finish early to choose another problem from the list to explore, or give them one of the following challenge problems: $n+12$, $n-11$, or $n-9$.

Exploring Tens and Ones on a 1-100 Chart 13

Teaching Notes

The lesson in Chapter 1, "Pairs of Squares on a 10-by-10 Grid," lays the foundation for this lesson. In that initial lesson, students explore the structure of a 10-by-10 grid without the interference of numbers. This lesson builds on that experience by using numbers to change the grid into a 1–100 chart.

Toward the end of Day 2 of the lesson, students consider what happens when they add eleven to any number (n). They investigate what happens to both digits in each pair of numbers and also how the positions of the pairs of numbers relate to each other on the 1–100 chart. For most pairs, the digits in the ones and tens places in the first number both increase by one. On the 1–100 chart, this creates a diagonal pattern. For some pairs of numbers, however, one of these patterns doesn't hold.

Consider pairs in which the first number has a 9 in the ones place; for example, adding 11 to 29 results in 40. The digit in the ones place changes from 9 to 0, while the digit in the tens place changes from 2 to 4, an increase of two. This occurs because adding 11 and 29 creates an additional group of ten with no ones remaining. However, the diagonal pattern on the 1–100 chart for 29 and 40 still holds.

If the first number in the pair has a 0 in the ones place, however, such as 20, then the diagonal pattern on the 1–100 chart doesn't hold. Adding 11 to 20 results in 31, which appears in the beginning of the next row on the chart. Working through this experience can help children more fully understand two important concepts: why numbers are "carried" and why a one that is carried isn't a one at all but is one group of ten.

Note that on Day 3, students will need to review the T-charts that you create on Days 1 and 2. For this reason, it's useful to use chart paper for recording the T-charts.

The Lesson

DAY 1

Before class, I placed the numerals from 1 to 100 sequentially in the pockets of a commercially made pocket wall chart. Then I turned the cards over so the numerals didn't show. I also cut two blank orange cards that fit into the pockets but that were about $\frac{1}{2}$ inch taller so they could be seen when they were placed behind a numeral card.

I gathered the children on the rug, asking them to be sure to sit so that they could easily see the pocket wall chart. I explained that I had placed cards with the numerals from 1 to 100 in order on the chart and then turned them over.

I placed one of the orange cards in the pocket with the number 4 card. "What number do you think is under the orange card?" I asked. I paused for a moment and then asked the students to show me the answer using their fingers. Most showed four fingers; four children held up three fingers. I continued, "I see some threes and some fours. How could we find out?"

"Count!" the students replied.

As we counted together, I pointed to the corresponding pockets on the chart, stopping at four when my finger touched the orange card. I pulled the number card from behind the orange card, turned it so the students could see that it was a 4, and replaced it in front of the orange card with the 4 showing.

I said to the class as I placed a second orange card in the pocket directly below the first and one row down, "What number do you think is behind the second orange card?" Conversations broke out among the students as they thought this over. When I called the class back to order, I said, "Tell me in a whisper voice."

"Fourteen," most students replied.

Jael was eager to share her thinking. "I just counted by ones. I started with four, then went across one square and that was five; I went across another square and that was six, and like that until I got to the second orange card. That was fourteen."

Sam said matter-of-factly, "From yesterday, I knew it took ten steps to go one square down, so I just did four plus ten. That's fourteen."

I then revealed that the hidden card was 14. The students cheered.

I removed both orange cards, but left the 4 and 14 showing so the students could use them as a reference. On chart paper, I drew a three-column T-chart. (I used chart paper so that I could have the T-chart available for reference over the next several days.) I labeled the left column n, explaining to the students that n was short for *number*. I labeled the middle column $n + 10$, explaining that this expression meant a number plus ten. I labeled the right column *Total*. Then I filled in the chart:

n	$n + 10$	Total
4	4 + 10	14

Next, I placed an orange card in the pocket holding the 3 and asked the students to predict what number it was covering. They easily figured that it was 3. I pulled out the number card, turned it over, and placed it in front of the orange card so the children could see the number 3. Then I placed the second orange card in the pocket directly below the 3 and one row down. The students easily guessed that the hidden number was 13. I filled in the T-chart and removed the orange cards, leaving the numbers 3 and 13 showing.

I repeated the process once more, first placing an orange card in the pocket holding the number card 27 and then placing the other orange card in the pocket directly below and one row down, covering the number 37. Some students still needed to count individual spaces, and others figured out the numbers using other strategies. After I revealed the numbers, I filled in the T-chart and removed the orange cards, leaving the 27 and 37 showing.

I repeated the activity for several other pairs of numbers—45 and 55, 19 and 29, and 84 and 94:

n	$n + 10$	Total
4	4 + 10	14
3	3 + 10	13
27	27 + 10	37
45	45 + 10	55
19	19 + 10	29
84	84 + 10	94

		3	4						
		13	14					19	
						27	29		
						37			
			45						
			55						
			84						
			94						

Doing this slowed down the activity and also revealed more information about the numbers on the chart as a reference for those students who were catching on more slowly than others.

Presenting Other Problems

I then said to the class, "I want to place an orange card in the pocket with sixty-three, but I'm not sure where sixty-three is. Who can help me?" The students thought quietly for a moment and then hands began to go up. When most hands were up, I called on Halley.

Halley said, "Start with where the three is. Sixty-three is just six more tens than three, so go down the chart six pockets, and that should be sixty-three." I did as Halley instructed and placed an orange card in the appropriate pocket.

"Who has another way of figuring out how to place the orange card in the pocket with sixty-three?" I asked.

"I know," Paul said. "Start with fifty-five and just count until you get to sixty-three." I followed Paul's directions, placing my finger on the pockets as I counted. I ended up at the same pocket that Halley had identified.

Kito had another idea. He said, "I know a tricky way. Start with forty-five. Go down the chart two pockets, and you're on sixty-five. Now go back to the left two, and that's sixty-three." I followed Kito's directions and again landed on the same pocket. I then pulled out the hidden number to verify it was 63. The students cheered, pleased with themselves. I placed the second orange card in the square directly below 63 and one row down, and the students quickly guessed the hidden number was 73. I turned over the card to verify and then recorded on the T-chart.

n	$n+10$	Total
4	4 + 10	14
3	3 + 10	13
27	27 + 10	37
45	45 + 10	55
19	19 + 10	29
84	84 + 10	94
63	63 + 10	73

I next said to the class, "Now I want to place an orange card in the pocket with thirty-six. Who can help?"

"Easy!" "I know that!" were some of the responses.

Sam explained how to locate 36 and I turned over the 36 number card. Then I placed the other orange card in the square directly below it. The students correctly predicted that it was 46, and I revealed the 46 number card.

I repeated the procedure for the number 81. The students all seemed to understand how to locate numbers on the chart and figure out the numbers directly below and one row down, so I moved on to the next part of the lesson.

Moving Toward a Generalization

I asked the students to watch as I wrote on the chart paper:

When 10 is added to a number (n), *the number in the ones place* _____.

I underlined the ones digit in the first four pairs of numbers on the T-chart and asked, "Why do you suppose I'm underlining these numbers?"

"They're the ones digits," Roberto explained. I nodded my agreement.

I continued, "What do you notice about the digits in the ones place of each number in the n column and its partner in the Total column? Talk with your partner about what happens to the digit in the ones place when ten is added to a number. First one of you shares for thirty seconds while the other listens. Remember, no interrupting. When I give you the signal, the first talker gets to listen and the first listener gets to talk. At the end of the second thirty seconds, I'll ask for your attention." The students began sharing ideas with their partners. At the end of thirty seconds, I reminded the students to change roles.

At the end of the second thirty seconds, I asked for the students' attention. "Who would like to read the sentence I started on the chart paper and complete it?" I asked. I called on Kito.

Kito said, "When ten is added to a number *(n)*, the number in the ones place will never change. It's that way on all the pairs on the chart." I recorded Kito's idea on the board.

Jillian shared next. "My way is like Kito's I guess, but I said it with different words. When ten is added to a number *(n)*, the number in the ones place will always stay the same." I added Jillian's thinking to the list on the board:

> *Kito*   *When 10 is added to a number* (n), *the number in the ones place will never change.*
>
> *Jillian*   *When 10 is added to a number* (n), *the number in the ones place will always stay the same.*

James explained, "When ten is added to a number *(n)*, the number in the ones place never changes."

Sam said, "The ones place number doesn't change."

Tina had one last idea. "When ten is added to a number *(n)*, the number in the ones place could never change."

While the children all had the same idea, I felt it was important to record everyone's version of it to help them understand that there are many ways of saying the same thing. The completed list of ideas looked as follows:

> *Kito*   *When 10 is added to a number* (n), *the number in the ones place will never change.*
>
> *Jillian*   *When 10 is added to a number* (n), *the number in the ones place will always stay the same.*
>
> *James*   *When 10 is added to a number* (n), *the number in the ones place never changes.*
>
> *Sam*   *When 10 is added to a number* (n), *the number in the ones place doesn't change.*

Tina   *When 10 is added to a number* (n), *the number in the ones place could never change.*

I asked, "Do you think this is true for adding ten to any number or just the ones showing on the pocket chart?" Some thought yes, the pattern was true for any number, while others weren't as sure.

I continued, "Study the chart again. This time look for what happens to the digit in the tens place when ten is added to a number." I wrote on the board:

> *When 10 is added to a number* (n), *the number in the tens place _____.*

The students thought quietly for a few moments and then began to talk among themselves. After a few minutes I asked for their attention.

Jillian shared first. "When ten is added to a number *(n)*, the number in the tens place is one ten higher. And the ones place still stays the same."

Olina shared the same idea using different words. "When ten is added to a number *(n)*, the number in the tens place adds one ten."

I recorded both Jillian's and Olina's versions on the board:

> *Jillian*   *When 10 is added to a number* (n), *the number in the tens place is one ten higher.*
>
> *Olina*   *When 10 is added to a number* (n), *the number in the tens place adds one ten.*

The period was now over and I told the students that we would do some more problems like these the next day.

DAY 2

Adding Eleven

Before class, I turned all the number cards facedown in the pocket wall chart. To begin class, I drew a T-chart on chart paper with three columns—*n*, *n + 11*, and *Total*.

n	$n+11$	Total

"Cool; today we get to explore with eleven," Vinay commented.

I turned the number card with 61 face-up and asked, "If n is equal to sixty-one, how much is n plus eleven?"

Isaac volunteered, "If n equals sixty-one, then n plus eleven is ten more, which is seventy-one, and then one more makes seventy-two. I had to add the last one because I had to add eleven, not just ten." I wrote on the board:

$61 + 11 = 72$

I said, "Put your thumb up if you agree that if n equals sixty-one, then n plus eleven is equal to seventy-two, put your thumb down if you disagree, and put your thumb sideways if you're not sure." Most students' thumbs were up and a few were sideways. I made a note to myself to keep a watchful eye on the few who weren't sure. Then on the pocket chart, I put my finger on 61, counted eleven spaces, and turned the number card in the pocket face-up to verify that sixty-one plus eleven equals seventy-two. I filled in the T-chart:

n	$n+11$	Total
61	61+11	72

I continued, "What if n equals thirty-five? Then what does n plus eleven equal?" I recorded 35 and $35 + 11$ on the T-chart.

Jael shared with a questioning voice, "Forty-six?"

"How do you know?" I asked.

Jael explained, "Eleven is like a ten and a one. Thirty-five and one more makes thirty-six and then add ten more and that's forty-six." The other students nodded their agreement. On the pocket chart, I turned over the number card with 35. Then I interpreted Jael's explanation on the chart: I counted to the right one to add one and then moved down one pocket to add ten more. I turned over the number card in the pocket to reveal 46. I recorded 46 on the T-chart.

I continued with the same procedure for the numbers 17 and 88.

n	$n+11$	Total
61	61 + 11	72
35	35 + 11	46
17	17 + 11	28
88	88 + 11	99

Then I asked, "What pattern do you notice about the pairs of numbers on the pocket chart?"

"It goes diagonally," Abel shared.

"Why?" I asked Abel.

"Because there is one ten in eleven, so you go down one pocket, and then there is one one in eleven, so you go right one square," Abel clarified.

I pointed to the T-chart and asked the class, "What seems to be happening to the ones place when eleven is added to n?"

"It goes up by one," Christopher explained and came to the board to point out his idea in the numbers on the T-chart.

Tina shared, "The tens place gets bigger by one ten, too."

I repeated the process with $n = 76$ and $n = 11$, each time asking the students if the diagonal pattern on the 1–100 chart continued and if the patterns shared by Christopher and Tina still worked.

n	$n+11$	Total
61	61 + 11	72
35	35 + 11	46
17	17 + 11	28
88	88 + 11	99
76	76 + 11	87
11	11 + 11	22

Presenting a Challenge

I had purposely avoided choosing first numbers that ended in 9—9, 19, 29, 39, and so on—for which the patterns in the ones and tens digits would be different because of the need to regroup when adding. Now, however, I presented this situation. I asked, "What would n plus eleven equal if n equaled twenty-nine?"

The students quickly replied that twenty-nine plus eleven would equal forty. I turned faceup the number cards for 29 and 40 and filled in the T-chart.

There were looks of surprise and animated discussions as the students realized that while the diagonal pattern on the pocket chart continued, the number patterns for the ones and tens places didn't seem to hold true.

"Something's fishy!" Kito stated. "The diagonal pattern on the chart keeps going, but look at the numbers on the T-chart. The ones place didn't go up one; it went down nine! And the tens place didn't go up one ten; it went up two tens!"

n	$n+11$	Total
61	61 + 11	72
35	35 + 11	46
17	17 + 11	28
88	88 + 11	99
76	76 + 11	87
11	11 + 11	22
29	29 + 11	40

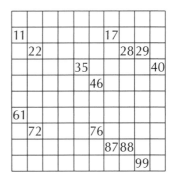

I asked, "What happened?" I paused to give Kito and the other students time to think.

Paul was excited. "I get it! I know what happened!" he said. "Take the one from eleven and put it with the nine from twenty-nine and that makes a ten right there. Then add the ten from eleven to the two tens in twenty and the ten you just made and that's forty."

I recorded on the board:

$$29 = 20 + 9$$
$$11 = 10 + 1$$
$$9 + 1 = 10$$
$$20 + 10 + 10 = 40$$

Sam added, "It's like if you have nine ones; you add one more one from the eleven to make a whole new ten. Then you have the ten from the eleven, so that means the tens place goes up two tens and the ones go to zero."

The students were quiet. I asked, "Who can give me another number for n so that the tens place goes up two tens, like it did when eleven was added to twenty-nine, and the ones place goes from nine to zero?" Several students raised their hands quickly, but I waited to give more students time to consider my question. When about half the students had their hands up, I called on Halley.

Halley shared, "I think forty-nine."

I asked the students to indicate with their thumbs their agreement or disagreement with Halley's suggestion. I turned the 49 number card faceup. Halley directed me to move to the right one for the one in

Exploring Tens and Ones on a 1-100 Chart   19

eleven and then to move down one for the ten in eleven. I turned the card in the pocket faceup. It was 60. I recorded *49* and *60* on the T-chart.

"It worked! I have another one," Kassidee said. "Eighty-nine. Add the one in eleven to eighty-nine, that's ninety. Add the ten in eleven to ninety and that's one hundred. There are ten tens in one hundred and eight tens in eighty. That means the tens place went up two tens. It works!" Our T-chart now looked like this:

n	$n + 11$	Total
61	$61 + 11$	72
35	$35 + 11$	46
17	$17 + 11$	28
88	$88 + 11$	99
76	$76 + 11$	87
11	$11 + 11$	22
29	$29 + 11$	40
49	$49 + 11$	60
89	$89 + 11$	100

Ben shared, "I think any number with nine in the ones place will have two more tens in the tens place when eleven is added. For example, one hundred thirty-nine plus eleven is one hundred fifty. And one hundred sixty-nine plus eleven is one hundred eighty. I think this is something like the regrouping stuff we learned last year . . . maybe."

"Oh, I know what Ben means. The little one we carried is the ten that happens from the one and nine, right?" Roberto asked. I nodded to verify to Roberto that his connection was correct.

Presenting Another Challenge

Next I had the children consider what happened to the patterns on the T-chart and with the digits when they added eleven to numbers that ended in zero—ten, twenty, thirty, and so on. Adding eleven to these numbers doesn't require regrouping and,

therefore, the pattern holds of increasing the digits in both the ones and tens places. But the visual pattern on the 1–100 chart is broken.

I asked, "What would n plus eleven equal if n was ten?"

It was easy for the students to figure that ten plus eleven would equal twenty-one. As I added this information the T-chart, Olina said, "Hey, it works again!"

"What works again?" I asked.

"The ones place goes up by one and so does the tens place, the same as for the numbers before you asked about the numbers that end in nine," Olina explained.

"Uh oh," Kassidee said. "There's a problem with the pattern on the chart." She had noticed that the diagonal pattern wouldn't appear. I turned faceup the number cards for 10 and 21 so others could see what Kassidee had visualized.

"Why is this so?" I asked.

The children were quiet for a moment and then hands began to go up. I called on Adama. She said, "I think it's because ten is at the end of the line, and if you go down one and over one you'll be off the chart, so you have to go to the next row down." The others agreed.

"Is this the same for all numbers that end in zero?" I asked. The students agreed that it was.

James said, "It's like they have their own pattern. If you start with a number at the end of a row and add eleven, then you get the first number on the next row."

With this comment, I ended the lesson for the day.

DAY 3

Introducing an Independent Exploration

My plan was to have students explore in pairs other addition and subtraction patterns using ten as a landmark as we had done on the previous days. Before class, I posted the T-charts from the first two days as a reminder to students of what we'd done before:

n	$n + 10$	Total		n	$n + 11$	Total
4	$4 + 10$	14		61	$61 + 11$	72
3	$3 + 10$	13		35	$35 + 11$	46
27	$27 + 10$	37		17	$17 + 11$	28
45	$45 + 10$	55		88	$88 + 11$	99
19	$19 + 10$	29		76	$76 + 11$	87
84	$84 + 10$	94		11	$11 + 11$	22
63	$63 + 10$	73		29	$29 + 11$	40
36	$36 + 10$	46		49	$49 + 11$	60
81	$81 + 10$	91		89	$89 + 11$	100
				10	$10 + 11$	21

When 10 is added to a number (n), the number in the ones place stays the same.

When 10 is added to a number (n), the number in the tens place goes up by 1.

I gathered the students on the floor. I explained, "Together we explored what happens when ten is added to a number and when eleven is added to a number. We used a one-to-one-hundred chart to help us see patterns and we used a T-chart to keep track of our information." I pointed to the information I'd posted before class. "In both cases we noticed patterns that occurred in the ones and tens places. Today you'll have the chance to do some exploring with a partner. Your partner will be the person sitting beside you. Here are some ideas for you and your partner to consider." I wrote on the board:

$n + 1$
$n + 9$
$n + 19$
$n + 20$
$n + 21$
$n - 1$
$n - 10$

Some of the choices were easier than others, allowing all students the opportunity to be successful. I continued to explain, "I included two choices that involve subtraction. That's something that those of you who like challenges might want to explore. When you do your investigation, you'll need to make a T-chart as I've done here." I pointed to the posted T-charts. "Be sure to label the columns as I have done. Include at least six pairs of numbers. Then look for patterns in the ones and tens places. Write about them as I did." I pointed to the two sentences I'd written beneath the T-chart about $n + 10$.

I asked if there were questions. Arin raised her hand. She said, "I don't get what to write."

I knew that Arin was not alone. Writing can be a daunting task for young students. To help Arin and others, I wrote on the board:

When __ is added to a number (n), the number in the ones place _____.
When __ is added to a number (n), the number in the tens place _____.
When __ is subtracted from a number (n), the number in the ones place _____.
When __ is subtracted from a number (n), the number in the tens place _____.

I explained, "Here are sentence starters to help you. What do you suppose should go in the first blank space?"

"The number you're adding or subtracting," Arin said, but she was stuck about what to write in the other blank. She called on Halley to help.

Halley explained, "The other blank is where you write about patterns you notice. Like when you add ten to a number, the ones place never changes." Arin nodded.

Vinay asked, "Even though we're working together, do we each do our own paper?" I nodded. There were no further questions.

Exploring Tens and Ones on a 1-100 Chart   21

I gave the students a few moments to make their decision about which problem to investigate. I showed students a pile of 1–100 charts they could use if they wanted to do so. I explained, "If you're also interested in looking at patterns on a one-to-one-hundred chart, come up and take a copy of the chart."

As I handed each pair of students two sheets of paper, I asked which problem they had chosen. This helped focus the students quickly on the task and gave me a way to suggest a change if I thought that students hadn't made an appropriate choice.

Observing the Students

Most students chose to investigate one of the following: $n + 19$, $n + 20$, or $n + 21$. A few chose $n + 1$ or $n - 1$.

Tina and Jael chose $n + 19$. I asked the girls why they didn't choose $n + 1$, $n - 1$, or $n - 10$. Jael shrugged, so Tina explained, "They're too easy. The ones place either goes up one if you add or down one if you subtract. The tens place only changes when you add enough times to get another ten or you subtract enough times to make a ten go away."

Tina continued, "With minusing ten, the ones place will never change. Zero has that effect on numbers. And the tens place will go down one ten. It's kind of like the opposite of adding ten, I think."

I stayed nearby the girls, observing as they worked. Tina was a shy child and Jael had many gaps in her understanding. I was impressed with the patience Tina showed Jael as she explained her reasoning. I was equally impressed with Jael's determination to understand. She stopped Tina at times to ask questions. After a little while I moved on to check on other students.

James and Jillian had also chosen to explore $n + 19$. As I approached, the two

were in a deep discussion about the patterns in the ones and tens places. Both children had written that when nineteen is added to a number, the digit in the ones place decreases by one. They had not yet discovered that when nineteen is added to a number ending with zero, the number in the ones place goes from zero to nine, appearing to break this pattern. They had noticed, however, that sometimes adding nineteen to a number increased the number in the tens place by one ten and sometimes by two tens. James had a clear idea of when this happened and was trying to explain it to Jillian. Finally Jillian said, "I can see that sometimes the tens place number goes up one ten and sometimes two tens. That's all I understand, so I'll write that." James nodded and each child wrote about what he or she understood. (See Figures 2–1 and 2–2.)

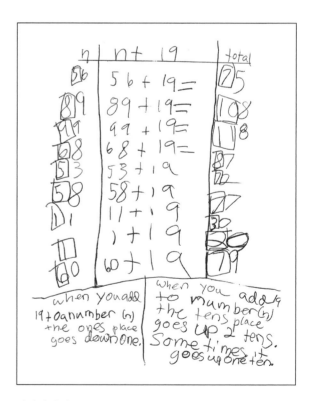

▲▲▲▲▲▲Figure 2–1 *Jillian wrote about her partial understanding of what happens when nineteen is added to a number* (n).

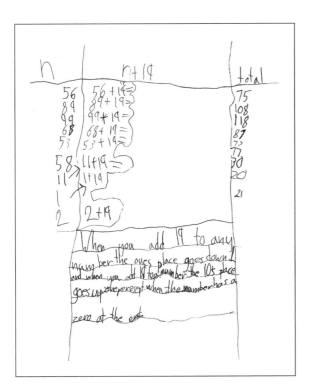

▲▲▲▲▲▲Figure 2–2 *James's understanding of what happens when nineteen is added to a number* (n) *included his observation that something different happens when nineteen is added to a number with a zero in the ones place.*

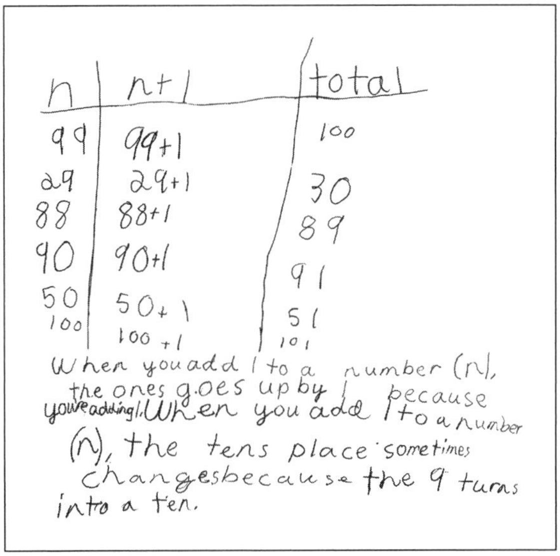

▲▲▲▲▲▲Figure 2–3 *Vinay's completed work showed understanding of what happens when one is added to a number with a nine in the ones place.*

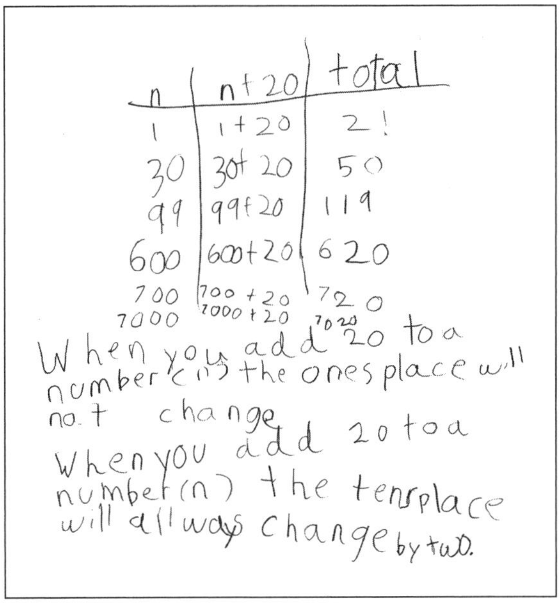

Vinay and his partner quickly finished $n + 1$. They figured out that when adding one to a number, the number in the ones place increases by one with no change in the tens place until there are enough ones to make a ten. (See Figure 2–3.) Vinay and his partner then chose a second problem to investigate.

Kito and Abel explored $n + 20$. They included numbers larger than 100. Initially the boys were struggling with how to write 7,020, the result of adding 20 to 7,000. They weren't sure where to put the digit 2. After some discussion, they used what they had learned about writing tens to help them write the number correctly. Kito explained, "We thought we should write it seven, two, zero, zero, but that didn't make any sense. Then we

▲▲▲▲▲▲Figure 2–4 *Kito explored adding twenty to some numbers larger than one hundred.*

remembered we added two tens to seven thousand, so it made sense to put two in the tens place to show we added two tens." Abel nodded his agreement. (See Figure 2–4.)

Exploring Tens and Ones on a 1-100 Chart   23

While Rachel and Keara were able to work together to complete their T-charts correctly for $n + 20$, their written explanations showed confusion. I sat down to talk with the girls so I could gain a clearer picture of what they did and did not understand. Keara struggled to see any patterns in the numbers. Rachel, however, was able to see patterns in both the ones and the tens places. She explained, "Because you always add zero to the ones place of the other number, the ones place won't change. And you're adding two tens, so the number of tens has to go up two." Rachel's struggle to get her ideas on paper reminded me of how very difficult it can be for young children to write and how important it is to also give them opportunities to explain their thinking orally. (See Figure 2–5.)

Jessie also had difficulty being precise in her written explanation although she was able to explain herself verbally. (See

Figure 2–6.) Karena, on the other hand, described very clearly what she saw. (See Figure 2–7.)

I checked back with Tina and Jael. To help Jael examine the effects on the ones place of adding nineteen to a number, both girls had meticulously underlined the ones in the Total column. In doing so, they discovered that the ones place decreased by one only sometimes when nineteen was added to a number. The girls also noticed that the tens increased by two tens "most of the time." Neither Jael nor Tina had any clear ideas why this was. (See Figures 2–8 and 2–9.)

As students finished, I gave them the option of choosing another problem from the list to explore independently or choosing from one of the following challenge problems: $n + 12$, $n - 11$, or $n - 9$. Ben, who loved big numbers, explored $n + 20$; Tina tackled $n - 9$; and Jillian explored $n + 12$. (See Figures 2–10 through 2–12.)

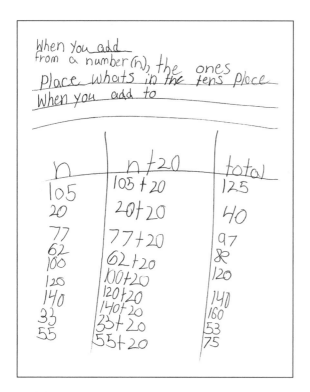

▲▲▲▲▲▲Figure 2–5 *Although Rachel was able to explain her thinking orally with clarity, her written explanation was confused.*

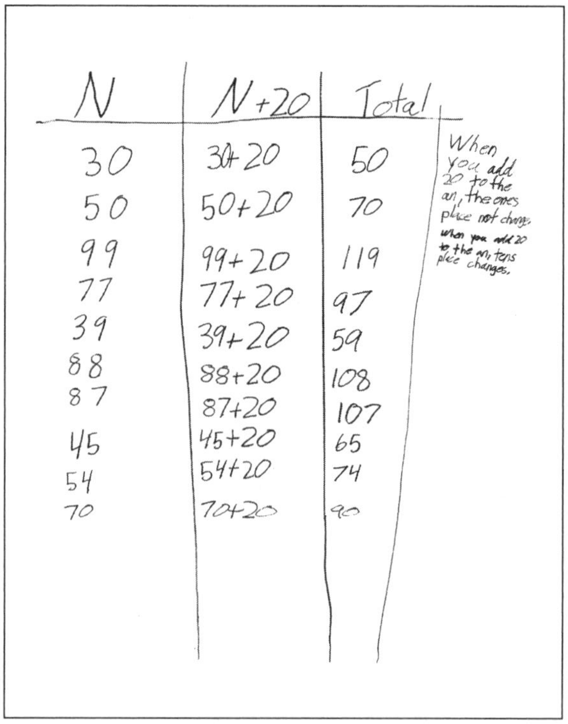

▲▲▲▲▲▲Figure 2–6 *Jessie completed her T-chart correctly but had difficulty using words to explain.*

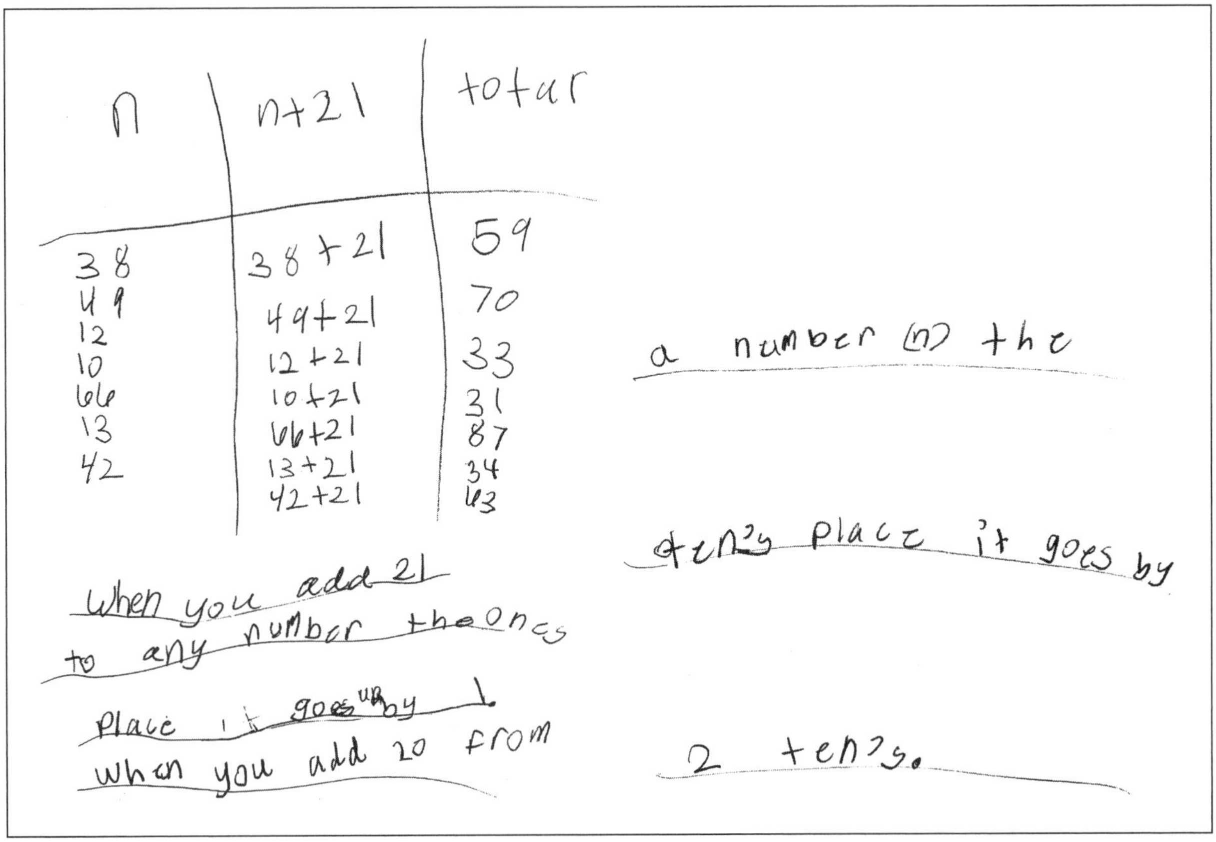

▲▲▲▲▲▲Figure 2–7   *Karena was able to use words to describe what she saw.*

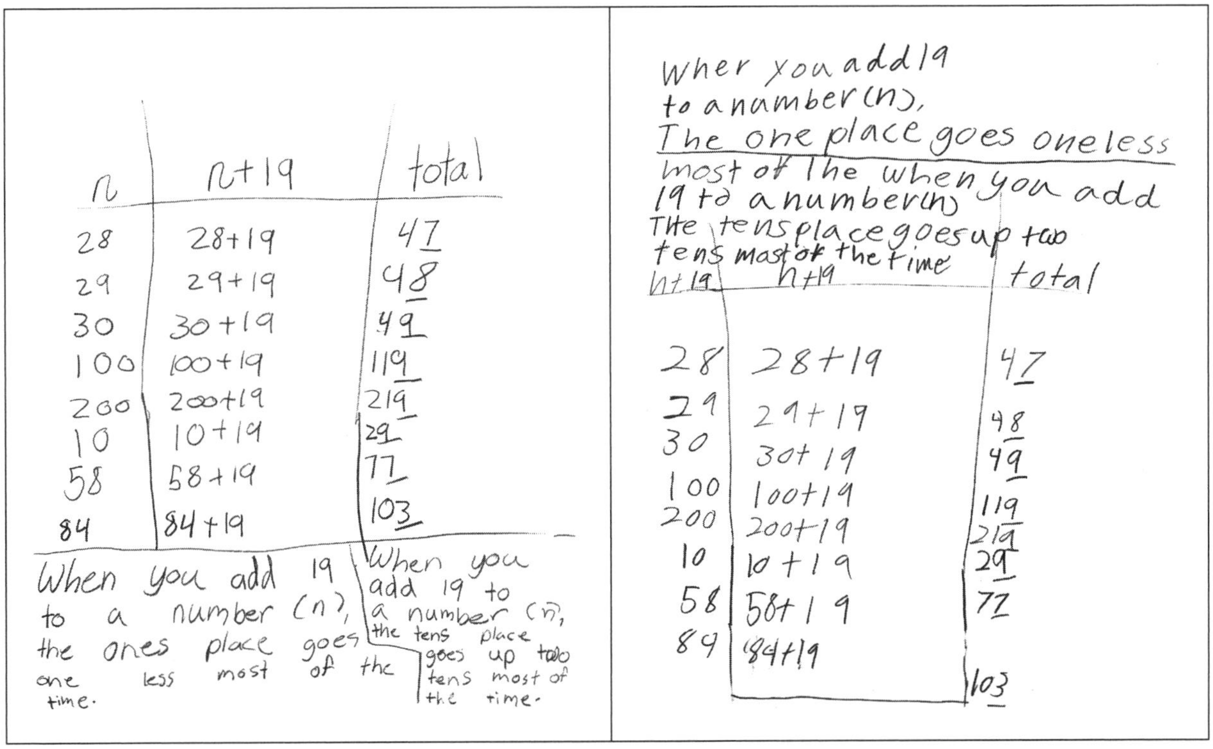

▲▲▲▲▲▲Figure 2–8 and Figure 2–9   *Tina and Jael persisted in their cooperative efforts and together made some discoveries about the effects of adding nineteen to a number.*

Exploring Tens and Ones on a 1-100 Chart   25

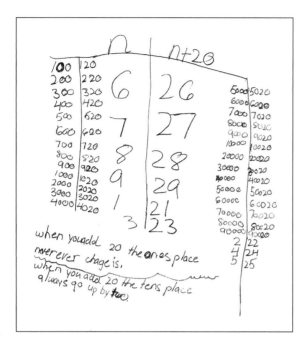

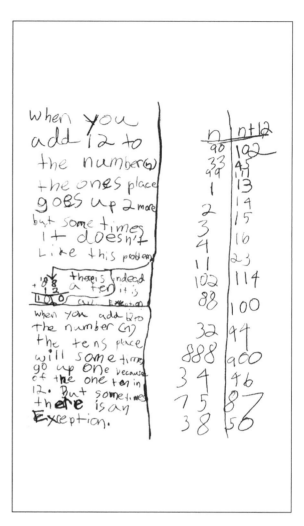

▲▲▲▲▲▲Figure 2–10   *Ben explored adding twenty to numbers less than ten and to larger numbers.*

▲▲▲▲▲▲Figure 2–12   *Jillian's understanding expanded to thinking about exceptions to patterns she noticed.*

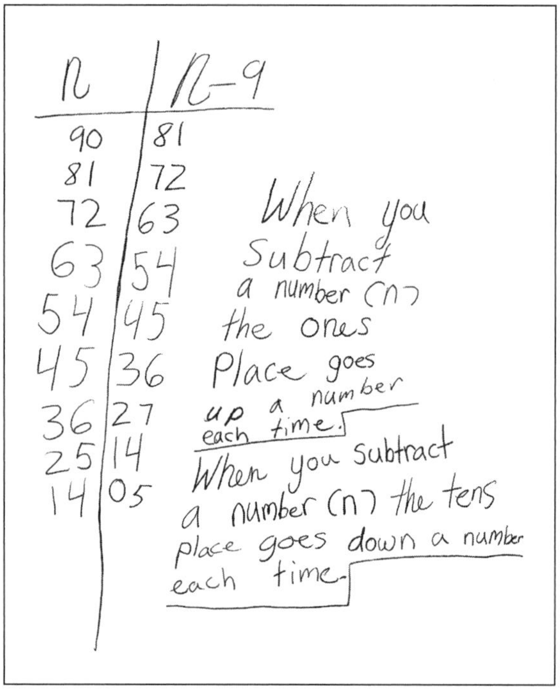

▲▲▲▲▲▲Figure 2–11   *Tina's written explanation showed emerging understanding. She made one error in her T-chart: 25 – 9 should be 16 rather than 14.*

EXTENSIONS

To push the students' thinking, ask them to add 10 to numbers in the bottom row of the 1–100 chart. On other days, ask students to explore adding or subtracting a larger number, such as 31, 29, or 32. Also, as students gain understanding and facility with this activity, introduce a chart with numbers from 101 to 200. Still later, children can explore the results of adding and subtracting numbers such as 100, 101, 99, and 110.

26   Lessons for Extending Place Value

Questions and Discussion

▲▲▲

▲ *Why did you use a three-column T-chart?*

Typically, T-charts have two columns. For this investigation, I think that the middle column helps focus children on what's happening numerically, thus making the activity more accessible for more students. I want as many children as possible to have access and success and to understand as fully as possible what is happening.

▲ *It seems that some of the children in your class needed the chart to figure answers while others were thinking numerically. Is this typical?*

Yes, some children need the support of the chart, which organizes the numbers for them. Others either have internalized the organization of the chart or have some other strategies for figuring. I try to give the children multiple ways to think about these problems.

▲ *How do you feel about using the numbers from 0 to 99 on the chart instead of from 1 to 100? Then zero is included, and all the numbers in a decade are in the same row.*

While I used the numbers from 1 to 100 with the class described, it's perfectly fine to use the numbers from 0 to 99 instead. As stated, using 0 to 99 provides the advantage that all numbers in the same decade are on the same row and, also, zero is recognized and used as a number. On the other hand, using 1 to 100 in the chart incorporates the important landmark number of one hundred and corresponds to the set of counting numbers, which starts with the number one.

In my situation, there were second language learners and special education students in my class who were very literal. For this reason, I chose to use the numbers from 1 to 100 so the numbering of the squares would more closely match their experience with numbers and counting.

CHAPTER THREE
EXPLORING ONES, TENS, AND HUNDREDS WITH BASE TEN BLOCKS

Overview

This lesson helps students cement and extend their understanding of how ones, tens, and hundreds relate to our number system. The children use base ten blocks to explore the relationship among ones, tens, and hundreds; represent the number 100 in various ways using different combinations of blocks; and figure out the value of different combinations of blocks. Then working independently in pairs, they explore ways to represent 72, and then 124, using different combinations of blocks.

Materials

▲ base ten blocks, about 25 ones cubes, 12 longs (tens), and 1 flat (hundred) per student
▲ optional: set of overhead base ten blocks
▲ optional: Base Ten Blocks sheet, 1 per student (see Blackline Masters)

Time

▲ one class period plus additional class periods for extensions

Teaching Directions

1. Before class, gather the base ten materials and distribute them to the students. See "Questions and Discussion" section at the end of this chapter for alternatives if base ten blocks are unavailable.

2. Allow a short period of time for students to explore the base ten blocks. Suggest to students that they try building the larger blocks using the smaller blocks in order to look for relationships among them.

28

3. Lead a discussion for students to share what they found out about the relationships among the blocks. During the discussion bring out the following:

Ten ones cubes are equivalent to one long.

Ten longs are equivalent to one flat.

One hundred ones cubes are equivalent to one flat.

4. Place one flat on the overhead projector and ask students: "How much is this worth?" (One hundred) Replace the flat with ten longs and ask again: "How much is this worth?" (One hundred) To reinforce that ten longs and one flat are equivalent, ask the students to count aloud with you as you count the longs by tens and rearrange them into the shape of a flat.

5. Remove the blocks from the overhead and replace them with nine longs and ten ones cubes. Ask students: "How much are these worth?" (One hundred) Have volunteers share their thinking. Then verify by rearranging the blocks into the shape of a flat.

6. Place one long on the overhead. Ask students: "How many ones cubes would I need to add to show one hundred?" Have volunteers share their thinking.

7. Place on the overhead projector eleven longs and two ones cubes. Ask students: "How much is this worth?" (112) Ask volunteers to share how they know. Record the students' ideas on the board.

8. Introduce an independent exploration. Write *72* on an overhead transparency and explain to students that they'll work in pairs to find ways of building seventy-two using base ten blocks. Model an example by placing on the overhead projector seven longs and two ones cubes. Ask students: "How much are these blocks worth?" Model for students how to record.

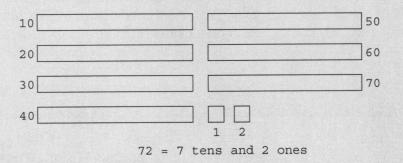

72 = 7 tens and 2 ones

9. As students work to find other ways to build seventy-two, circulate through the room, observing, helping, and answering and asking questions as appropriate.

10. When students complete their investigation of 72, have them next explore ways to build 124.

11. As a way of sharing with the whole group and summarizing the lesson, ask each table group, one by one, to send a representative to the board to draw one way of building seventy-two using base ten blocks that is different from the ones already on the board. After each person records, ask the rest of the students to indicate by raising their hands if the way shared is also one of their ways.

12. If time allows, repeat Step 11 for the number 124.

Teaching Notes

Many children in the third grade can identify the digits in the ones, tens, and hundreds places in numbers. But when asked, many children cannot explain the meaning of the digits. Base ten blocks provide children a concrete model of how ones, tens, and hundreds relate to one another. Experiences with the blocks strengthen students' number sense, build their understanding of regrouping, and help them learn to add and subtract accurately and efficiently. Also, the experiences support students' later learning about thousands, ten thousands, and larger numbers and provide a foundation that will help children learn about multiplication, division, and decimals.

The following vignette describes what occurred in one class period. After an introduction to the blocks, students explore different ways to use the blocks to represent the number seventy-two. Similar experiences from time to time with other numbers are beneficial for children. The activity can be made simpler for children by using smaller and more familiar numbers, or it can be made more challenging by using larger and less familiar numbers.

A note about terminology for the base ten blocks: In the following vignette, I initially refer to the smallest base ten block as a "ones cube," to the ten block as a "long," and to the hundred block as a "flat." These labels are easy for children to remember because they relate to the shapes of the blocks. However, I alternate these labels with "ones," "tens," and "hundreds," using the terminology interchangeably to help reinforce the link between the blocks' descriptive labels and their mathematical values. Hearing both used regularly in the context of activities supports children's learning.

The Lesson

Before class, I gathered the base ten blocks and enough baskets so there was one basket for each group of four children. I placed in each basket about one hundred ones cubes, about forty-five longs, and five or six flats.

To begin the lesson, I held up a basket of blocks and said, "Raise a hand if you've used blocks like these before." About half of the students raised their hands. So that we could communicate easily about the blocks, I held up each type of block and named it for the students, using names that related to their shapes—ones cube, long, and flat. On the board, I drew a sketch of each and wrote the name underneath.

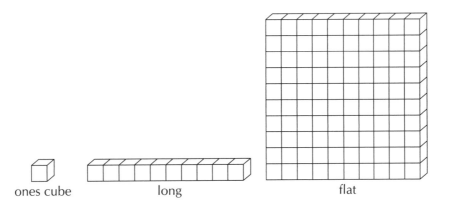

ones cube   long   flat

Whenever I introduce materials that are new for some or all of the students, I feel it's important to provide time for the students to explore the materials before I begin using them for instruction. In this instance, to structure this exploration, I asked the students to explore the blocks and figure out the relationships among them. I suggested, "You can try building the bigger blocks with the smaller blocks." Also, I reminded the students that they were to share the materials in the baskets among their group members and that grabbing or tossing the blocks was unacceptable. The students were eager to get to work and didn't have comments or questions.

I circulated throughout the room, answering questions, reinforcing proper behavior, and giving occasional reminders to focus the students. After about five minutes, I asked the students for their attention.

When the students were quiet, I said, "Raise your hand if you'd like to share something you noticed about the relationships among the blocks." Hands quickly filled the air. To provide all students with the opportunity to share at least one idea, I asked the students to turn to their partners. I explained, "Each of you will have thirty seconds to share your thinking. First one of you will talk and the other will listen. Then after thirty seconds, I'll give you a signal

and the first talker will get to listen and the first listener will get to talk." After thirty seconds, I reminded the students to switch roles. At the end of another thirty seconds, I called the students to attention for a class discussion.

Jade shared first. "I noticed that it takes ten little cubes to make a long one."

I responded, "Raise a hand if you also discovered what Jade shared." Everyone raised a hand.

Olina added, "It takes ten longs to make the flat block." She pointed on her desk to where she had built a flat using ten longs. As I did when Jade had reported, I asked who else had discovered Olina's idea, and again everyone raised a hand.

Kassidee said, "You could also make the flat with one hundred little cubes." Most students raised their hands to show that they agreed.

Isaac then said, "Hey, I just thought of something! The little cubes are like ones and the longs are like tens!"

I nodded and said, "Yes, we can also call the ones cube a one, the long a ten, and the flat a hundred." I added these labels to what I had already written on the board (see page 32) and used them interchangeably with the others for the rest of the lesson. Using terminology in the context of an activity helps students become familiar and comfortable with it.

Exploring Ones, Tens, and Hundreds with Base Ten Blocks   **31**

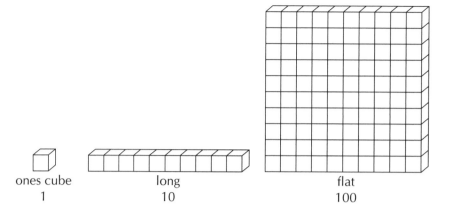

ones cube
1

long
10

flat
100

Vinay had a slightly different idea. He said, "You could use five longs and fifty cubes to make a flat."

I said, "Tell us a little more about your idea."

Vinay explained, "Five longs makes half of the flat, and that's the same as fifty ones. You can prove it because each long is ten. Count by tens for each long, and that's fifty if you use five longs. Then you can cover the other half of the flat with fifty cubes. Five longs and fifty cubes make one hundred, and that's the same as a flat."

I was pleased that Vinay shared his idea, as it provided an opportunity for children to think more flexibly about how to compose numbers. However, I didn't follow up on it at this time because I planned to introduce the idea later in the lesson.

BUILDING ONE HUNDRED WITH DIFFERENT COMBINATIONS OF BLOCKS

I turned on the overhead projector and placed on it one flat. "How much is this worth?" I asked.

"One hundred," the children chorused.

"What about this?" I asked. I removed the flat and replaced it with ten longs, counting aloud from one to ten as I placed

them so it was clear that there were ten longs in all.

"One hundred," the children chorused again.

"Let's count them by tens to be sure," I said. Together we counted as I pointed to each, "Ten, twenty, thirty, forty, fifty, sixty, seventy, eighty, ninety, one hundred." Then I arranged the longs so that they looked like a flat to reinforce visually the equivalence of ten tens and one hundred.

I removed the blocks and said, "Watch as I project another combination of blocks." This time I counted out nine longs and then ten ones cubes. "Talk to your neighbor about how much these are worth altogether," I said. After a few moments, I called the students to attention and asked for their answer in a whisper voice.

"One hundred," they whispered.

"Who would like to explain?" I asked.

I called on Adama and she said, "I counted the longs and I got to ninety. Then I counted on the ones—ninety-one, ninety-two, like that—and I got to one hundred."

Jessie added, "I did it kind of the same. The longs are ninety altogether, and the little cubes are ten, so ninety plus ten more is one hundred exactly."

Tina, who always referred to things visually, said, "You can push them together

32 **Lessons for Extending Place Value**

and then you can see that it's one hundred." I did this, arranging the nine longs and ten ones cubes into the shape of a flat.

Vinay said, "It's like what I did before, but I used five longs and fifty little cubes."

"You're absolutely right," I said, acknowledging Vinay's earlier contribution by replacing the blocks on the overhead projector with five longs and fifty ones cubes.

I cleared the projector again and put up just one long. I asked, "How many little cubes would I need to add to show one hundred?" The students were clear that I would need ninety ones cubes.

FIGURING THE VALUE OF ELEVEN TENS AND TWO ONES

I cleared the projector once more. I again put up longs, counting by ones as I did so until there were eleven longs. Then I also placed two ones cubes on the projector. I asked the students, "How much is this worth altogether?" They raised their hands quickly.

Adama explained, "You have eleven longs, so that's one hundred ten, and two ones cubes, so that's one hundred twelve altogether." Other students indicated their agreement with Adama's thinking by putting their thumbs up. I wrote on the board:

11 tens and 2 ones is 112.

I then asked, "Did anyone have another way of figuring out that these blocks together are worth one hundred twelve?"

I called on Tina and she explained, "Ten longs can make a flat, so you can push them together to make a flat, or you can take them away and put a flat instead. That's one hundred. Then the one long that's left makes one hundred ten. Then add on the two ones and that's one hundred twelve." I did as Tina instructed, carefully counting and pushing together ten of the longs on the projector.

I laid a flat on top of them to show that they were equivalent amounts and then removed the ten longs, leaving the flat in their place. There were a few looks of surprise along with a few comments, such as "Wow!" and "Hey, there can either be eleven tens or one hundred and one ten!" I wasn't surprised by these comments. Many students leave second grade able to identify the ones, tens, and hundreds places but not understanding the meaning of the digits in those places. Children need many experiences to develop this understanding. I wrote on the board, adding this idea to what I had already recorded:

11 tens and 2 ones is 112.
1 hundred and 1 ten and 2 ones is 112.

Several children had their hands raised, eager to share more ideas. I called on Tanya and she said, "You could make one hundred twelve with one hundred twelve ones cubes!" She giggled as she continued, "I don't think I'd want to do that because it would be a pain to count all those cubes right!"

I said to the class, "Who would like to explain either why Tanya's idea makes sense or why it doesn't?" Again hands waved wildly in the air. This was an idea that made sense to the children, and they were eager to share their thoughts.

James explained, "What Tanya said is good because it takes ten ones to make a ten. There are eleven tens, so count by ten eleven times and that's the same as one hundred ten ones. Then add the two ones and that's one hundred twelve ones." I pointed to the base ten blocks as the class counted by tens, as James had suggested, and then added the two ones. I added to what I had recorded on the board, this time shifting to using an equals sign instead of the word *is*.

11 tens and 2 ones is 112.
1 hundred and 1 ten and 2 ones is 112.
112 ones = 112

Exploring Ones, Tens, and Hundreds with Base Ten Blocks 33

Rachel had another way of thinking. She explained, "The flat is equal to one hundred ones. That's a hundred. The long is equal to ten ones. Add one hundred with ten and you have one hundred ten ones. Then, like James said, add the last two ones and that's one hundred twelve." I recorded Rachel's idea with only mathematical symbols, not words.

11 tens and 2 ones is 112.
1 hundred and 1 ten and 2 ones is 112.
112 ones = 112
100 + 10 = 110
110 + 2 = 112

INTRODUCING AN INDEPENDENT EXPLORATION

I wrote *72* on the overhead and said, "In a few minutes, you and a partner will be exploring different ways to show seventy-two using the tens and ones blocks. But first I'll show you how to record your ideas on paper." I placed seven longs and two ones cubes on the overhead projector. I pointed to the blocks and asked, "How much are these blocks worth?" As I watched, many children pointed to the projected overhead blocks while counting to themselves. When all hands were up, I asked the children to whisper their answer.

"Seventy-two," they chorused in whisper voices.

On the board, I modeled for the children how to record this way of representing seventy-two.

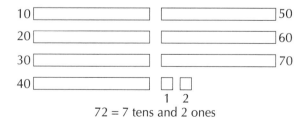

72 = 7 tens and 2 ones

Abel had a question. "Can we just draw a straight line for the tens sticks?"

"Yes," I agreed, nodding. Then I added, "You and your partner are to build seventy-two with other combinations of the tens and ones blocks, the way we built one hundred in different ways. Record each way you find as I did for the example I showed."

"Hey, Abel just made me think of something!" Tobias exclaimed. "Some ways of making seventy-two need a lot of ones. Can I just make Xs instead of little boxes?" Again I nodded.

"I think I know a lot of ways to do this," Jade said.

I continued with the instructions for the exploration. "You'll work with your partner, but each of you will record on your own piece of paper. You'll have to share blocks with the other people at your table because there may not be enough for everyone to have his or her own. After I hand you your paper, please put your name and the date at the top, write *Seventy-Two* as the title, and copy onto your paper the way we made seventy-two together. Remember to record your ideas using a picture and with numbers." I pointed to my recording on the board once again. I handed each student a sheet of paper and the students got to work on the exploration.

Observing the Students

As the students worked, I circulated through the class, watching for problems and answering questions. Tobias's table was in the process of dividing the base ten blocks equally among the partners. I suggested to them that it might be better to leave the blocks together and take them as they needed them. Ben's table had already divided the blocks and the students were starting to argue with one another as they discovered they didn't have enough. With a look of frustration on his face, Ben said to his group, "Stop! I told you there weren't enough. Mrs. Wickett said there weren't enough. Now we know there aren't enough! Just put the blocks back in the middle so we can use them when we need them!"

While the others agreed with Ben and returned their blocks to the center of the table, Jade wouldn't give up her blocks. The other children got mad at Jade and were starting to yell at her, but Tina patiently asked Jade, "Why won't you cooperate and just put your blocks back so we can all get to work?"

Jade thought about Tina's question a moment and then responded, "No one ever shares with me. I don't want to share."

Tina replied, "Well, I'll share with you— I promise." Jade looked at Tina intently for a moment and then put her blocks back in the center of the table. The group then got to work.

After working through a few initial problems, the students worked well together and came up with multiple ways to build seventy-two using the base ten blocks. The exploration was accessible to all of the students but was more difficult for Karena than for most other students. I sat with her and gave her individual help while the other students completed the task. I started by giving Karena smaller numbers to think about. Together we explored different ways to use the base ten blocks to make twenty, then twenty-three, and finally thirty-four. By the time we finished working on thirty-four, she wanted to work on seventy-two without my help. I had found that with Karena I often had to go back to a simpler related problem to reinforce prior knowledge or develop a concept and then carefully build step-by-step to the level of the rest of the students.

Arin, another student who often had difficulty, was thrilled with her work. She worked very hard and carefully and found three ways to make seventy-two using the base ten blocks. Her work was correct and she was gaining confidence in her understanding and ability in math. (See Figure 3–1.)

Jessie came up with a unique way of thinking about the investigation. She started with a flat, subtracted three longs, or thirty, and then added two ones. She couldn't figure out how to represent her idea on her paper, but she used the materials to show her thinking to me. She finally decided to use words to record her idea on her paper. (See Figure 3–2.)

Sam waved his hand. He explained, "I think I found a pattern. Every time the tens go down by one, that adds ten to the ones pile. I wonder if it would always work that way for any number?" (See Figure 3–3.)

I asked Sam's partner if she agreed. Jael indicated she did. I looked at Sam's work and could see how he was thinking. I decided to give them an additional challenge that would also go along with what he was wondering. I said, "Together, explore one hundred twenty-four and see if Sam's idea works for that number." Sam jumped up to get two sheets of paper and then he and Jael got to work.

Vinay, who was sitting across the room, had the same idea as Sam. He wrote about it on his paper. (See Figure 3–4.)

Jillian showed her understanding of tens and ones as she showed her ideas with pictures and numbers. (See Figure 3–5.)

As the students finished, I looked over their papers, asked for further clarification when needed, and then gave them the same challenge problem I'd given Sam and Jael—to find as many ways as possible to make 124 using base ten blocks.

Ben and Vinay worked together on the challenge. Initially, Vinay's work reflected his earlier thinking as he systematically explored the possibilities by reducing the number of tens by one and increasing the number of ones by ten. He recognized that when he got to thirty-four ones and nine tens, he no longer could use a hundreds flat. (See Figure 3–6.)

Exploring Ones, Tens, and Hundreds with Base Ten Blocks   35

▲▲▲▲▲▲Figure 3–1   Arin showed her growing understanding by making seventy-two in three ways.

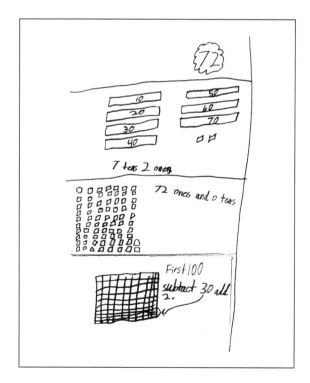

▲▲▲▲▲▲Figure 3–2   Jessie had difficulty showing her third idea using a picture, but she was able to explain it orally and with words.

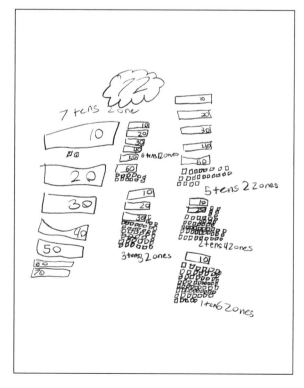

▲▲▲▲▲▲Figure 3–3   Sam used pictures to represent a pattern of tens and ones.

36   Lessons for Extending Place Value

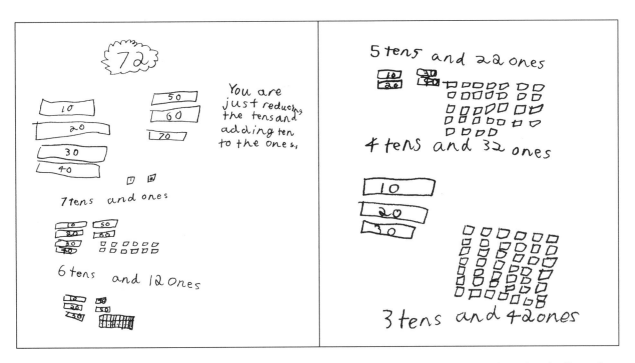

▲▲▲▲▲▲Figure 3–4 *Vinay discovered the same pattern as Sam. His written explanation indicated clear understanding.*

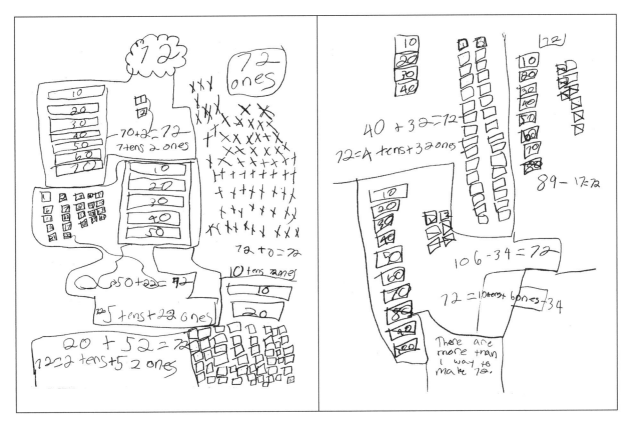

▲▲▲▲▲▲Figure 3–5 *Jillian showed flexibility in her unique ways of thinking about seventy-two.*

Exploring Ones, Tens, and Hundreds with Base Ten Blocks 37

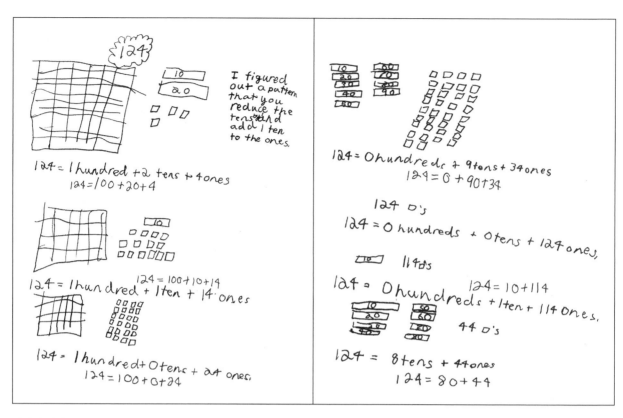

▲▲▲▲▲▲Figure 3–6   *Vinay applied the pattern he noticed earlier to the more challenging problem of making 124. He also used expanded notation to represent his words and pictures.*

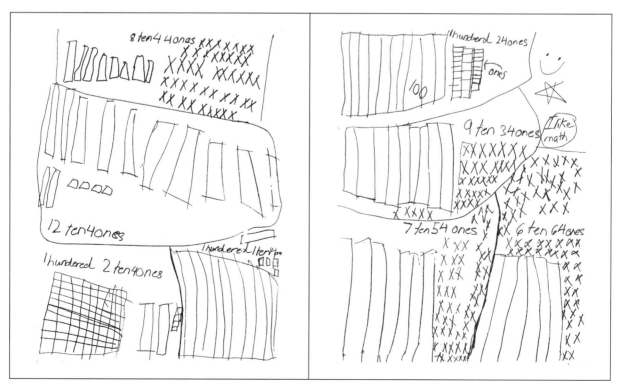

▲▲▲▲▲▲Figure 3–7   *Ben's paper showed many ways of using base ten blocks to make 124.*

38   Lessons for Extending Place Value

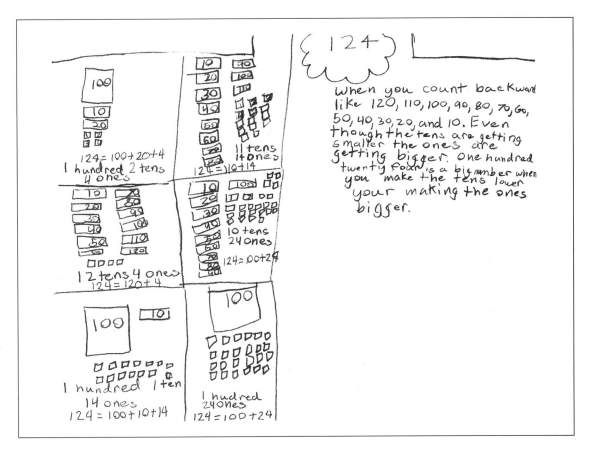

▲▲▲▲▲Figure 3–8   *Sam concluded that as he decreased the number of tens, the number of ones increased.*

Although the two boys talked about their ideas as they worked, Ben's paper revealed a more random approach than Vinay had taken. (See Figure 3–7.)

Sam was pleased to see that his idea worked; that is, decreasing the tens by one ten always results in an increase of ten in the ones. (See Figure 3–8.)

While the students initially worked together in pairs, as they got more involved in the exploration and shared the blocks, they also shared ideas with their entire table group.

I gave the students a five-minute warning. When the five minutes were up, I asked them to return the blocks to the baskets. Then as a way of summarizing and sharing with the whole group, I asked each table group, one by one, to send a representative to the board to draw one way of building seventy-two with the base ten blocks that

was different from the ones already on the board. After each person recorded, I asked the rest of the students to indicate by raising their hands if the way shared was also one of the ways they had found.

EXTENSIONS

To give students additional practice, build their number sense and confidence, and deepen their understanding of the base ten number system, repeat this experience for other two-digit numbers, such as 54, 63, and 87. To provide more of a challenge, ask students to represent with base ten blocks three-digit numbers such as 105, 136, and 221. (**Note:** The size of the three-digit numbers you assign will depend on the amount of flats you have available for students to use.)

Exploring Ones, Tens, and Hundreds with Base Ten Blocks   39

Questions and Discussion

▲▲

▲ *What suggestions do you have if the number seventy-two seems too easy or too difficult for my students?*

There is nothing magical about the number seventy-two. If seventy-two seems too difficult for your children, chose a smaller number, such as twenty, twenty-four, or thirty-two, that's easier for students to visualize.

I suggest, however, that you start with seventy-two even if it you think it will be easy for your students. This can provide access and success for all, will reinforce previous learning, and will strengthen the students' foundation of understanding. Then move to three-digit numbers. Sometimes children bump into difficulty when counting beyond one hundred, especially when counting by tens.

A nice aspect of this lesson is that once you are confident children understand what to do, you can assign them different numbers—smaller, more familiar numbers for those needing additional support, reinforcement, and experience and larger numbers for those needing a challenge.

▲ *I don't have access to base ten blocks. What are some alternatives?*

If you don't have access to base ten blocks or don't have enough, and if borrowing them is not an option, there are a few alternatives that work for this lesson.

One alternative is to use the Base Ten Blocks Blackline Master in the back of this book to make copies of base ten blocks on tagboard. Ask a parent volunteer, older students, or your own students to cut them out carefully. For this lesson you'll need at least twenty-five ones, twelve longs, and one flat per student. If you expect to use numbers beyond 150, you'll need additional longs and flats. Quart-size zip-top bags work well for storage.

If your school has a die cutter, you may be able to get a set of base ten cutters. One issue with this method is the lines are not on the longs and flats, making the relationships among the blocks more difficult for students to determine.

Some publishers have inexpensive plastic sets of ones, tens, and hundreds available. Also, when it comes time to explore thousands, these same publishers also have cardboard thousand cubes available at inexpensive prices.

▲ *Why do you suggest children explore with a material prior to using it for instructional purposes? Isn't this a waste a valuable instructional time?*

Providing time for exploration of a new material prior to instruction allows most children to satisfy their curiosity about the material, which in turn allows them to better focus on the instruction. Exploration of a material is not a waste of time, particularly if the exploration is structured, as it is in this lesson. My request that students investigate the relationships among the blocks as part of their exploration actually served as the foundation for the instruction that followed.

▲ *If Jade wasn't satisfied after Tina had assured her that she would share the blocks with her, would you have intervened?*

I was pleased that the group was able to resolve the issue of sharing blocks without intervention from me. However, I most certainly would have intervened if this hadn't been the case. An issue such as this one is important to resolve early in the year. I have many discussions with the students to help them learn how to work together, cooperate, and be sensitive to one another's needs.

40   Lessons for Extending Place Value

CHAPTER FOUR
THOUSANDS AND BEYOND
EXPLORING LARGER NUMBERS

Overview

In this lesson, students use base ten blocks to grapple conceptually with larger numbers. First students use the base ten blocks to review relationships among ones, tens, and hundreds. Then, building on these ideas, they use the blocks to represent one thousand and then ten thousand.

Materials

▲ base ten blocks, 11 one-thousand cubes, and at least 10 each of ones cubes, longs, and flats
▲ 5 4-by-6-inch or larger cards folded in half and numbered as follows: 1; 10; 100; 1,000; 10,000

Time

▲ one class period

Teaching Directions

1. Review the relationships among the base ten blocks.

2. Place base ten blocks as shown so that all students can see them (see page 42). Discuss that 10 ones cubes make 1 long, 10 longs or 100 ones cubes make 1 flat, and the blocks increase in size order by ten times.

41

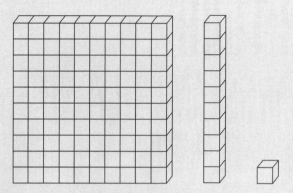

3. To introduce the one-thousand cube, ask students to predict what the next larger block will look like and how many blocks it will take to make it. If a student suggests it, build the one-thousand cube using ten flats. If no student makes this suggestion, do it as a way to introduce the one-thousand cube.

4. Write on the board *1,000* and tell students ten hundreds, or ten flats, equal one thousand. Ask students: "How many longs, or tens blocks, are needed to make a one-thousand cube?" As the students think about this, write the following on the board beneath the 1,000:

> *10 hundreds (flats) = 1,000*
> *? tens (longs) = 1,000*

5. Lead a discussion for students to share their ideas about the number of longs in one thousand. When students agree it takes one hundred tens to equal one thousand, change the question mark shown in Step 4 to *100*.

6. To help students understand that one thousand ones cubes are equivalent to the one-thousand cube, count by hundreds the flats needed to make a one-thousand cube.

7. Ask students: "Does ten hundred equal one thousand?" Lead a class discussion on this point to guide and cement students' understanding that ten hundred is equivalent to one thousand. Add the following to the information already on the board:

> *1,000 ones = 10 hundreds = 1,000*

8. Add the one-thousand cube to the sequence of blocks from Step 1. Label each block with the appropriate number card. Discuss any new patterns children see in the sequence, the relative sizes of the blocks, the numerals, or the block shapes. Record any patterns students share on the board.

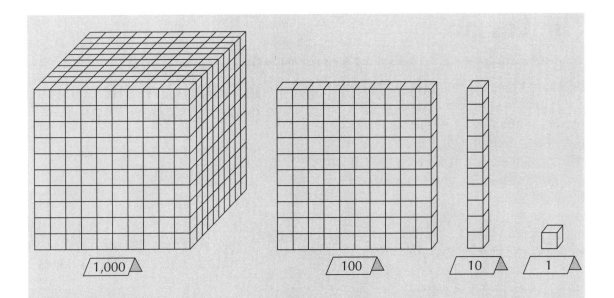

9. Explain to the students they are going to be block designers. Ask them to think about what the next larger block could look like and then share with a partner. Ask volunteers to share their ideas with the whole group. Help students come to the conclusion that the next block is a ten-thousand long. Use ten one-thousand cubes to build the ten-thousand long and label it as you did with the ones, tens, hundreds, and thousands blocks.

Teaching Notes

Students should have previous experience with Chapter 3, "Exploring Ones, Tens, and Hundreds with Base Ten Blocks." This prerequisite lesson provides the foundation for the big ideas in this lesson.

When placed in size order, each base ten block is ten times larger than the previous block. For example, a long is equivalent to ten ones cubes, a flat is equivalent to ten longs, and a one-thousand cube is equivalent to ten flats. Also, the introduction of the one-thousand cube can reveal to students that the shapes of the blocks begin a pattern that will continue for larger blocks: cube, long, flat, cube, and so on. Later in the lesson, students discover that a block that represents ten thousand can be constructed from ten one-thousand cubes, making a larger long block.

The students in the vignette were beginning third graders and had little or no previous experience with multiplication. As this lesson progressed, however, they began thinking and talking with ease about the blocks in terms of multiplication, recognizing, for example, that ten groups of ten equal one hundred and that one hundred groups of ten equal one thousand. This lesson supported the development of children's thinking about multiplication.

Thousands and Beyond   43

The Lesson

▲▲

I gathered the students on the floor in a circle and brought out a supply of base ten blocks. In the middle of the circle, I placed a ones cube, a long, and a flat so all students could see them. I asked the students, "What do you know about these base ten blocks?"

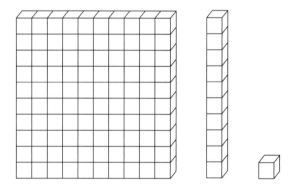

Kassidee volunteered, "I know it takes ten little cubes to make the long."

Abel added, "And it takes ten longs to make a flat. You can get ten longs and lay them on top of the flat to prove it. The ten longs and the flat will match exactly." I handed Abel a flat and a handful of longs so he could prove his point to the rest of the students.

Jael said, "I think it takes one hundred of the little blocks to equal the flat one, but I'm not really too sure."

Jessie jumped in, "Jael's right, I'm sure. There are ten ones in a long and ten longs in a flat, so that makes ten tens in one hundred. Count by ten, ten times and you'll be on a hundred." Many students nodded their agreement.

The students were confident and comfortable in their knowledge of how these base ten blocks related to each other.

INTRODUCING THE ONE-THOUSAND CUBE

I then asked the class, "What do you think the next larger base ten block will look like?" Some students' hands immediately shot up while other children, whose experience was more limited, needed a few moments to consider my question. I waited until most children had their hands up and called on James.

James explained with some hesitation, "Maybe it will be some flats laid in a row."

I asked James, "Why do you think you'll need flats for the next block?"

"Well," James began and then paused. "It seems like each bigger block uses the block that's just before it. Like the tens block uses ones blocks, and the hundreds block uses tens blocks." Several students nodded their agreement, but Halley wasn't convinced that she completely agreed with James.

Halley said, "I think James is partly right, but he's missing something. You can make a flat with ten longs like he said, but you can also make it with one hundred cubes or even some cubes and some longs."

"Oh yeah!" James agreed. "But still, you can make the next bigger block with just ten of the blocks before it."

Connor came alive. "James just gave me a really smart idea. Each new block is ten times bigger than the block before it! It takes ten blocks to make the next bigger block. Ten ones make a ten, and ten tens make a hundred."

Connor's comment generated nods from several other students although many looked uncertain. To reinforce the idea that the blocks increased ten times in size and to give those who were unsure another perspective on Connor's idea, I said to the children, "Who would like to explain Connor's idea in your own words?" I called on Jillian.

Jillian explained, "If you put the blocks in order from littlest to biggest, each time you make a bigger block, it takes ten of the blocks that were just before it."

I asked, "So we could build the next larger block with flats?" Jillian and others nodded.

"How many flats would we need?" I asked, directing this question to the class. "Raise a hand if you think you know." While I knew that this was obvious to some of the children, I wanted to check that others were also sure that we'd need to use ten flats to build the next larger block. I called on James to respond.

"Maybe six," James said. I was surprised by his answer, especially because of what he had contributed earlier about needing ten blocks to build the next size.

"Why do you think six?" I probed. James shrugged, unable to explain. I called on Arin.

"Ten," Arin said, but she also couldn't explain why.

I said to the rest of the class, "Who else thinks ten?" Many hands went up. "Who would like to explain your thinking?" Most hands stayed up. I called on Olina.

Olina explained, "I think ten because with the other blocks, like we said earlier, it takes ten of the block before it to make the next bigger block." The other students nodded their agreement.

Roberto had had his hand up, patiently waiting to share his thoughts. I didn't call on him earlier as I knew he had lots of previous experience with base ten blocks, and I wanted to provide others the opportunity to think and share their ideas. But now I called on him. Roberto explained, "I know what the next bigger block is. Can I share?" I nodded. He continued, "It's ten flats piled on top of each other. They make a big cube."

I asked Roberto to show his idea using the blocks. He carefully stacked ten flats.

"How much are these ten flats worth altogether?" I asked the rest of the students. "Talk about this with your neighbor." The class got noisy and then quieted down as children raised their hands to report.

"Let's say the answer together in whisper voices," I said.

"One thousand," many said.

"Who can explain how you figured that out?" I asked.

Tanya explained, "You can count by hundreds because each flat is one hundred ones." To verify Tanya's thinking, I pointed to each of the stacked flats as she counted aloud by hundreds.

Then I showed the students a one-thousand cube and set it next to the stacked flats to verify that the cube and the stacked flats were equivalent.

"Hey, it's like a big ones block!" Isaac said.

There was a flurry of comments from the students, such as "Wow!" "Oh yeah!" and "I see that!"

I wrote *1,000* on the board. I pointed to it and explained, "This is how to write one thousand. It takes ten hundreds to make one thousand."

I paused a moment and then I asked, "How many blocks do you think I'd need if I wanted to make a one-thousand cube using just longs, the tens blocks?" I paused to give students time to consider my question. As the students thought about my question, I wrote on the board:

10 hundreds (flats) = 1,000
? tens (longs) = 1,000

I gave the students a few moments to talk among themselves and then asked for their attention. Many had their hands raised, eager to share. I called on Tina.

Tina said, "To make a one-thousand cube with tens, I think you need one hundred longs."

I said to the other students, "Put a thumb up if you agree with Tina's idea, put a thumb down if you disagree, or hold your thumb sideways if you're not certain." Most students held their thumbs up. I asked Tina to explain her reasoning.

Tina continued, "It takes ten longs to make a flat, or a hundred, and there are ten flats, or ten hundreds, so ten times ten is one hundred."

I asked the class, "Who would like to restate Tina's idea using your own words?"

Vinay volunteered to restate Tina's thinking. "There are ten flats in a thousand cube. You can trade the flats for ten longs for each flat. Ten longs for one flat, twenty for two flats, thirty for three, and like that until you trade in all the flats for longs. There are ten flats, so ten times ten, and that's one hundred longs."

Adama was eager to show Tina and Vinay's idea using the base ten blocks. She carefully stacked ten flats to form the cube, then compared it with the one-thousand cube to be sure they were equivalent. Next she used her finger to indicate where the longs were drawn on the flat, proving there were ten longs on a flat. Finally she counted the flats by tens to figure the number of tens.

I pointed to what I had written on the board and replaced the question mark with *100*:

10 hundreds (flats) = 1,000
100 tens (longs) = 1,000

I then said to the class, "I think it would take one thousand of the little cubes, the ones, to build the one-thousand cube. It would be very hard to build because the little cubes would keep falling and moving." I pointed to the stack of ten flats that Adama had built. "But we can

count using these," I continued. "There are one hundred ones cubes in a flat. Let's count by hundreds." The children counted along with me as I pointed to each flat in the stack. "One hundred, two hundred, three hundred, four hundred, five hundred, six hundred, seven hundred, eight hundred, nine hundred, ten hundred." While I and some of the children said "ten hundred," most of the students said "one thousand."

I asked, "Does ten hundred equal one thousand? Show me with a thumb up if you think yes, a thumb down if you think no, or a thumb turned sideways if you aren't sure." Some students put their thumbs up, some put their thumbs down, and some put their thumbs sideways. Even though I'd written on the board that ten hundreds equal one thousand, I wasn't surprised with the variety of their responses and was glad for the opportunity to explore this further. I know that writing information on the board as I had done is helpful to some but not all students, and further exploration is often needed.

I pointed to where I'd written 1,000 on the board. I explained, "This is how to write one thousand. When we counted by hundreds, after nine hundred some of us said ten hundred. Is ten hundred the same as one thousand? Who would like to share your thinking?" Several students raised their hands. I called on Keara.

Keara said, "I don't think you can say ten hundred, so I don't think there's any such number as ten hundred."

Jael commented, "I think the way we counted by hundreds to ten hundred is right, but I haven't heard the number ten hundred. I thought it was one thousand, like nine hundred ninety-nine and then one thousand. I think I'm confused."

Tanya said, "I think ten hundred and one thousand are the same. If you look at how one thousand is written on the board, the first two digits say ten and the last two zeros are the hundred part, so ten hundred. I think it's like when we were making one hundred twenty-four a few days ago. One hundred twenty-four could be made with a flat, two tens, and four ones, or it could be made with twelve tens and four ones. You could see where the twelve tens is written in one hundred twenty-four." Tanya was referring to a lesson we'd recently done, described in Chapter 3, "Exploring Ones, Tens, and Hundreds with Base Ten Blocks."

Kito shared, "I think ten hundred and one thousand are the same. You can think of it like money. A little cube is like a penny, and then a long is a dime, and a flat is one dollar, and that's a hundred pennies. You could have ten one-dollar bills, which is like having ten flats or ten hundreds.

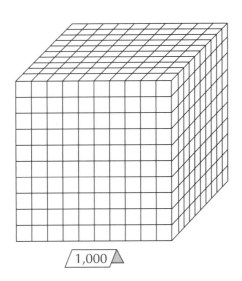

1,000

Each dollar is like one hundred pennies, so that's ten hundred pennies. Or you could have one thousand pennies. It's the same thing. Really!"

No one else wanted to share. I said, "Ten hundred and one thousand are two ways of describing the same number. We usually don't say ten hundred, but we could." I then added to what I'd written on the board:

10 hundreds (flats) = 1,000
100 tens (longs) = 1,000
1,000 ones = 10 hundreds = 1,000

BEYOND THE ONE-THOUSAND CUBE

To reinforce for students how to write the numbers represented by the base ten blocks, I arranged one of each block in size order, starting with the one-thousand cube on the left, followed by a hundreds flat, a tens long, and a ones cube on the far right. I placed the appropriate number card in front of each block. Third graders often have difficulty reading and writing numbers beyond one hundred and I wanted to help them connect a concrete representation of each number to the numerals.

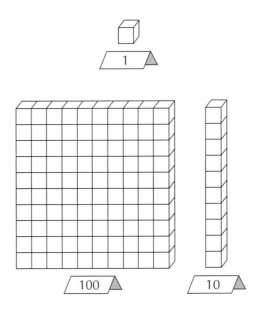

1   100   10

Sam said, "The blocks go cube, long, flat, cube."

Connor restated his earlier observation that consecutive blocks were ten times larger than the one before it when going from smallest to largest.

I wrote both ideas on the board:

Sam   The blocks go cube, long, flat, cube.

Connor *When going in order from smallest to largest, each block is ten times larger than the block just before it.*

If Sam and Connor or some other students hadn't shared these ideas, I would have drawn them out with questions.

Next I said to the class, "Today, you'll be the base ten block designer. Using Sam's and Connor's ideas, think quietly to yourself about how you would design the next block and what number it would represent." I paused for a few moments to give the students time to think. I continued, "Share your ideas with your partner. First one of you talks while the other listens without interrupting. Then, after thirty seconds, the first talker listens and the first listener talks." The children erupted with ideas. After thirty seconds, I gave a signal for the children to switch roles. At the end of the second thirty seconds, I asked for the children's attention. The students were eager to share their ideas with the group. I called on Ben.

Ben said, "Maybe the next block should be a cube. I'm not sure why; it just seems like it should be a cube."

I asked Ben, "How many will be in your next block?" He shrugged.

Christopher shared next. "I'm not sure, but I think if the blocks go cube, long, flat, cube, like Sam said, then I think the next block should be a long. It follows a pattern."

"Hey, he took my idea!" Jillian blurted.

I responded, "So Jillian had the same idea as Christopher. Did anyone else have the idea that the next block could be a long?" Many of the students raised their hands to indicate they had had the same idea. Ben looked puzzled; then he smiled and waved his hand to get my attention.

Ben said, "I think my idea was wrong. I just thought there would be cubes from now on. I forgot to think about what Sam said. If the last block was a cube, then the next one should be long. Now what I don't get is how long it will be!" If Ben or another student hadn't posed this question, I would have. Many hands were up. I called on Olina.

Olina said, "I think there should be six one-thousand cubes to make the long." I was surprised by Olina's idea.

I asked, "Why do you think that six of the one-thousand cubes are needed?"

"Well," Olina began, "there are six sides on a cube, so I just thought there must be six cubes to make a long."

As I responded, I corrected Olina's mathematical language and restated what I understood her to say: "I agree there are six faces on a cube. Are you saying that for each face, you need a cube to make the long?" Olina nodded.

Jessie said, "I disagree. So far it always takes ten of the block before to make a new block. I think it will take ten of the one-thousand cubes to make the new block. I think it will be a really long block."

"How many ones would be in your new block?" I asked Jessie.

Jessie said hesitantly, "Um, maybe ten thousand?"

"Hey! Yeah, that works!" Connor said. "Can we build it to be sure?"

"Yeah!" "Cool!" "Can we do it?" others blunted out enthusiastically.

I didn't have enough one-thousand cubes for the children to explore independently or even in pairs or small groups. I said to the students, "There aren't enough one-thousand cubes for you to each do this, or even to do it in pairs or small groups, so we'll build it together. We seem to agree the new block should be a long, and many of you think it should have ten of the one-thousand cubes. Picture in your minds for a moment what the block might look like and how you might build it."

I paused, and then I asked Tobias and Karena to build it. Together they placed ten of the one-thousand cubes side by side on the floor to create a long block. The other students agreed. We counted by thousands, one one-thousand cube at a time, to confirm that the block represented ten thousand. I placed the card with 10,000 written on it beside our new construction.

"Hey, the number just added another zero to one thousand," Arin noticed.

With Arin's comment, I ended the class.

Questions and Discussion

▲▲▲

▲ *When you wrote 1,000 on the board, you put in the comma. But sometimes we don't use the comma. Is it always necessary?*

It isn't always necessary, but I think it's helpful to use the comma to begin the pattern of using it in larger numbers. Being consistent helps reinforce the idea of how commas are used in large numbers. But you also may want to let your students know that it's not mandatory to use a comma with numbers that have only four digits, but it is required for numbers with more than four digits.

CHAPTER FIVE
COUNTING TO TEN THOUSAND

Overview

This lesson begins and ends with the book *Count to a Million* by Jerry Pallotta. The book explores how numbers in the base ten number system grow and compares the relative sizes of numbers. During the lesson, the students work together to draw and gather ten thousand tally marks. First, each student draws as many tally marks as possible in one minute, then each student asks an adult at home to do the same, and finally another class helps out by doing the activity. The students gather tally marks until they have collected ten thousand. Along the way, students solve addition and subtraction problems involving large numbers.

Materials

▲ *Count to a Million: 1,000,000,* by Jerry Pallotta (New York: Scholastic, 2003)
▲ 30 3-by-24-inch sentence strips cut into thirds to make 3-by-8-inch strips, or construction paper cut into 90 3-by-8-inch strips
▲ clock with a second hand, a stopwatch, or some other way to time one minute

Time

▲ three class periods

Teaching Directions

1. Share the first page of *Count to a Million,* by Jerry Pallotta, which states, "If you can count to ten, you can count to one million." Discuss with students how this is possible. Then continue reading the book aloud, stopping to discuss questions and comments as appropriate.

2. Ask and discuss with students: "Do you think if we worked together, we could draw a million tally marks?" Then ask: "How many tally marks do you think you could draw in one minute?" Record on the board students' estimates.

3. Model for students on the board how to draw tally marks in groups of five

$$\cancel{||||}$$

and then in rows of ten.

$$\cancel{||||} \ \cancel{||||}$$
$$\cancel{||||} \ \cancel{||||}$$

4. Ask the students to time you for one minute. Using a 3-by-8-inch strip turned vertically, draw tally marks in rows of ten.

5. Allow students to revise their estimates.

6. Give each student a 3-by-8-inch strip. Write on the board:

I predict I can draw _____ tally marks in one minute.

Have the students copy and complete the sentence on one side of the sentence strip.

7. Ask students to turn their sentence strips over and to turn them vertically. Time one minute as they draw tally marks.

8. Discuss strategies for students to use to count their tally marks. Have each student use a strategy that makes sense to him or her to count the tally marks. Ask each to record his or her total on the back under the prediction.

9. After students have figured their individual totals, have each table group figure the total number of tally marks the group drew. Record on the board each group's total. Together figure the class total and how many more tally marks are needed to make ten thousand.

10. Ask students to cut off any unused part at the bottom of their strips. Give each group a long piece of tape and ask them to tape their strips together vertically, making sure that their first strip has at least one hundred tally marks. Finally, making sure the first strip has at least one hundred tally marks, tape each group's strips together to form one long class strip. Write the total tally marks shown on the class strip next to the bottom row.

11. Lead a class discussion to help students understand how numbers in the base ten number system grow. Beginning with the first strip, which should have at least one hundred tally marks, circle the first tally mark on the class strip of tally marks and tell the children the tally mark represents one. Then draw a line around the entire first row.

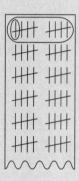

Say: "This is ten. Ten is ten times bigger than one. What is ten times bigger than ten?" (One hundred) Draw a line around the first ten rows of ten on the class strip. Ask students: "Do we have enough tally marks on our class strip to have ten times one hundred?" (It takes one thousand.) Ask students: "How many rows of ten are needed to make one thousand?" (One hundred) Count and draw a line around ten groups of ten rows to show one thousand.

12. For homework, give each student a 3-by-8-inch strip. Ask each student to time one minute as an adult or older brother or sister makes tally marks.

13. On Day 2, have students figure their group totals of homework tally marks. Record each group's total on the board and figure the class homework total.

14. Figure the sum of the class total and the homework total.

15. Repeat Step 10 to make a homework tally mark strip for the class. Compare the class strip and the homework strip. Then tape the two strips together to create one long strip. Write the total tally marks for both strips next to the last row on the strip.

16. With the students, figure the number of tally marks still needed to reach ten thousand.

17. Decide how to gather the remaining tally marks needed to reach ten thousand. In the following vignette, another class helped out.

18. Return to *Count to a Million.* Relate the picture of the planet Earth to the circled first tally mark on the ten-thousand strip. Relate the ten ladybugs to the first circled row of tally marks. Continue connecting the ideas in the book to the ten-thousand strip.

19. Display the completed ten-thousand strip for students to admire and to reinforce their learning during the lesson.

Teaching Notes

Count to a Million, by Jerry Pallotta, shows children how they can count to a million if they can count to ten. He briefly explains place value in the base ten number system followed by pleasing, colorful illustrations showing how each new place in numbers is ten times larger than the place immediately before it. The illustrations delight children, clarify how numbers grow, and serve as a springboard for discussion. The book begins by showing a picture of the planet Earth, representing the number one, and ends by representing one million with screaming sports fans in ten stadiums, or groups, of one hundred thousand.

During the lesson, children gain understanding of the relative sizes of 1, 10, 100, 1,000, and 10,000. The students each draw as many tally marks as they can in one minute, count them, and then combine their totals for a class total. This experience builds students' number sense as they continue to count and combine until they have 10,000 tally marks.

In the following vignette, there were thirty children in the class. Gathering ten thousand tally marks required all thirty children to draw tally marks, most of them to repeat the experience at home with their parents, and another third-grade class of thirty students to draw tally marks. If you have a class smaller than thirty students, you may need to repeat drawing tally marks in one minute a fourth time before you have ten thousand.

It's important to have children turn their strips vertically and draw tally marks in rows of ten. Doing so makes the tally marks easier to count by tens, thus relating to the base ten number system.

The Lesson

DAY 1

"I'd like to have a million dollars!" Olina stated as I held up the book *Count to a Million,* by Jerry Pallotta.

"I think a million pizzas would be good," Christopher added. "And I'd eat them all!" Christopher and the others giggled.

"Or a million Hershey's kisses. I love Hershey's kisses!" Ana said.

After a few more students shared their ideas about having a million of something, I settled the class and began to read the first page, "If you can count to ten, you can count to one million." I asked the students, "How do you think this is possible?" The students thought quietly for a few moments and then hands began to go up. When most students had their hands up, I called on Jael.

Jael shared, "Maybe it means you could count to one million by tens. I think that would take a very long time."

Jillian had a different idea. She explained, "I think it means if you can count to ten, you just keep doing it over and over again. The ones place just keeps repeating, like one, then two, then three, like that." Jillian sighed and seemed to be searching for words to express her thinking. "The ones place when you count goes one, two, three, four, and so on. When it gets to nine, the tens place adds one and the ones place starts again . . . oh, I don't know, it's too complicated to explain!"

I appreciated Jillian's effort and struggle to express herself. Rather than comment on what she'd said or attempt to paraphrase her words to clarify her thoughts for her and the others, I decided to continue reading the next two pages knowing the information presented there could support Jillian. When the students saw the next spread, showing ten ladybugs, Roberto noticed that the dots on the backs of the ladybugs went from one to ten. The students immediately noticed on the following spread that this pattern carried over to each of the ten groups of ten ladybugs.

I continued to read and share the book, encouraging students to share their comments and thoughts as we went. They were particularly intrigued by the spreads showing how ten thousand people grew to one hundred thousand people and one hundred thousand people grew to one million people.

"A million people is really a lot!" Connor commented.

Estimating How Many Tally Marks We Could Draw

I said to the students, "I agree with Connor: a million is a lot. I wonder how many tally marks we could draw as a class in one minute if each of us drew tally marks as fast as we could?" Excited chatter spread as students speculated among themselves.

After a few moments, I settled the students and asked, "Do you think if we worked together, we could draw a million tally marks in one minute?" Many students shook their heads, indicating they didn't think so, but several nodded, showing that they thought this was possible.

James said, "I don't think we can draw a million tally marks in a minute or even five minutes." Several students nodded, indicating their agreement with James's thinking. James continued, "There are twenty-nine of us here and Mrs. Wickett. That's thirty. If we only get one minute, I think drawing a million tallies would be impossible! If we each made one hundred that would be thirty times one hundred, or thirty hundreds. That's not even close to one million."

I asked James and the other students, "What's another way of saying thirty hundreds?" James shrugged.

Vinay said, "Thirty hundreds and three thousand are the same. You write thirty hundreds with a thirty and then two zeros after the thirty to show they are hundreds."

I wrote *3,000* on the board and then asked Vinay, "Is this what you mean?" He nodded.

Vinay continued, "You write three thousand with a three to tell how many thousands and then three zeros to show that the three means thousands." I wrote on the board *3,000*, and again Vinay nodded his agreement with what I'd written.

I was curious about what the students thought about the number of tally marks they could draw in one minute. I asked, "How many tally marks do you think you could draw in one minute?" Waving hands clearly indicated the students' eagerness to share. Each student who wanted to do so shared an estimate of how many tally marks he or she could draw in one minute. I recorded each guess on the board; their estimates ranged from twenty-three to one thousand.

The students' wide range of estimates indicated that they needed additional information on which to base their guesses. Also, I wanted to model for the students how they would draw their tally marks. I said, "I'm going to find out how many tally marks I can draw in one minute. Watching me will give you some information that might help you make a more accurate estimate about how many tally marks you can draw in one minute. I'll draw tally marks in groups of five by making four vertical lines crossed by a fifth horizontal line, like this." To model for the students, I drew on the board:

I continued, "Also, I am going to put my tally marks in rows of ten, with two groups of five in each row, like this." I continued drawing on the board:

The students were eager for me to get started. I decided instead of asking just one student to time me for one minute, I'd have the entire class tell me when to begin and when to stop. I explained to the students, "When the second hand reaches the twelve, say, 'Go!' I'll draw tally marks as fast as I can. When the second hand reaches the twelve a second time, say, 'Stop!' That will be one minute. Then we'll count how many tally marks I wrote." As the students turned their attention to the classroom clock, waiting with anticipation for the second hand to reach the 12, I quickly taped a 3-by-8-inch strip to the board vertically.

When the second hand reached the 10 on the clock, several students began a countdown until the second hand arrived at the 12. When they said, "Go!" I began making tally marks on the sentence strip. At the end of one minute the students said, "Stop!" Together we counted the tally marks I'd made, counting by tens. There were 176.

I gave the students the opportunity to revise and share their new estimates, again recording them on the board. The range of their guesses narrowed from 23 to 1,000 to 120 to 270.

Drawing Tally Marks

I gave each student a 3-by-8-inch strip and I wrote the following on the board:

I predict I can draw _____ tally marks in one minute.

I asked the students to copy what I'd written onto one side of their strips and to complete the sentence by filling in the blank with their best guesses. When all the students had done this, I asked them to turn their strips to the other side and turn them vertically. I explained to them, "It's important that your strip is turned vertically. This makes drawing tally marks in rows of ten easier and it will be easier for you to count them quickly and accurately." I also knew that we would tape the strips together later in the lesson and it would be useful to have all of the tally marks oriented in the same way on the strips.

I pointed to the board and the strip I'd used to model the activity. I said, "Remember, you'll have one minute to draw as many tally marks as you can. I'll tell you to start when the second hand gets to twelve." The students were poised with pencils and sentence strips ready to go, and their eyes were glued to the clock. The excitement built as the second hand approached the 12. I said, "Go!" and the students leaped into action, drawing tally marks as fast as they could. At the end of one minute I said, "Stop! Pencils down." Pencils were slapped down on the desks as the students immediately started talking among themselves and comparing tally marks.

I asked for the students' attention. When they were once again quiet, I said, "Please count your tally marks and record the total on the other side of your strip. Is it necessary for you to count the tally marks by ones?"

"No," the students chorused.

Ana said, "If you remembered to do them in groups of five, you can count by fives, and that's a lot faster."

Ben added, "An even faster way is to count them by tens because we made them in rows of ten."

Adama suggested, "Maybe we should count them twice to be sure we're right. The first time we could count by fives and the second time by tens. Or you could do it the other way around."

Arin said with worry in her voice, "If I want to, can I count them by ones?" I nodded.

Vinay said, "You could just use multiplication. You count the number of groups of five and multiply by five, or you count the number of rows of ten and then multiply by ten. Multiplying by ten is even easier than multiplying by five."

There were no more comments or questions and the students quickly got to work.

Figuring the Class Total

It took the students only a few minutes to figure the number of tallies they each had drawn. While they counted, I circulated, observing how they counted and reminding some to write the total on the back of the sentence strip. Several expressed surprise at how close or far they were from their estimates.

Most students counted by tens, several counted by fives, and some counted both ways. The number of tally marks the children drew ranged from 73 to 203.

I asked for the students' attention and gave the following instructions: "When everyone at your table has finished counting his or her tally marks, your next task will be to figure the total for your table group. You'll need to work together to find out how many tally marks altogether the members of your table group drew in one minute."

There were no questions and the students immediately began to figure the total tally marks for their table groups. Adding four or five three-digit numbers is a challenging task for some third graders, but the students cooperated well and had little trouble. Since the students were sitting in groups of four or five, I estimated that their table totals would be somewhere around five hundred. As groups found their totals, I quickly checked to be sure each answer seemed reasonable and then suggested that they check their work by finding the total a second way. Had a table had an unreasonable answer, I would have asked the students to give me an estimate of what they thought their total should be. Then I would have compared their estimates with what they had actually gotten, guiding them to see that their initial answer wasn't reasonable.

After several minutes, I called the students to order. I went around the room, asking each table group to report its total as I recorded on the board:

$$528$$
$$473$$
$$635$$
$$550$$
$$633$$
$$523$$

I said to the students, "How can we figure our class total?" All hands were up. I was interested to see the variety of ways the students would suggest. I called on Jael first.

Jael said, "Start with the ones and add all those up. Then do the tens and then the hundreds."

I said, "Put your thumb up if you think Jael's idea will work." All thumbs were up. I asked Jael to come to the board and figure the total using her idea. She did so using the standard addition algorithm, but she forgot to carry from the ones to the tens column and arrived at 3,322 for the answer. Jael had, however, correctly carried from the tens to the hundreds column, so I assumed her error was because of carelessness, not lack of understanding.

After a few moments, Ben raised his hand. He said, "Jael's way will work, but

she forgot to carry the two tens from the ones to the tens column. Carrying messes me up, so I start with the hundreds and figure out all the hundreds. I write that down. Then I figure out all the tens and write that down and then do the same thing with the ones. That way I don't have to do carrying." I invited Ben to come to the board and show us his thinking. He did so. His work looked as follows:

$$528$$
$$473$$
$$635$$
$$550$$
$$633$$
$$523$$
$$3100$$
$$220$$
$$22$$
$$3342$$

Finally, I asked Halley to get a calculator and find the sum. Her total agreed with Ben's total. By that time, Jael had added again at her desk and agreed that 3,342 was correct.

I said, "We are trying to get to ten thousand tally marks. So far, we have made three thousand three hundred and forty-two. About how many more do we need to make ten thousand?" I gave the students a moment to think. When most hands were up, I called on Keara.

Keara explained, "I think a little less than seven thousand, because we already have a little over three thousand, and seven thousand and three thousand equals ten thousand."

Sam added, "I think it's about six thousand seven hundred. Six thousand seven hundred plus three thousand three hundred equals ten thousand."

Tina figured the exact number. She said, "I think the answer is six thousand six hundred fifty-eight." A few others nodded their agreement with Tina's thinking while others looked confused. I asked Tina to explain further how she had figured.

Counting to Ten Thousand **57**

Tina clarified, "Three thousand three hundred plus six thousand seven hundred equals ten thousand, like Sam said, but our total is actually a little more than three thousand three hundred. It's three thousand three hundred plus forty-two more. So I have to take out forty-two from the six thousand seven hundred. That would be six thousand six hundred fifty-eight."

I recorded Tina's thinking on the board:

$$3,300 + 6,700 = 10,000$$
$$(3,300 + 42) + (6,700 - 42) = 10,000$$
$$3,342 + 6,658 = 10,000$$

"Ten thousand sure is a lot!" Arin said. The others agreed.

I suggested, "Let's see how long a strip we would have if we taped all three thousand three hundred forty-two tallies together." This excited the students. I settled them and continued, "First, you'll need to cut off the part of your strip you didn't use. Cut just below your bottom row of tally marks. While you are doing that, I will put a long piece of tape on your table so you can tape your table's strips together."

Adama asked, "Do we tape them together at the short end or along the long side?"

I replied, "Please tape them together at the short end to make one long, skinny strip. Also, be sure that the first strip of your table strip has at least one hundred tally marks." There were no other questions. As the students got to work cutting their strips, I put long pieces of tape at each table. After a few minutes the job was done. Making sure that the first strip of the class strip had at least one hundred tally marks, I taped the table strips together into one long strip and placed it on the floor. Then I wrote the total number of tally marks after the last row of tally marks. When I was finished, we had a strip that went about two-thirds of the way across our classroom.

"Wow! That's a long strip and it's still a long way from ten thousand!" Abel exclaimed.

Understanding How the Numbers Grow

I gathered the students together around the taped strip. I circled just the first tally mark and said to the class, "Here is one." Next I drew a line around the first row. "This is ten. Ten is ten times bigger than one."

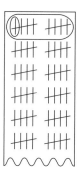

I paused a moment and then asked, "What is ten times bigger than ten?"

"One hundred," the class instantly replied.

I counted the first ten rows of ten on the class strip and drew a line around them. I said, "Ten is ten times bigger than one, and one hundred is ten times bigger than ten. Do we have enough tally marks on our class strip to have ten times one hundred?"

"Is ten times one hundred a thousand?" Arin asked. I nodded. Students indicated with thumbs up that we had enough tally marks to have ten times one hundred.

"Hmm," I said to the students. "Most of the tally marks are in rows of ten. How many rows of ten will I need to make one thousand?" The students thought quietly for a few moments and then began talking with one another. I asked for their attention.

Roberto said, "I think you need a hundred rows of ten."

I asked Roberto to explain his thinking, but he only shrugged. I said to the other students, "Who agrees that one hundred rows of ten are needed for one thousand?" Most students raised their hands. "Who would like to explain why?" I called on Tobias.

Tobias said, "There are ten tens in one hundred. There are ten hundreds in one thousand. Ten times ten is one hundred."

Jenae said, "You could count by tens ten times because there are ten tens in one hundred. Ten, twenty, thirty, forty, fifty, sixty, seventy, eighty, ninety, one hundred."

Vinay said, "What Tobias and Jenae said are really the same thing. Ten times ten is like counting by ten, ten times."

I nodded to show my agreement with Tobias, Jenae, and Vinay and then continued. I said, "I agree that one hundred rows of ten are needed to show one thousand. I'm going to start with the first row, but I don't actually have to count the first ten rows again because I already drew a line around them to show ten rows of ten equal one hundred. I'm going to continue counting rows of ten and drawing a line around each group of ten rows. I'll keep doing this until I have drawn a line around ten groups of ten rows of ten. As Vinay, Jenae, and Tobias shared, ten groups of ten rows will equal the hundred rows of ten needed to make one thousand." I drew lines around groups of ten rows of ten, skipping rows that had fewer than ten tally marks.

"Wow!" Adama said when I was finished. "Ten times bigger is sure getting a lot bigger now than at the beginning of our strip."

James said, "We can't do ten times bigger with one thousand. That would be ten thousand, and we only have three thousand three hundred forty-two."

I said, "James is right. For homework tonight, I want you to ask your parents for help on our project. Explain to them that we are trying to make a strip with ten thousand tally marks, and so far we have only three thousand three hundred forty-two. I'm going to give each of you a strip to take home. Your job is to ask one of your parents to draw as many tally marks

as possible while you time for one minute. Then bring back your strip tomorrow. Maybe with your parents' help we'll have ten thousand tally marks."

Kito said, "I'm not going to see my mom tonight. What should I do?"

I replied, "Ask the person taking care of you to help us out." Kito nodded.

I handed each student one 3-by-8-inch strip to take home and ended math class for the day.

DAY 2

Working with the Homework Tally Marks

Most of the students returned the next day with their strips full of tally marks. I again asked the students to work with their table groups to figure the total of the tally marks for each table. I reminded the class that even those students who didn't have tally marks from home should help in the process of figuring the total for their table group. As the students figured their totals, I circulated through the class, noting who had and had not done their homework. Also, I looked to see how the number of tally marks drawn by the parents compared with those drawn by the children. While the number of tally marks the children had drawn in one minute ranged from 73 to 203, the number of tally marks drawn by the parents ranged from 105 to 256. Since some students didn't do the homework, I guessed the total of the parents' tally marks would be similar to the students' total even though the parents had drawn more tally marks. After a few moments the groups had their totals. I asked for the students' attention and then began a discussion.

As I had done the day before, I went around the class, asking one member of each table group to report the total for that group. I recorded on the board and together we found the total. The parents had contributed 3,691 tally marks toward our goal of 10,000.

Next, we added the 3,691 tally marks to the 3,342 from the previous day for a total of 7,033.

"Oh, man!" Sam said. "Are we ever going to reach ten thousand?"

Tanya wondered aloud, "If we tape together all the strips from our parents, I wonder how much longer it will be than our class strip?"

I had planned on taping the strips together as I'd done the day before. Again, I gave each group a long strip of tape to share so they could tape their strips together. Then I collected each group's strip and put them together in one long homework strip. We compared the two strips, and the homework strip was longer, as the children had expected it would be. Then I taped the two strips together and noted the total of 7,033 tally marks next to the last row of tallies. Since the strip was now longer than the length of our classroom, I rolled it up and set it on a table.

I said to the students, "We have seven thousand thirty-three tally marks. How many more will we need to make ten thousand?" The students thought about this quietly for a few moments and then hands began to go up.

Karlee said, "I think we need less than three thousand."

I probed, "Why do you think less than three thousand are needed?"

Karlee thought for a moment and then said, "Well, if we added three thousand to seven thousand thirty-three, the answer would be over ten thousand."

I asked, "What would be the sum of seven thousand thirty-three and three thousand?"

"Ten thousand thirty-three," Karlee replied quickly.

I asked, "How much over ten thousand do you think it would be?"

Karlee replied, "Thirty-three."

So the other students could more easily follow what Karlee was explaining, I wrote on the board:

$7,033 + 3,000 = 10,033$

Hands danced in the air. I called on Vinay.

Vinay said, "All you have to do is subtract the thirty-three extras from three thousand and that will tell you how much to add to seven thousand thirty-three to make ten thousand. Three thousand minus thirty-three is . . . two thousand . . . nine hundred and sixty-seven."

I recorded on the board:

$3,000 - 33 = 2,967$

I asked, "How can we check Vinay's idea?"

Jillian said, "Add thirty-three to two thousand nine hundred sixty-seven and it should equal three thousand." Jillian paused a moment to think and then continued. "It's right. I know because sixty-seven plus thirty-three is one hundred and one hundred plus nine hundred is one thousand. One thousand plus two thousand is three thousand."

I recorded on the board:

$$2,967 + 33 = 3,000$$
$$33 + 67 = 100$$
$$100 + 900 = 1,000$$
$$1,000 + 2,000 = 3,000$$

I said, "It looks like we need two thousand nine hundred sixty-seven more tally marks. How can we get them?"

"I know!" Tobias said with excitement. "Let's get Mrs. Martin's class to help us. They can make tally marks!"

The students liked Tobias's idea. I told the students I would talk with Mrs. Martin after class and invite her class to help us. On that note, I ended math class for the day.

DAY 3

Getting Help from Another Class

Before we started math class the next day, Mrs. Martin, whose classroom was directly across the hall, had her students complete the task of drawing tally marks for one minute and compute the totals. Her class total was 3,021. She did not, however, have the students tape the strips together.

To begin class, I wrote on the board:

Our class:	*3,342*
Our parents:	*3,691*
Total	*7,033*
Mrs. Martin's class	*?*

The students chatted among themselves about what I had written. Many remembered that we still needed 2,967 tally marks. I said, "Mrs. Martin's class helped us out. Each student drew tally marks for one minute. Her class drew three thousand twenty-one tally marks. Will that be enough?" I replaced the question mark with *3,021*. The students broke out with cheers.

Sam said with great excitement, "Finally! We have more than ten thousand. Seven thousand thirty-three plus three thousand is ten thousand thirty-three. Mrs. Martin's class actually had three thousand twenty-one, so add twenty-one more to ten thousand thirty-three and that's ten thousand fifty-four."

Abel added, "If you want exactly ten thousand tally marks, you can leave off fifty-four tally marks and that will be exactly ten thousand."

Olina said, "Let's tape Mrs. Martin's strips to ours and see how long ten thousand tally marks really is." Had Olina or another student not suggested this, I would have done so. The students worked together to trim the unused space off each strip, and then we taped all but fifty-four of Mrs. Martin's class's tally marks to ours. When we finished, the strip reached from the far wall across our classroom, out the door and across the hall, and halfway into Mrs. Martin's classroom. This delighted all students in both classes.

Connecting Tallies to the Book

To bring closure to the lesson, I brought the strip back to our classroom and folded it accordian style to gather it together, returned to the book *Count to a Million,* and asked the students to sit where they could see it. When the students were settled and quiet, I opened the book to the spread showing the planet Earth and the number 1. I said to the students, "In this book, the idea of one is shown with one planet Earth. Where is the idea of one on our ten-thousand strip?" Hands flew up.

Ana pointed to the first tally mark I had circled on the ten-thousand strip. The students showed their agreement with Ana with thumbs up.

Next I showed the students the spread with the ten ladybugs. I said, "In the book, the idea of one group of ten is shown with these ten ladybugs. Where did we show the idea of one times ten, or one group of ten, with our tally marks?"

Kito pointed to the first row of ten that I had circled earlier in the lesson. I turned to the next spread, showing ten groups of ten ladybugs, and again asked the students where this idea was represented on the ten-thousand strip. Kassidee pointed to where I'd drawn a line around ten rows of ten, or one hundred tally marks. I turned to the page showing ten groups of one hundred gumballs, and this time Christopher pointed out where I had drawn lines around ten groups of ten rows to show one thousand on the ten-thousand strip. Finally I turned to the spread showing ten groups of one thousand ants. Olina shared, "Each group of one thousand tally marks on our ten-thousand strip would be like each group of one thousand ants in the book. Our whole entire ten-thousand strip is like the ten groups of one thousand ants in the book." The others showed their agreement with Olina's thinking with thumbs up.

Counting to Ten Thousand 61

Tobias commented, "We have all those tally marks and we would need one hundred more strips like the one we just made to have a million."

Jessie replied, "That's amazing!"

I ended math class for the day. I unfolded our ten-thousand strip and stapled it across the front wall above the chalkboard, continuing on the adjacent wall.

Questions and Discussion

▲ *What books other than* Count to a Million *would work with this lesson?*

If *Count to a Million* is unavailable to you, *Can You Count to a Googol?* by Robert E. Wells (Morton Grove, IL: Albert Whitman, 2000), is a good alternative. The structure and format of the book is similar and will work well with this lesson.

▲ *In this lesson, the students' homework was an important part of the lesson. What did you do about students who did not return their strips?*

In an activity such as this, students' interest and enthusiasm typically result in returned, completed homework. Sometimes there are a few students who have not done the homework or have done it and forgotten it. In either case, the students are expected to join in the work of the group to figure the group total. If a large number of students fail to return their homework, students may need to repeat the experience of drawing tally marks for one minute. The purpose of gathering tally marks for homework is to give students and parents an opportunity to be involved together in an enjoyable mathematical activity.

CHAPTER SIX
1,001 THINGS TO SPOT

Overview

1001 Things to Spot in the Sea, by Katie Daynes, presents a colorful array of water-related scenes and an I-spy challenge for children. The book also provides the context for helping students use place value ideas to add with regrouping. The lesson involves students in using first interlocking cubes and then base ten blocks to figure out how many things they spot in each scene and then in the entire book. The lesson also focuses on strategies for combining the numbers. In addition, the lesson incorporates an individual assessment.

Materials

▲ *1001 Things to Spot in the Sea,* by Katie Daynes (London: Usborne, 2003)
▲ interlocking cubes, about 100
▲ base ten blocks, about 50 unit cubes and 10 longs per pair of students, plus 10 flats and 1 one thousand cube
▲ chart paper, 1 piece
▲ 12-by-18-inch construction paper, 7 pieces

Time

▲ about ten class periods, spread over several weeks

Teaching Directions

1. For several weeks prior to beginning this lesson, make the book *1001 Things to Spot in the Sea,* by Katie Daynes, available for students to explore.

2. After students are familiar with the book, gather them on the floor so they can see the book, ask them what they thought about the book, and read aloud the introductory page across from the contents, titled "Things to spot."

3. Turn to the first scene, "Open sea," and hold the book so students can study the scene. After a few moments, ask: "How many things to spot do you think there are in this scene?" Have volunteers share and explain their estimates; record their estimates on the board.

4. Point to the humpback whale shown in the border of "Open sea." Then take one interlocking cube, tell the children that it represents the one humpback whale they are to spot in the scene, and place the cube on the chalkboard tray.

5. Ask a student to use interlocking cubes to represent how many there are of the next animal to spot (ten sea nettles) and ask another student to represent the next animal (eight halfmoon fish). Have them stand the finished trains of cubes on the chalkboard tray. Ask: "How many cubes do we have in all?" After the children have shared, together count the cubes to verify there are nineteen.

6. Repeat Step 5 for the remaining animals to spot—3 ocean sun fish, 4 blue sharks, 8 squid, 10 mackerel, 9 flying fish, 7 little tunnies, and 3 gannets. Count the cubes to figure the running total each time a child places a new train on the chalkboard tray, ending with a grand total for the scene of 63.

7. Write above each cube train the number of cubes in it.

$$1 + 10 + 8 + 3 + 4 + 8 + 10 + 9 + 7 + 3$$

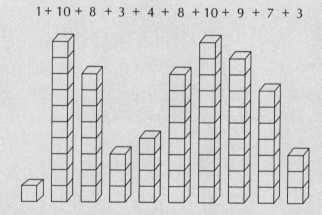

8. Focus on the tens and ones structure of sixty-three. First ask students to use their fingers to show how many tens are in sixty-three. Then say, "I don't see six tens in the cube trains. How do you know that there are six tens in the number sixty-three if we don't have six trains with ten cubes in each?" Ask volunteers to share their ideas. Next, rearrange the trains of cubes into trains of ten, representing what you do numerically. For example, when you combine a train of three and a train of seven into a train of ten, record as shown.

$$1 + 10 + 8 + 3 + 4 + 8 + 10 + 9 + \underset{\smile}{\overset{\displaystyle 10}{\textcircled{7} + \textcircled{3}}}$$

9. Record on a sheet of chart paper:

1,001 Things to Spot in the Sea

Open sea   63

10. Begin Day 2 by showing the children the scene "Water sports." Post a chart listing the things to spot in this scene.

Water sports

4 speedboats
10 flippers
5 jet skis
9 yellow life jackets
3 rubber rings
9 red buoys
6 striped sails
10 herring gulls
5 windsurfers
7 boogy boards

Ask volunteers to share their estimates of how many things there are to spot in "Water sports," record their estimates, and ask them to explain their reasoning.

11. Use base ten blocks to represent the things to spot in this scene. On the floor, lay out a line of four unit blocks to represent the four speedboats. Record a *4* on the board. Then ask a student to use base ten blocks to represent the ten flippers. Record on the board: *4 + 10*. After students figure the total so far (fourteen), continue for the other items to spot, adding to the addition expression and figuring the total as you go. The total for the scene is sixty-eight and the final addition expression will be *4 + 10 + 5 + 9 + 3 + 9 + 6 + 10 + 5 + 7.*

12. Ask: "How many tens are in sixty-eight?" With the help of the students, verify there are six tens by combining the numbers in the final addition expression. Then use the base ten blocks to show how to combine units into longs and represent the numerical figuring. Add the total for "Water sports" to the chart started on Day 1.

1,001 Things to Spot in the Sea

Open sea   63
Water sports   68

13. On Day 3, show the students the scene "Icy north" and post a chart listing the things to spot.

Icy north

10 capelin
4 arctic terns
8 ringed seals
10 harp seals

8 seal pups
4 polar bears
9 arctic cod
5 white parkas
3 killer whales
9 arctic charr

Have the children work in pairs to figure how many things there are to spot in "Icy north." Students may use interlocking cubes or base ten blocks to help them figure, and each student should make his or her own recording sheet. Then discuss their results and add the day's total to the chart.

1,001 Things to Spot in the Sea

Open sea	*63*
Water sports	*68*
Icy north	*70*

14. Begin Day 4 by asking: "How many things have we spotted already in the first three scenes? How could we use the base ten blocks to figure that out?" Using base ten blocks, represent each scene's total, then combine the scene totals. Record on the chart.

1,001 Things to Spot in the Sea

Open sea	*63*	
Water sports	*68*	
Icy north	*70*	*201*

15. Ask students: "If we keep counting and using base ten blocks, what blocks should we wind up with after we've spotted a thousand and one things?" Have students share their ideas first with their partners and then in a whole-group discussion.

16. On the chart, list the remaining scenes.

1,001 Things to Spot in the Sea

Open sea	*63*	
Water sports	*68*	
Icy north	*70*	*201*
Coral reef		
By the seashore		
Underwater forest		
On a cruise		
Deep down		
Sea village		
Lost city		
Chilly south		
Grassy seabed		
Shipwreck		
At the aquarium		

17. Then have students individually figure out how many things there are to spot in the next scene, "Coral reef." (See Assessment section, page 206, for further details.)

18. Over the next several weeks, devote time for students to find the sums in the remaining scenes. Represent each new scene with base ten blocks; then combine them with the blocks already cumulated to find the grand total of 1,001.

Teaching Notes

1001 Things to Spot in the Sea, by Katie Daynes, is a colorful, engaging book that's appropriate for students who need support for understanding and applying place value near the beginning of the year. *1001 Animals to Spot,* a children's book in the same series, is used for a lesson that is more appropriate for students closer to the end of third grade (see Chapter 10). One important difference between the lesson in this chapter and the lesson in Chapter 10 is that this first lesson has a greater focus on linking concrete materials to their more abstract numeric representations.

1001 Things to Spot in the Sea shows thirteen scenes with animals and water activities from around the world. It begins with an introductory page called "Things to spot." This page explains to the reader that in each scene there are things to find and count. Small pictures of the things to be found appear in the borders of the scene, along with a number showing how many of each item to find. The page also introduces Billy, a photographer, and challenges readers to find Billy's camera in each scene. Following the thirteenth scene, a page titled "At the aquarium" shows sea animals from the book and challenges the reader to find the scenes in which they appear and count them. The total number of things to find in the thirteen scenes is 899, and there are 102 animals to find from "At the aquarium," resulting in a grand total of 1,001.

1001 Things to Spot in the Sea and the book in Chapter 10, *1001 Animals to Spot,* are part of a series of five books that also includes *1001 Things to Spot in Town, 1001 Things to Spot on the Farm,* and *1001 Things to Spot Long Ago.* A note of caution: The things to spot in the three other books do not total 1,001. (There are 988 things to spot in *1001 Things to Spot Long Ago,* 975 things in *1001 Things to Spot in Town,* and only 773 things in *1001 Things to Spot on the Farm.*)

For several weeks prior to teaching this lesson, make the book available for the students to explore at their leisure. Being familiar with the I-spy nature of the book will allow students to focus on the mathematics of the lesson when the time comes.

Before teaching Day 2 of this lesson, use a sheet of 12-by-18-inch construction paper to make the following chart:

Water sports

4 speedboats
10 flippers
5 jet skis
9 yellow life jackets
3 rubber rings
9 red buoys
6 striped sails
10 herring gulls
5 windsurfers
7 boogy boards

Before Day 3, use another sheet of 12-by-18-inch construction paper to make the following chart:

Icy north

10 capelin
4 arctic terns
8 ringed seals
10 harp seals
8 seal pups
4 polar bears
9 arctic cod
5 white parkas
3 killer whales
9 arctic charr

Also use five 12-by-18-inch sheets of construction paper folded in half lengthwise to make the following charts. You can write one list on each half.

By the seashore	*Underwater forest*	*On a cruise*
8 oystercatchers	10 garibaldi fish	3 lifeboats
4 sandwiches	8 turban snails	7 life rings
5 fishing nets	5 black rock fish	8 deck lights
7 hermit crabs	9 kelp crabs	5 tables
9 groups of mussels	8 kelp bass	4 yachts
3 blue sunhats	4 sea otters	6 yellow loungers
10 gobies	10 sea urchins	10 palm trees
8 shore crabs	6 sea fans	8 striped loungers
6 black-headed gulls	2 leopard sharks	9 ship's officers
8 red buckets	9 kelp fish	4 pairs of binoculars

Deep down	*Sea village*	*Lost city*
10 lantern fish	5 huts	9 greeneye fish
9 vent shrimps	9 oysters	5 jars
8 spook fish	10 durian fruits	7 seabream
10 vent crabs	7 canoes	8 gold coins
7 black smokers	5 red-footed boobies	10 cardinal fish
5 gulper eels	10 paddles	6 octopuses
6 angler fish	8 white T-shirts	9 whelk shells
9 deep-sea jellyfish	10 coconuts	10 bullet tuna
5 dumbo octopuses	6 ladders	1 white stone head
1 submersible	4 dogs	7 divers

Chilly south	*Grassy seabed*	*Shipwreck*
1 whale-watchers' tour boat	10 mullet	10 barracudas
5 elephant seals	8 yellow winkles	5 carnation corals
9 chinstrap penguins	9 catfish	9 squirrel fish
8 albatrosses	3 sea cows	10 surgeon fish
3 whale tails	7 seeds	7 sweetlips
6 backpacks	9 snappers	2 writing slates
10 king penguins	5 roseate spoonbills	9 banner fish
10 penguin chicks	8 blue crabs	4 moray eels
9 brown skuas	7 terrapins	1 anchor
4 hourglass dolphins	10 butterfly fish	8 cow fish

At the aquarium

10 emperor fish
7 bottlenose dolphin
7 moon jellyfish
10 walruses
3 tripod fish
10 red sea anemones
8 macaroni penguins
1 blue-spotted ray
3 loggerhead turtles
2 napoleon wrasses
8 seahorses
9 picasso fish
6 lion fish
6 spiny lobsters
7 butterfly blennies
5 sun stars

The Lesson

▲▲

DAY 1

For several weeks prior to teaching the lessons in this chapter, I made the book *1001 Thing to Spot in the Sea,* by Katie Daynes, available to the children and encouraged them to explore it. It's hard for all students to see the creatures to spot when the entire class is gathered to look at the book together, so this way the children could become familiar with the book's format on their own before the whole-class lesson.

To begin the lesson, I gathered the children on the floor. As they settled, I held up the book and suggested they sit where they could see it. When the children were quiet I said, "Raise your hand if you've looked at this book." Almost all students raised their hands. I continued, "What did you think of it?" Hands waved in the air. I called on Jack.

Jack said, "It's really cool! There are all kinds of pictures about water. My favorite one is the 'Icy north.' There's a big picture and you have to find and count certain things in the big picture."

Andrea continued, "You know what you have to find in the big picture because there are little pictures all around it that show what you have to find and how many."

I then opened the book to the introductory page, after the contents, titled "Things to spot." Besides demonstrating to readers how to spot and count things, "Things to spot" also introduces Billy, an underwater photographer, and challenges readers to find his camera in each scene.

After reading the introduction, I turned to the first scene, "Open sea." I held it up so all the students could study it. They all took great pleasure in locating Billy's underwater camera. After a few moments, I asked the students, "How many things do you think there are to spot altogether in this scene?" Immediately the students started to talk among themselves; some shared estimates while others pointed and counted aloud the objects to be spotted. I settled the class and then led a class discussion for the students to share their estimates.

Tamra said, "I think there are thirty or maybe thirty-one. There are ten sea nettles and ten mackerel. That's twenty. There are seven little tunnies and three gannets. Seven and three make another ten. Twenty and ten more makes thirty. Then there are some other things. So I think maybe thirty-one."

While Tamra's estimate wasn't close to the answer, I was pleased that she was using a friendly number—in this case ten—and making groups of that number to help her start to think about finding the total things to spot in the scene. Without comment, I recorded her estimate of *31* on the board.

Len shared next. He said, "I think maybe there are seventy or so things to spot. I'm not sure exactly why; it's just an estimate." I recorded Len's estimate on the board under Tamra's and also recorded the estimates of all others who wanted to share:

31
70
61
65
63

I then said, indicating a container of interlocking cubes, "I thought maybe we could use the cubes to help us figure out how many things there are to spot in the 'Open sea' scene. I'm going to ask Becky to hold the book. Gather around her so you can see." Becky placed the book on the floor in front of her as the others gathered around.

I asked for the students' attention, held up one cube, and explained to the class, "I'm going to use this one cube to represent the one humpback whale we're supposed to spot." I turned, placed the cube on the chalkboard tray, and then asked, "How many cubes will I need to represent the next creature listed on the page, sea nettles?" Hands shot into the air.

Maria responded, "You need ten."

I asked Maria to build a train of ten cubes to represent the ten sea nettles. As Maria was doing this, I continued to the next item in the list and asked the others, "How many cubes do we need to represent the halfmoon fish?" Viktor responded that eight cubes would be needed, and he then began snapping together a train of eight cubes.

Meanwhile, Maria had finished her train of ten cubes. She placed it on the chalkboard tray beside my one cube. As Viktor worked, I asked the class, "When Viktor finishes his train of eight cubes and puts it with the other two trains of cubes, how many cubes do you think we'll have in all?" Viktor then finished his train and placed it on the tray with the others. Now we had three trains—a train of one, a train of ten, and a train of eight.

Kelly explained, "Maria's train has ten. Viktor's has eight, and one more is nine. Ten and nine ones make nineteen cubes." Together, we counted the cubes by ones to confirm that there were nineteen in all.

Next I asked, "How many will we have if we add the ocean sun fish?" The border indicated that there were three ocean sun fish to find. Soon most hands were up.

"Tell me in a whisper voice," I said.

The students whispered, "Twenty-two." I asked Molly to make a train of three to represent the ocean sun fish and then asked Natalia to make a train of four cubes for the blue sharks. They stood their trains next to the others. The children now understood that we were combining the numbers of animals to spot. Most counted on to figure out that we now had spotted twenty-six in all.

Tamra waved her hand in the air. "Can I change my guess?" I nodded. Tamra continued, "I think instead of thirty-one, there are a little more than sixty."

To encourage Tamra to explain her thinking, I said, "Tell us why you think that."

Tamra paused and then said, "Well, we have twenty-six so far, and I see that we still have lots more to go."

I nodded and read the creatures listed across the top border. "We still have to add on eight squid, ten mackerel, nine flying fish, seven little tunnies, and three gannets. Let's build trains for each." I asked five children each to build one of the trains. As they were doing so, I said to the others, "So we have twenty-six so far. How many will there be after we add on the eight squid?"

Most children counted on their fingers and in a moment hands were up. Again I had them answer in a whisper voice.

"Thirty-four," they whispered in unison.

By that time the children had completed building their trains. I stood the train of eight next to the others and pointed to the cubes as the children counted aloud. Then I stood up the train of ten for the mackerel. I waited for hands to go up and called on Miguel.

"That's easy," he said. "Thirty-four and ten more makes forty-four." Others nodded. As I pointed to each of the cubes in the train, we started with thirty-four and counted up to verify that Miguel's answer was correct.

I continued in this way with the last three trains—standing them up one by one; asking the class to figure the total; calling on a child to report; and then counting the cubes to verify. We arrived at a grand total of sixty-three.

Connecting to Grouping by Ten

Then, above each train, I recorded the number of cubes in it.

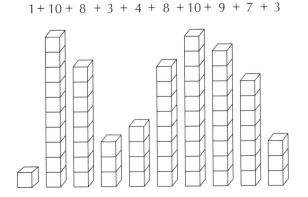

$$1 + 10 + 8 + 3 + 4 + 8 + 10 + 9 + 7 + 3$$

I asked, "So how many cubes are there altogether?"

"Sixty-three," the students chorused.

I paused for a moment to study the cubes and then said, "How many tens are in sixty-three? Use your fingers to show me." I looked around and most students were holding up six fingers.

I then said, "I don't see six tens in the cube trains. How do you know that there are six tens in the number sixty-three if we don't have six trains with ten cubes in each?" The children looked puzzled for a moment, and then they began to share their ideas with their neighbors. After giving them a few moments to discuss their thinking, I called them back to attention. As they quieted, students eagerly waved their hands in the air. I called on Justin.

Justin explained, "You could put the cubes together into trains of ten."

To encourage Justin to further explain his thinking, I replied, "Give me an example so I can better understand your idea."

Justin said, "You could put the train of three and the train of seven together. That would make a ten."

I did as Justin suggested, combining the train of three and the train of seven to make a train of ten and placing this new train of ten back on the chalkboard tray. To help the children see how to represent with numbers what I had done with the cubes, I drew the following on the board, circling the numbers I'd combined to make ten:

$$1 + 10 + 8 + 3 + 4 + 8 + 10 + 9 + \underset{\underset{10}{\diagdown}}{(7) + (3)}$$

Alberto said, "I see another way to make two trains into a train of ten. Put together the one and the nine. That makes ten, too."

I asked Claire to show with the cubes what Alberto had suggested. She did so and then stood her train of ten on the chalkboard tray. I asked for a volunteer to come to the board and show the rest of us how to represent with numbers what Claire and Alberto had done as I had done before to show Justin's idea. Victoria came to the board and recorded the following:

$$①+ 10 + 8 + 3 + 4 + 8 + 10 + ⑨ + ⑦ + ③$$
with 9, 7, 3 grouped to make 10, and 1 grouped with the sum to make 10.

"How many tens do we have now?" I asked. Together, we counted four trains of ten cubes. I recorded on the board to help keep track of which numbers we'd used to make trains of ten.

$$①+ \boxed{10} + 8 + 3 + 4 + 8 + \boxed{10} + ⑨ + ⑦ + ③$$
with 9, 7, 3 grouped to make 10, and 1 grouped to make 10.

Nicholas lit up. He squirmed and waved his hand to get my attention. "I have a way cool idea! You could split the four into two groups of two. Then there would be two groups of two and two groups of eight. Put one eight with each two and that would be two more groups of ten. Can I show with the cubes?" I nodded and Nicholas came to the chalkboard tray. He broke apart the train of four into two twos and put one of the twos with each of the eights.

I asked the students, "How many tens do we have now? Tell me in a whisper voice."

"Six," they whispered.

I called on Amanda to come to the board and record numerically what Nicholas had just done. Initially she was a bit puzzled about how to show breaking four into two groups of two. After a moment she got an idea and recorded.

$$①+ \boxed{10} + 8 + 3 + ④ + ⑧ + \boxed{10} + ⑨ + ⑦ + ③$$
with 10 above the 8 and ②+② grouping, 8, another 10, and 9 7 3 making 10.

Jack observed, "That just leaves the three. We have six tens and three ones, so that's sixty-three, just like we figured. You can see it in the cubes and on the board."

"That's pretty cool!" Nicholas commented.

"I like how we could make tens. It's really easy to figure out that way," Kami added.

Melissa said, "I liked Nicholas's idea of splitting the four into two twos and then putting one with each of the eights. I also liked how Amanda showed it on the board."

No one wanted to add any other comments. Before ending class for the day, I recorded on a piece of chart paper:

1,001 Things to Spot in the Sea

Open sea   63

DAY 2

Before class, I listed on a sheet of 12-by-18-inch construction paper the things to spot in the next scene in the book, "Water sports."

Water sports

4 speedboats
10 flippers
5 jet skis
9 yellow life jackets
3 rubber rings
9 red buoys
6 striped sails
10 herring gulls
5 windsurfers
7 boogy boards

I posted the chart and again gathered the children. I opened the book to the "Water sports" scene and held it up so that

72   **Lessons for Extending Place Value**

all the children could see the scene. I said to the students, "For the 'Open sea' scene, we used interlocking cubes to help us figure out that there were sixty-three things to spot. Today, we're going to use base ten blocks instead." I pointed to a nearby tub of base ten blocks. I changed the manipulatives for several reasons. One was that I knew that the total of the first two scenes would be more than one hundred, and it is less unwieldy to show one hundred with base ten blocks. Also, using different materials to represent situations and solve problems helps children become flexible in their problem-solving approaches.

The children were excited. As I had done on Day 1, I invited the children to estimate how many things there were to spot in the scene, recorded their estimates on the board, and asked them to explain their reasons. Several indicated they had made groups of ten.

Then I said to the students, "I know that I can use four unit cubes from the base ten blocks to represent the four speedboats." I laid four units in a line on the floor where the students could easily see them and recorded a *4* on the board. I continued, "Using base ten blocks, how could we show ten flippers?" All hands were up. I called on Cody.

Cody explained, "You could use a long."

"I know another way," Molly said. "You could also use ten units. A long and ten units equal the same thing."

I nodded my agreement with Molly and said, "I agree with Molly; there's another way to make ten. But let's use the fewest number of blocks possible to represent the ten flippers. What would be the fewest number of blocks?"

"A long," the children quickly responded. I asked Cody to place a long beside the line of four units and I recorded on the board:

4 + 10

"How many do we have so far?" I asked.
"Fourteen," the students chorused.

I called on Jacinto to represent five jet skis. He counted out five unit cubes and arranged them in a line next to the other blocks on the floor. I recorded on the board:

4 + 10 + 5

"Do we have enough unit cubes to exchange for a second group of ten?" I asked. Most students took a moment to count the units and then raised their hands.

Grace explained, "There are only nine units. We need one more before we have enough for another ten."

"We have nineteen now," Amanda added.

I continued on the page. Next, Viktor made a line of nine units to represent the nine yellow life jackets, Casey made a line of three units to show the rubber rings, and Tori made a line of nine for the red buoys. Each time I added to the numerical expression on the board and had the students figure the total, counting the blocks.

4 + 10 + 5 + 9 + 3 + 9

I then said, "So our total so far is forty. How many tens are there in forty? Show me with your fingers." I checked and saw that most children were holding up four fingers. For the few children who weren't sure, I held up four of my fingers and counted by tens, pointing to them as I did so: "Ten, twenty, thirty, forty. Four tens make forty."

I then said, "Let's check this by combining the numbers into tens to see if we wind up with four tens, or forty. How could we do this?"

Andrea said, "I see only one ten—the ten flippers. But I do see a double, two nines. That's eighteen. Eighteen and the ten make twenty-eight." Andrea paused and looked confused about what to do with the remaining three numbers. "Can I call on somebody for help?" I nodded. She called on Natalia.

Natalia began to explain, "There's still a four, a five, and a three. Four plus five is nine, so now we have three nines." She paused for a minute. "Oh, I know! Then we take the three and split it up so we make each nine into a ten. That makes four tens, and that's forty," she announced with a smile.

I refocused the students on the book, saying, "There are still four more groups of things to spot in the scene." Kami represented the six striped sails with six units; Cyrus used a long for the ten herring gulls; Tori counted out five units for the windsurfers; and Justin counted out seven units for the boogy boards. As the students laid the base ten blocks on the floor, I recorded the numbers on the board. The final addition expression looked as follows:

$$4 + 10 + 5 + 9 + 3 + 9 + 6 + 10 + 5 + 7$$

I asked the students, "How many are there altogether in the scene? What strategies can we use to figure the total number of things to spot in the 'Water sports' scene?" Most showed their eagerness by waving their hands in the air. To give more students the opportunity to share their thinking aloud, I said, "Turn to you neighbor and share your idea. First one of you talks for thirty seconds while the other listens carefully. When I give the signal, the first talker gets to listen while the first listener gets to talk. Remember not to interrupt your partner." The students immediately decided who would talk or listen first. At the end of thirty seconds, I gave the signal to change roles. At the end of another thirty seconds, I called for the students' attention. Hands were again raised. I called on Becky.

Becky said, "I used to start with the first number and just add the numbers together in order. But I see numbers that can make groups of ten and some doubles. You can put the fives together and it makes a group

of ten and is a double." I recorded Becky's suggestion on the board:

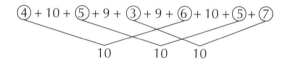

Kelly said, "You can make another group of ten. Add the three to the seven and that will make another ten."

Grace added, "Four and six also makes a ten." I recorded Molly's and Grace's ideas.

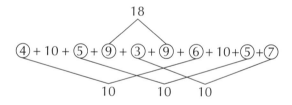

Len said, "I see another double. How about the two nines? They make eighteen."

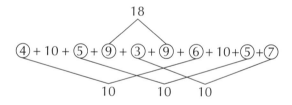

"It's so easy to figure out this way!" Cyrus said. "Now all you have to do is count up five tens and add eighteen or start with eighteen and add five tens. Either way, it's sixty-eight."

Connecting the Numbers to the Base Ten Blocks

I said, "Earlier Becky said to put the fives together. How can we show that using the blocks?" I pointed to where the students had placed the lines of base ten blocks to represent the numbers of objects to be found. When all hands were up, I called on Jack. Jack combined the two lines of five into one line of ten and exchanged the ten units for a long. Then he came to the board and indicated the two fives that he had combined.

74   Lessons for Extending Place Value

Victoria combined the line of six and the line of four into a line of ten, exchanged, and then showed on the board where these had been combined.

Maria combined the lines of three and seven, exchanged them for another long, and pointed to these numbers on the board.

Jacinto combined the two lines of nine into eighteen. As he did so, he commented, "If I wanted to, I could actually make the eighteen into a ten and a line of eight. Then we'd have another long and eight units." He did this and then, on the board, showed the nines that he had combined. We now had six longs and eight units. Together we counted the base ten blocks, the first time beginning with the eight unit cubes and counting on by tens—8, 18, 28, 38, 48, 58, 68. The second time, we first counted tens and then added on the eight unit cubes—10, 20, 30, 40, 50, 60, 68.

To end the class, I recorded the total for this scene on the chart paper below where I had recorded the first total:

1,001 Things to Spot in the Sea

Open sea	*63*
Water sports	*68*

DAY 3

I gathered the children on the floor and showed them the next scene, "Icy north." As I had done for the previous scene, I posted a chart listing all the things to spot in this scene.

Icy north

10 capelin
4 arctic terns
8 ringed seals
10 harp seals
8 seal pups
4 polar bears
9 arctic cod
5 white parkas
3 killer whales
9 arctic charr

I said, "Today you'll figure out how many things there are to spot in the 'Icy north' scene. You'll work with a partner, but you each need to record your thinking on your own piece of paper. You may use the cubes, the base ten blocks, or any other way that makes sense to you and your partner." I decided that this time I would pair the children randomly by pulling Popsicle sticks. At the beginning of the school year, I had written the name of each child on a Popsicle stick and then placed the Popsicle sticks in a jar. When I need to choose children randomly, it's quick to pull pairs of Popsicle sticks from the jar. As I did so, I instructed the children to get two sheets of paper and any materials they needed. Soon the room hummed with conversations as the children worked.

I circulated through the room, carefully listening and observing as the students worked to learn what strategies the students would use. Claire and her partner, Grace, were using cubes to figure the answer. Claire explained, "First Grace and I made all the groups. I drew those on my paper, see?" She indicated her paper, which showed the groups of cubes.

Then Grace picked up the explanation. "Then we put the groups together to make tens. We took apart one of the fours and made it into groups of two. We put one group of two with one eight and then the other two with the other and that made two tens. I started to draw the tens on my paper."

Claire continued, "We noticed that if we put the group of five and the other group of four together, that would be another group of nine. That would leave three groups of nine and one group of three. We took apart the group of three and made it into three ones. We put one with each nine. Voilà! We had three more groups of ten. That made seven groups of ten altogether. Grace drew the seven groups of ten on her paper." Both girls pointed to Grace's paper. While neither paper had a complete explanation, I accepted their work. It was clear to me as I listened that both girls understood the process and were comfortable making groups of ten as a way to solve the problem. (See Figures 6–1 and 6–2.)

Natalia was working with Humberto, a second language learner. To help him better understand, Natalia and Humberto used base ten blocks to represent each object to be found in the "Icy north scene." Then, together, Natalia and Humberto counted by ones to find the total of seventy. Then Natalia showed me using the base ten blocks how she could regroup the blocks into seven groups of ten. I suggested she show me this on her paper. (See Figure 6–3.)

As I walked by, Melissa commented, "I didn't do this on my paper, but I can see

three eights. There are two groups of eight and then I could put the two groups of four together to make eight."

I asked Melissa, "How many is three groups of eight?"

Melissa paused and thought for a few moments. She began, "Well, I know that two eights is sixteen." Then she counted on her fingers, stopping at twenty-four. She announced the total was twenty-four and then said, "I think the first way I did it was easier. Making tens and adding them up is easier than adding up eights."

The work done by Natalia, Claire, and Grace was typical of the other students.

I called for the students' attention for a short discussion. I began by asking the students to share their totals. Most students had figured the total to be seventy although one pair found a total of sixty-nine while another thought the total was seventy-two.

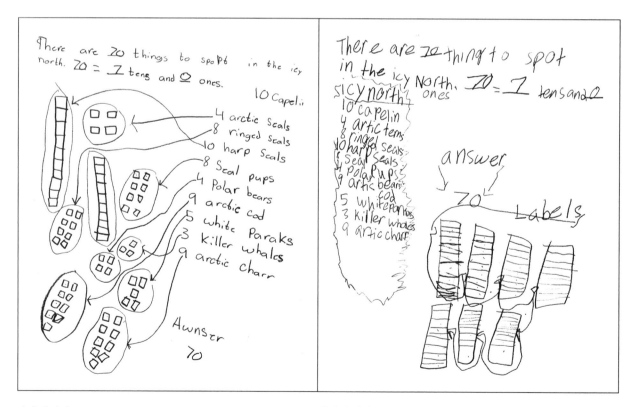

▲▲▲▲▲▲Figure 6–1   *Claire's paper showed how the girls represented the problem with blocks.*

▲▲▲▲▲▲Figure 6–2   *Grace's paper showed the result of combining the groups Claire had drawn to make tens and solve the problem.*

76   Lessons for Extending Place Value

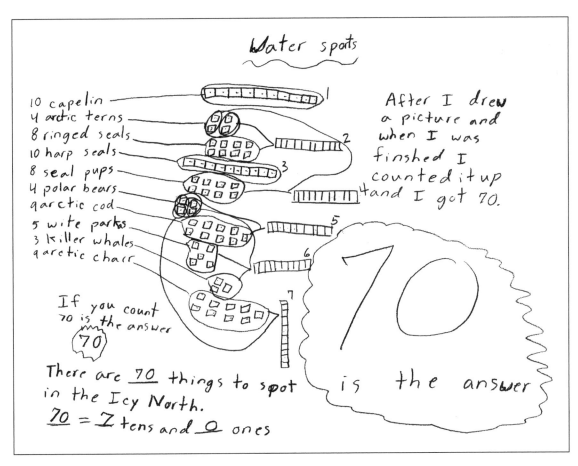

Water spots

10 capelin
4 arctic terns
8 ringed seals
10 harp seals
8 seal pups
4 polar bears
9 arctic cod
5 wite parks
3 killer whales
9 arctic chair

After I drew a picture and when I was finshed I counted it up and I got 70.

If you count 70 is the answer (70)

70 is the answer

There are 70 things to spot in the Icy North.
70 = 7 tens and 0 ones

▲▲▲▲▲▲Figure 6–3   *Natalia used base ten blocks, first counting by ones to find the total of seventy. Then Natalia showed how she combined the unit cubes to make longs.*

Cody shared that when he tried to figure it out with just numbers, he got fifty-four, but when he checked with cubes, he got seventy. Then he added the numbers again and got seventy. Most students indicated that they used either the base ten blocks or the cubes to help them find the sum.

I added the day's total to the chart paper:

1,001 Things to Spot in the Sea

Open sea	*63*
Water sports	*68*
Icy north	*70*

DAY 4

To begin the next part of the lesson, I asked the class, "So how many things have we spotted already in the first three scenes? How could we use the base ten blocks to figure that out?" At the students' suggestions, we first represented each day's total with longs and units.

Then Andrea said, "We have enough longs to make a flat." The others watched as she took the six longs from the sixty-three, counted out four more longs from the sixty-eight, arranged the ten longs on top of a flat, and then exchanged them for the flat. That left us with one flat, three units left from the sixty-three, two longs and eight units left from the sixty-eight, and seven longs from the seventy.

Len said, "Uh oh; we can't make another flat. We need one more long."

Jack added, "Look, we can get another long from the eight little units and the three little units. Put two with the eight and that makes ten. Then there's just one unit left over." He did this and then exchanged ten longs for another flat. Now we had two flats and one unit.

"How much is this worth altogether?" I asked.

"Two hundred one," several students answered. I wrote *201* on the board.

Connecting the Base Ten Blocks to 1,001

"So we've spotted two hundred one things in the first three scenes," I said. "How many things are we supposed to spot in the entire book?"

"One thousand and one," Miguel answered.

"We've got a lot more to spot," Maria said, rolling her eyes.

I then asked, "If we keep counting and using the base ten blocks, what blocks should we wind up with after we've spotted a thousand one things? Talk to your neighbor about this." After a few minutes, most children were ready to report. I called on Natalia.

She said, "We think that you could have ten flats and one unit or one thousands cube and one unit." The others nodded their agreement.

"Do you think we'll count exactly one thousand one things?" I asked. Some thought yes; others thought no; still others weren't sure.

"There are eleven more scenes in the book," I continued. I listed the scenes on the chart I had started and the cumulative total for the first three:

1,001 Things to Spot in the Sea

Open sea	*63*	
Water sports	*68*	
Icy north	*70*	*201 (so far)*
Coral reef		
By the seashore		
Underwater forest		
On a cruise		
Deep down		
Sea village		
Lost city		
Chilly south		

Grassy seabed
Shipwreck
At the aquarium

I then said, "Now I'd like each of you to figure out how many things there are to spot in the next scene, 'Coral reef.'" I posted the list of things to spot in the scene and used this task as an individual assessment. (See the Assessment section, page 206, for details.)

The next day, after I had reviewed the children's papers, we discussed their results and I added the total to the chart.

EXTENDING THE EXPERIENCE

Over the next few weeks, I devoted class time for the children to find the sums for the other scenes in the book. I continued to encourage them to focus on the numbers and use addition strategies, but I also had them verify their answers with base ten blocks. It was helpful to have the students work in pairs to figure out the total for each scene and then for pairs to compare answers and strategies before we talked together as a whole class. Sometimes, I had different pairs of students work on different scenes so that we could progress through the book more quickly.

Also, we kept track of the cumulative totals as we worked through the book. Each time we had a cumulative total, I saved the blocks for the next time. Then, after representing each new scene with base ten blocks, we'd combine them with the blocks already cumulated, make exchanges, and record the total so far on the chart. Finally, we had a thousand cube and a unit cube with the base ten blocks and had posted the following on the chart:

1,001 Things to Spot in the Sea

Open sea	63	
Water sports	68	
Icy north	70	201
Coral reef	73	274

By the seashore	68	342	Lost city	72	693
Underwater forest	71	413	Chilly south	65	758
On a cruise	64	477	Grassy seabed	76	834
Deep down	70	547	Shipwreck	65	899
Sea village	74	621	At the aquarium	102	1,001

Questions and Discussion

▲▲▲

▲ *Why did you begin the lesson using interlocking cubes rather than base ten blocks?*

I used interlocking cubes for the first day because I think it's important for children to have the kinesthetic experience of physically putting together the cubes to form a connected train of ten cubes. This physical experience provides another way to support children's learning and deepen their understanding. Also, using more than one material to represent a concept or idea helps students become flexible thinkers.

CHAPTER SEVEN
THE 512 ANTS ON SULLIVAN STREET

Overview

The 512 Ants on Sullivan Street, by Carol A. Losi, gives students the opportunity to think about what happens to the magnitude of numbers when they double over and over again and about how doubling relates to addition and multiplication. The book also provides a context to present subtraction problems to students that engages them in applying their understanding of the role of ones, tens, and hundreds in our place value system. In addition, the lesson models how to organize instruction so that it's possible to provide help for children who are struggling while providing meaningful work for the others.

Materials

▲ *The 512 Ants on Sullivan Street,* by Carol A. Losi (New York: Scholastic, 1997)

Time

▲ one class period

Teaching Directions

1. Read aloud the first two spreads of *The 512 Ants on Sullivan Street,* by Carol A. Losi.

2. Ask students to predict the number of ants on the next page and to explain their thinking.

3. Read the next two pages to verify the students' predictions. To help the students see the pattern of how the ants increase, record on the board:

Number of Ants

1

2

4

80

4. Discuss again the patterns students see emerging. If a student doesn't point it out, lead them to discover the doubling pattern: $1 + 1 = 2, 2 + 2 = 4, 4 + 4 = 8$. Record on the board:

Number of Ants

1

2 = 1 + 1

4 = 2 + 2

5. Ask students: "What's a way we can show a doubling pattern using multiplication?" Record on the board:

Number of Ants

1

2 = 1 + 1 = 2 × 1

4 = 2 + 2 = 2 × 2

6. Continue to have children predict the next number of ants. Verify their predictions by reading aloud the story, and then record on the board.

7. When you get to thirty-two ants, ask the students: "If I wanted to put the ants into groups of ten, could I do so? Would I have any ants left over?" Allow students a few moments to discuss this among themselves; then lead a class discussion.

8. Finish reading aloud the story and recording on the chart.

Number of Ants

1

2 = 1 + 1 = 2 × 1

4 = 2 + 2 = 2 × 2

8 = 4 + 4 = 2 × 4

16 = 8 + 8 = 2 × 8

32 = 16 + 16 = 2 × 16

64 = 32 + 32 = 2 × 32

128 = 64 + 64 = 2 × 64

256 = 128 + 128 = 2 × 128

512 = 256 + 256 = 2 × 256

9. Use the story context to pose a problem. Ask students: "There are thirty-two ants. How many more to make fifty ants?" Discuss students' thoughts and record them on the board.

10. Write on the board a second problem:

At a nearby picnic, 64 ants want to carry away a huge dill pickle. Although the ants try their best, they can't move the pickle. They decide that 100 ants could do the job. How many more ants are needed?

Ask the students to work on the problem independently. Provide to each child paper, and then observe the children as they work to see what strategies they use and how accurately and efficiently they apply their number sense and knowledge of tens and ones.

11. Present a third problem:

512 ants have discovered a watermelon. 1,000 ants are needed to carry it away. How many more ants are needed?

12. Observe the students as they work on the third problem, or if useful, provide small-group or individual help for those needing it.

Teaching Notes

The 512 Ants on Sullivan Street, by Carol A. Losi, tells a tale of cooperation and thievery as a colony of ants steals a picnic lunch. First, 1 ant grabs a crumb, followed by 2 ants who steal some plum. Next 4 ants carry off a barbecued chip and 8 ants take a bacon strip. The number of ants doubles as the items stolen get larger and heavier until, finally, 512 ants escape with the fudge cake. When the owners return to enjoy their lunch, nothing remains, but down in their hole, the ants on Sullivan Street have a lovely feast.

The doubling pattern of the ants provides an opportunity for children to predict the next number of ants and practice doubling and multiplying by two mentally. Parts of the story are repetitive, and the students enjoyed joining in as they heard these parts. Also, at the end of the book, there are several activities that focus on number sense, doubling, and square numbers.

One important objective I had for this lesson was to provide students with an opportunity to use tens and ones to find differences between numbers. Some of the children used subtraction while many used a counting-on strategy—that is, they started with the smaller number and counted on to the larger number to find the difference between the two. From this lesson, I hoped to assess how individual students were applying their knowledge of hundreds, tens, and ones to compute efficiently and accurately.

During this lesson, four children needed a considerable amount of extra help. One left to go to speech class, but the structure of the lesson was such that I was able to work with the other three in a small group while the rest of the students worked independently on a different and more challenging problem.

The students in the vignette had previous experience with using ones, tens, and hundreds to solve addition and subtraction problems. They also had experience with doubling numbers. They were just beginning their study of multiplication and just beginning to make the connection between doubling numbers and multiplying by two.

The Lesson

▲▲▲

The students gathered around me, chatting excitedly about the book I was holding, *The 512 Ants on Sullivan Street*, by Carol A. Losi. Jessie commented as she sat down, "Five hundred twelve sounds like a lot, but not when it comes to ants. There's at least that many in our room!" I, along with the other students, giggled at Jessie's comment. Our school has constant problems with ants.

Adama added, "Maybe the book should be called *The 512 Ants of Room 19.*" Again giggles erupted and Adama was pleased with her cleverness.

I settled the students and then read aloud the first two spreads of the book, which introduce one ant walking away with a crumb and two ants taking part of a plum. I asked the children to predict the number of ants on the next page that would be involved in taking food from the picnic basket. Some students thought perhaps it would be three ants, stating that there could be a pattern that increased by one ant each time. Others thought perhaps there would be four ants, suggesting there was a doubling pattern. A few thought there was no pattern to the number of ants at all.

I continued reading and we learned that next, four ants make off with a barbecued chip. I recorded on the board:

Number of Ants

1

2

4

As I finished recording, students waved their hands, eager to share. I called on Jessie.

Jessie said, "It's a doubling pattern. One plus one equals two. Two is the next number. Two plus two equals four. And four is the next number. I think the next number after that will be eight because four plus four equals eight."

I added Jessie's idea to the list I had begun:

Number of Ants

1

2 = 1 + 1

4 = 2 + 2

The students agreed with Jessie. I read the next spread to verify that eight ants come along next, this time carrying off a bacon strip. The students also noticed the repetition in the story and started to chant those parts aloud as I read them.

I said to the students, "It seems as if there is a doubling pattern. What's a way we can show a doubling pattern with multiplication?" Although none of the students brought up the idea of multiplying by two as another way of doubling, the question was easy for the class. I called on Karena.

"That's easy! Doubling is like timesing by two," Karena replied with confidence.

To be sure Karena understood the connection between doubling and multiplying by two, I gently pushed her to explain further. I said, "It would be helpful to me and the others if you could explain your thinking and give an example."

Karena explained, "Well, the times sign means groups of. And doubling means two of something. So instead of one plus one, you could think of it as two groups of one. You'd write that with a two, then a times sign, and then a one. That equals two just like one plus one equals two."

I recorded Karena's idea on the board and then pointed to 2 + 2 = 4. I asked the students, "How would I write this as a multiplication sentence?"

Christopher replied, "Two times two equals four. There are two twos, so that's two groups of two or two, two times."

The 512 Ants on Sullivan Street   83

With the students' help, the recording soon looked as follows:

$$1$$
$$2 = 1 + 1 = 2 \times 1$$
$$4 = 2 + 2 = 2 \times 2$$
$$8 = 4 + 4 = 2 \times 4$$

The children continued to make predictions about subsequent numbers of ants, I verified by reading the story, and then I continued to record on the board. When we got to thirty-two ants, I asked, "If I wanted to put the ants into groups of ten, could I do so? Would I have any ants left over?" I gave the students a few moments to discuss these questions with their partners and then called the class to order. Hands were up. I called on Karlee.

Karlee said, "There will be ants left over, but I'm not exactly sure why."

I said, "Put you thumb up if you agree that there will be ants left over if we put thirty-two ants into groups of ten. Put your thumb sideways if you're not sure, and put your thumb down if you think there will be no ants left over." All thumbs were up. I said, "Raise your hand if you'd like to explain why there will be leftover ants."

Olina shared, "If there's exactly a group of ten, the number ends in zero. Like ten has one group of ten and ends in zero. Twenty has two groups of ten and ends in zero. Thirty-two doesn't end in zero. It has three groups of ten and two leftover ants."

Tobias said, "You can use multiplication. Three times ten equals thirty and four times ten equals forty. Thirty-two gets skipped. I agree with Olina; there will be two ants left."

Ana added, "Just count by tens. Ten, twenty, thirty. Then you need two ones to get to thirty-two."

I continued reading the story to the students and together the students and I finished the chart we'd started showing the patterns of doubling both by adding and by multiplying by two.

Number of Ants

$$1$$
$$2 = 1 + 1 = 2 \times 1$$
$$4 = 2 + 2 = 2 \times 2$$
$$8 = 4 + 4 = 2 \times 4$$
$$16 = 8 + 8 = 2 \times 8$$
$$32 = 16 + 16 = 2 \times 16$$
$$64 = 32 + 32 = 2 \times 32$$
$$128 = 64 + 64 = 2 \times 64$$
$$256 = 128 + 128 = 2 \times 128$$
$$512 = 256 + 256 = 2 \times 256$$

SUBTRACTION WITH REGROUPING

I used the context of the story to pose another question. "Remember in the story when thirty-two ants hauled a wing and a leg?" I asked. The students nodded. "What if they needed fifty ants for that job?" I continued. "How many more ants would they need?" When most of the students had their hands up, I called on Adama.

Adama said, "You need eighteen. The problem could be fifty minus thirty-two, but all you have to do is start with thirty-two and count up to fifty. Thirty-two plus ten equals forty-two; then eight ones make fifty. Fifty minus thirty-two equals eighteen."

I recorded on the board:

Adama $50 - 32 =$
$$32 + 10 = 42$$
$$42 + 8 = 50$$
$$50 - 32 = 18$$

Roberto said, "You could start with thirty-two and add eight ones to make forty and then one group of ten to make fifty. Eight and ten equal eighteen, so thirty-two plus eighteen equals fifty."

I recorded on the board:

Roberto $32 + 8 = 40$
$$40 + 10 = 50$$
$$10 + 8 = 18$$
$$32 + 18 = 50$$

Tina said, "You could start with fifty and go back ten to forty and then back eight

84   Lessons for Extending Place Value

more to get to thirty-two. Fifty minus eighteen equals thirty-two. That means you'd need eighteen more ants to have fifty ants if you started with thirty-two."

I recorded:

Tina   50 − 10 = 40
       40 − 8 = 32
       10 + 8 = 18
       50 − 18 = 32

A SECOND SUBTRACTION PROBLEM

I wrote on the board:

At a nearby picnic, 64 ants want to carry away a huge dill pickle. Although the ants try their best, they can't move the pickle. They decide that 100 ants could do the job. How many more ants are needed?

After the students thought about this quietly for a few moments, I explained that they would now work on solving this problem. I explained, "I'm interested in knowing what each of you thinks and understands, so please do your own work." As I handed each student a sheet of paper, I answered questions.

While the students got to work, I circulated through the class, observing carefully. My goal was to gain a clearer understanding of what strategies the students were using and what misconceptions they might have had. I also was very interested to see which students had

access to the problem and which didn't, which students would use their understanding of place value, and which would rely on the standard algorithm or another means of figuring. I was also interested in which students would solve the problem using subtraction and which would choose addition.

Roberto wrote the problem as a subtraction problem: *100 − 64*. His written explanation stated, *I add to 64 to 100 and it took me 36 fingers. That's 3 tens and 6 ones. 36.* As I came by Roberto's desk, he was in the process of verifying his answer using base ten blocks. He had first laid out a hundred flat and then laid on top of it six tens and four ones. He was counting the uncovered spaces on the hundred block. He found that there were thirty-six spaces left uncovered, thus verifying his answer.

Keara used subtraction and her knowledge of place value to solve the problem. Although she subtracted, she did not use the standard algorithm. She subtracted the tens first and then the ones. (See Figure 7–1.)

Adama first solved the problem using addition; then she used the standard algorithm as a check. (See Figure 7–2.)

Several students used an approach similar to Jessie's. Jessie counted on from sixty-four, using tally marks grouped in tens to help her find an answer. (See Figure 7–3.)

Tobias also counted on. He started with 64 and counted up by tens until he got to 104, for a total of four tens, or forty.

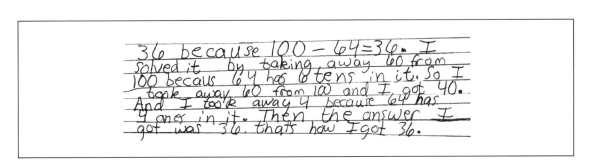

▲▲▲▲▲▲Figure 7–1   *Keara used her knowledge of place value to successfully solve the problem.*

The 512 Ants on Sullivan Street   85

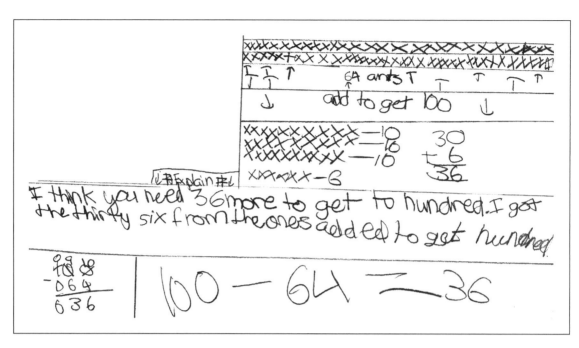

▲▲▲▲▲Figure 7–2   *Adama counted on using tens and ones to find the solution.*

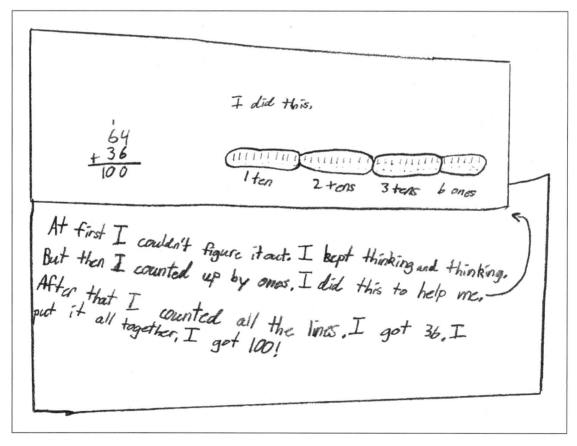

▲▲▲▲▲Figure 7–3   *Jessie used tallies and added on groups of tens and ones to help her solve the problem.*

86   Lessons for Extending Place Value

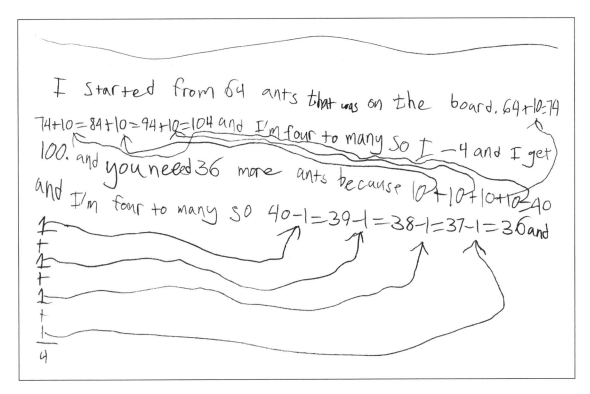

▲▲▲▲▲▲Figure 7–4   *Tobias successfully solved the problem.*

Then he counted four back from 104 to get to 100. Finally, he subtracted four from the four tens, or forty, to get thirty-six. (See Figure 7–4.)

Jael was stuck. She asked if she could use cubes to help her solve the problem. I nodded and asked how she planned to use the cubes. She shrugged and got up to get a tub of cubes. She started to count the cubes out by ones. When she got to twenty-one, she lost track. I said, "If you put the cubes in trains of ten, it might make it easier to keep track as you count."

Jael smiled and replied, "Oh yeah!"

"How many trains of ten will you need to make sixty-four?" I asked.

Jael paused, appearing to be deep in thought, and then said, "I think six trains with ten and then four extra." I nodded my agreement and moved on as Jael began to make trains of ten cubes.

As I walked by Jenae's desk, she was deeply involved in solving the problem.

She had carefully drawn sixty-four dots enclosed with a rectangle. The dots were arranged in six rows of ten with a seventh row of four dots. She was now working on figuring the number of dots needed to make one hundred. She explained that she arranged the dots in tens and ones. "Sixty-four is six tens and four ones." She pointed to her work in progress and said, "So far I have eighty-four dots. Sixty-four on the top and two tens on the bottom, so that's eighty-four." Jenae often struggled and I was pleased to see that she was using her understanding of tens and ones as a tool to solve this problem with confidence and understanding. My next challenge with Jenae was to help her find more efficient yet still meaningful ways to solve problems like this one. (See Figure 7–5.)

When I checked back with Jael, she had finished making a pile of sixty-four with six trains of ten cubes and four ones. She had also made a second pile with

The 512 Ants on Sullivan Street   87

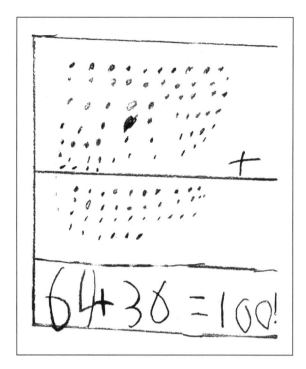

three trains of ten cubes and six ones. She explained, "The sixty-four ants need thirty-six more ants to have one hundred." Jael seemed to be slowly making sense of the problem and how to use place value to help her solve it.

Jade drew a picture. She made an error in counting and got thirty-seven for her answer rather than thirty-six. Also, her work did not indicate that she was using place value as a tool to solve this problem as most of the other children had done. (See, for example, Ben's work in Figure 7–6.) My next step for Jade was to give her additional experiences in which place value would be a useful tool for problem solving. (See Figure 7–7.)

Only a few students seemed to have difficulty with this activity.

▲▲▲▲▲Figure 7–5   *Jenae's strategy of drawing dots and counting on was successful but inefficient.*

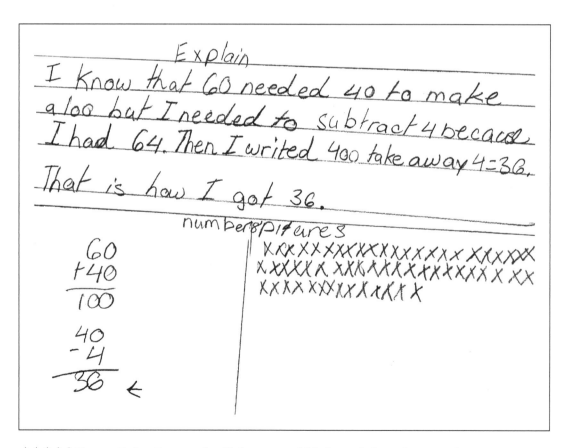

▲▲▲▲▲Figure 7–6   *Ben made efficient use of his knowledge of tens and ones.*

88   Lessons for Extending Place Value

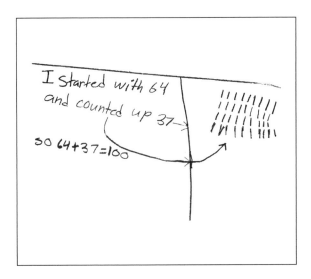

I started with 64 and counted up 37 →

so 64+37=100

▲▲▲▲▲Figure 7–7   *Jade showed no use of tens and ones and made a counting error.*

A THIRD PROBLEM AND SMALL-GROUP ASSISTANCE

As the students finished, I looked over their work. All but three were successful. These three as well as Jenae needed additional assistance. To create time so I could help them, I presented a third, challenge problem for the others.

I wrote the third problem on the board:

512 ants have discovered a watermelon.
1,000 ants are needed to carry it away.
How many more ants are needed?

As most of the class began work on the new problem, I gathered Jenae, Jade, and Rachel in a small group on the floor. (Jael also needed help, but she had left to go to speech class.) Jenae had successfully solved the previous problem, but her only approach had been to use dots to represent the problem. This strategy is slow, tedious, and leaves many opportunities for errors. Further, Jenae's strategy would have been even less efficient and practical for the problem the other students were now solving. Jenae's picture and verbal explanation

did indicate an understanding of tens and one. I hoped that I could build on this understanding and help her start to represent her thinking with numbers rather than dots.

Jade showed little application of place value ideas in her work. She counted on by ones from sixty-four, using tally marks to keep track of her counting. She thought thirty-seven was the answer rather than thirty-six. I wanted to help Jade see the usefulness of counting on by tens and ones rather than counting on using ones only.

Rachel was very confused. Her verbal explanation for the previous problem made sense and showed she could apply ideas of place value to solve the problem accurately. However, when she recorded her work on paper, she became confused and stated that ninety ants were needed, even though in her verbal explanation she stated thirty-six ants were needed to make one hundred. (See Figure 7–8.)

To begin, I asked the girls, "What was it you were trying to figure out in the last problem?"

Jenae was clear on this. She explained, "There were sixty-four ants. We needed one hundred. We had to figure out how much more ants were needed."

I said to Rachel, "Can you say what Jenae said using your own words?"

Rachel paused a moment and then said, "We have to figure out how many ants there are from sixty-four to one hundred."

I asked Jenae, "Do you agree with Rachel?" Jenae nodded.

Jade explained it as follows: "What's the difference between sixty-four and one hundred?"

I asked both Rachel and Jenae, "Did Jade say your idea in her own words?" They nodded.

Rachel shared with us, "I really got confused. I started with sixty-four and I used

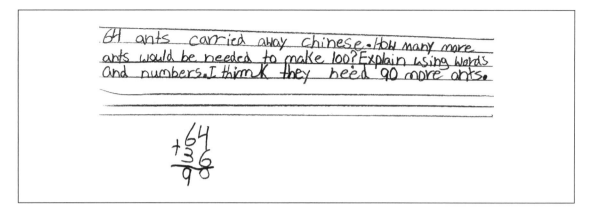

▲▲▲▲▲▲Figure 7–8 *Rachel's written work showed confusion.*

my fingers to add tens and then ones, and I got thirty-six. I even checked by going sixty-four plus ten is seventy-four plus ten more is eighty-four plus ten more is ninety-four." As Rachel explained, she kept track of the number of tens on her fingers. Looking at her fingers carefully, she said, "I have three fingers up for tens, so that was thirty. Then to go to one hundred, I counted by ones from ninety-four. Ninety-five, ninety-six, ninety-seven, ninety-eight, ninety-nine, one hundred. That's six fingers, so that means six ones. Three tens and six ones is thirty-six. But when I wrote sixty-four plus thirty-six on my paper and added it up, it equaled ninety. I don't get it."

Rachel had explained her thinking to me twice. Both times her verbal explanation indicated she could use place value as a tool to find the difference between two numbers. However, when Rachel attempted to put her thinking on paper, she used the standard addition algorithm incorrectly. Her results were incorrect and unexpected; consequently, she was no longer able to make sense of what she was doing. Her answer that ninety more ants were needed to make one hundred made no sense numerically or within the context of her oral explanation.

To begin, I asked her to restate what she was trying to figure out. She correctly stated she wanted to find the number of ants needed to make one hundred if there were already sixty-four. Next I asked her why she added sixty-four and thirty-six.

Rachel thought a moment and then said, "I'm not sure. I think I was trying to see if sixty-four and thirty-six equal one hundred. They should, but instead it was ninety and then I got very confused and thought ninety more ants were needed."

With a clearer understanding of Rachel's thinking, I decided to ask her and the others to consider the reasonableness of her answer. Since 64 ants is more than halfway to 100, and 90 is close to 100, adding 90 to 64 to make 100 ants is unreasonable. I asked the girls, "Is ninety close to one hundred or far from it?"

Rachel replied, "It's really close. It's only ten away." Jenae and Jade nodded their agreement.

I continued, "What about sixty-four? Is it close or far away from one hundred?"

Rachel said, "It's sort of in the middle."

Jenae added, "Sixty-four is more than halfway between zero and one hundred because it's bigger than fifty. Fifty is halfway."

Jade commented, "Sixty-four is closer to fifty than to one hundred."

90 Lessons for Extending Place Value

I asked Jenae and Rachel, "Do you agree or disagree that sixty-four is closer to fifty than to one hundred?" Neither was sure.

I said, "Let's make a number line to represent the numbers from zero through one hundred." On a sheet of paper, I quickly drew a line and marked *0*, stating, "This is where zero goes. Where should one hundred go?"

Jade made a mark near the end of my line and labeled it *100*.

I said, "Now that zero and one hundred are marked on the number line, where should fifty go?"

"Halfway!" Jenae said and correctly marked and labeled 50 on the number line.

Rachel got excited. She said, "I think I know how to put seventy-five and twenty-five on the number line. Twenty-five is half of zero to fifty and seventy-five is half of fifty to one hundred." She correctly marked and labeled on the number line *25* and *75*. Rachel continued, "Sixty-four has to be closer to fifty than one hundred because it is less than seventy-five and seventy-five is halfway between fifty and one hundred."

Next, I said, "If sixty-four is somewhere between fifty and seventy-five, does it seem reasonable that ninety more ants will be needed to make one hundred?"

Rachel shook her head while saying, "Ninety doesn't make sense at all. I know that thirty-six is the number of ants, but I don't understand why I got ninety when I added thirty-six and sixty-four." She studied her paper a moment and then started to use her fingers to keep track as she counted on from sixty-four once more. Again she got thirty-six. As Rachel thought about her dilemma, she glanced over at Jenae's paper, noticing the dots Jenae had drawn. She quickly counted the thirty-six dots Jenae had added to the sixty-four and commented that Jenae had gotten thirty-six

also. Next she counted all of Jenae's dots, first counting the nine groups of ten and then the ten ones. Rachel said with surprise, "I know what happened." She pointed to Jenae's sixty-four dots and continued, "This group is six tens and four ones, or sixty-four, which is right here on my paper but in numbers instead of dots. And then Jenae did thirty-six more dots and I wrote it in numbers. I counted nine groups of ten in Jenae's picture, but the six ones and the four ones make one more ten, which is ten tens altogether. On my paper I didn't put in the ten from when I added six and four, so I only got nine tens, or ninety!"

I was delighted that Rachel made the connection between the numbers she used and the dots that Jenae drew and was able to recognize she hadn't carried the one ten when she'd tried the standard addition algorithm. Jenae beamed because her work had helped Rachel to better understand. To use Rachel's learning as a bridge for Jenae, I pointed to her first group of sixty-four dots and asked, "What number could you use instead of all these dots?"

Jenae quickly replied, "Sixty-four."

"Where in your dots is the sixty-four?" I pushed.

"Oh, that's easy," Jenae replied. "There are six groups of ten dots. That's the sixty part. There are four more dots and that's the ones part. That makes sixty-four."

"What number could you use instead of your second group of dots?" I asked.

"Thirty-six. Three tens and six ones," Jenae explained.

I asked Jenae, "What number could you use to show the total of sixty-four and thirty-six?"

Jenae explained, "Three tens and six tens make nine tens. Four ones and six ones make ten ones. That's enough for one more ten. So that's ten tens, or one hundred ants. One hundred is the number I could use."

The 512 Ants on Sullivan Street   91

I was pleased with the progress the girls were making, but I felt I needed to check on the other students. I gave the girls another problem to solve while I checked on the rest of the class. This time they had to figure how many more ants would be needed to make one hundred if they had forty-two ants. I explained they could work together and use cubes, base ten blocks, a number line, or any way that made sense to them to solve the problem.

When I checked on the girls a while later, they had correctly solved the problem. Jenae and Jade used base ten blocks. Jenae laid out a flat, and on top of it, she placed four longs and two ones cubes. She then counted the uncovered tens and

ones. Jade laid out four longs and two ones cubes. Then she added longs counting by tens as she did so, until she got to ninety-two. From ninety-two, she added ones cubes until she reached one hundred. Rachel used her fingers and counted on, first by tens to ninety-two, then by ones until she got to one hundred. They agreed that fifty-eight more ants were needed.

Observing the Students Solve 1,000 − 512

I then went to check on the others, who were finishing up figuring how many ants needed to be added to 512 to make 1,000.

Jillian had written that her estimation was 488 but gave no explanation about

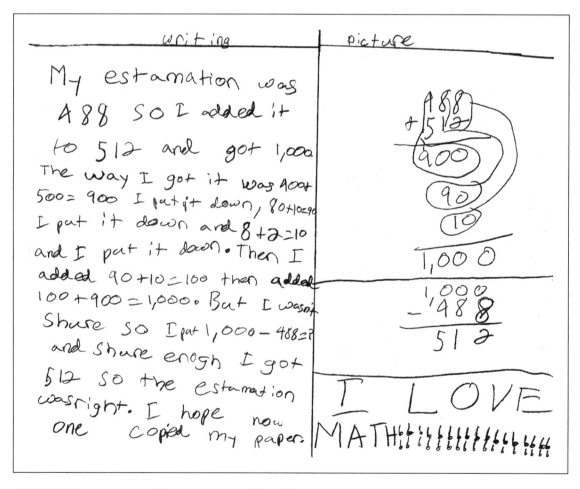

▲▲▲▲▲Figure 7–9 *Jillian represented her thinking using words and numbers.*

92   Lessons for Extending Place Value

how she arrived at that estimate. I asked her to explain. She said, "I knew adding five hundred to five hundred twelve was too much. That would make one thousand twelve. So I knew the answer was four hundred something. I added four hundred with the five hundred and that was nine hundred. Then I thought about the tens. There is one ten in five hundred twelve. That leaves four hundreds and nine tens. Then I thought about the two ones in five hundred twelve. I can change in one of the nine tens for ten ones. Take out the two ones for five hundred twelve and that leaves eight ones. That means there are four hundreds, eight tens, and eight ones, or four hundred eighty-eight. That's how many ants are needed to make one thousand." (See Figure 7–9.)

Tina used a guess-and-check method. First she doubled 512 and found that that

was too big. Next she chose a smaller number, 498, to add to 512. This put her only 10 away from 1,000. She subtracted 10 from 498 to get 488 and when she added 488 to 512, the sum was 1,000. (See Figure 7–10.)

Vinay indicated his awareness that the order of numbers matters in subtraction. He correctly used the subtraction algorithm to figure the answer. (See Figure 7–11.)

While Jessie got an incorrect answer, she used her number sense and place value ideas. I was sure that with more experience, her answers would be more accurate. (See Figure 7–12.)

I gave the students a two-minute warning. At the end of the two minutes, I asked the students to get ready for lunch while I collected their papers, ending class for the day.

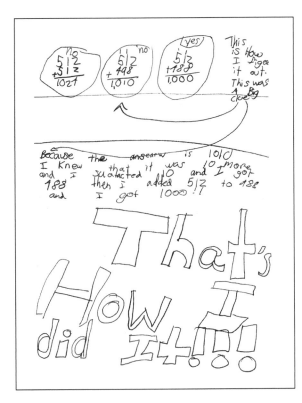

▲▲▲▲▲▲Figure 7–10 *Tina used a guess-and-check approach.*

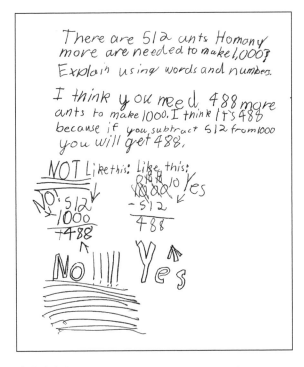

▲▲▲▲▲▲Figure 7–11 *Vinay showed an awareness that the order of numbers matters in subtraction.*

The 512 Ants on Sullivan Street   93

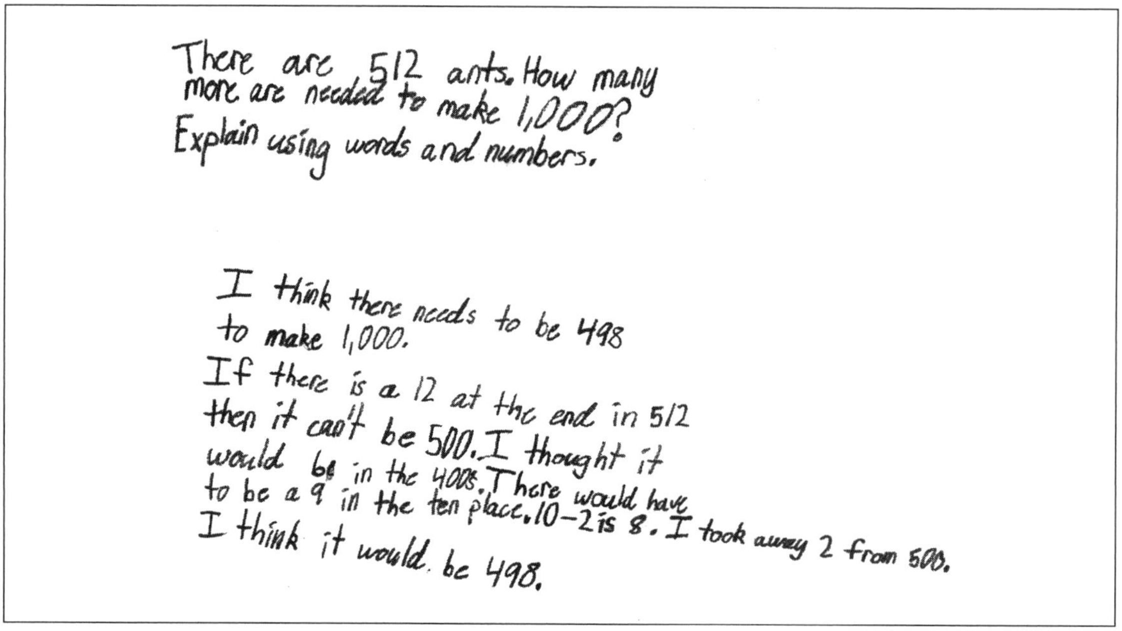

There are 512 ants. How many more are needed to make 1,000? Explain using words and numbers.

I think there needs to be 498 to make 1,000.
If there is a 12 at the end in 512 then it can't be 500. I thought it would be in the 400s. There would have to be a 9 in the ten place. 10-2 is 8. I took away 2 from 500.
I think it would be 498.

▲▲▲▲▲▲Figure 7–12 *Jessie used good number sense but showed confusion about how to account for the ten in twelve when she subtracted twelve from five hundred.*

Questions and Discussion

▲▲

▲ *How did you determine what to do to help Rachel, Jenae, and Jade?*

My instructional decisions were based on careful observation and listening as I questioned the girls and they responded and worked. As I'd hoped, my questions revealed what the girls did and did not understand. The discussion provided input for the girls as they listened to one another, and using a number line and providing base ten blocks gave them additional support that was visual and kinesthetic. In this case, Jenae's picture helped Rachel and Rachel's explanation helped Jenae. If Jenae's picture hadn't been available, I would have drawn one or used base ten blocks or cubes to help Rachel see what was happening in the problem.

▲ *How do you help students like Jael when they have to miss class?*

Sometimes it's difficult to provide help to children who need it, particularly when they miss class. However, in this case, I was able to work with Jael later that same day while the other students were involved in silent reading. On other days, this isn't possible, so I have to find time to work with such students the following day or whenever possible.

CHAPTER EIGHT
FINDING DIFFERENCES

Overview

Applying place value ideas to figure differences between two numbers is the main focus of this lesson. Partners play the game of *Finding Differences,* using two dice of different colors to randomly generate two-digit numbers. One color die determines the number of tens while the other determines the number of ones. Each player rolls the dice and records the two-digit number represented by the numbers that come up; then the pair compares their two-digit numbers and figures the difference. After three rounds, the players total their numbers and figure the difference between their totals.

Materials

▲ 2 dice of different colors per pair of students
▲ optional: *Finding Differences* recording sheet 1 per student (see Blackline Masters)
▲ optional: *Finding Differences* rules (see Blackline Masters)

Time

▲ one to two class periods plus additional class periods for the extensions

Teaching Directions

1. Tell the students that they will be learning a new game, *Finding Differences*, and draw on the board a sample recording chart.

95

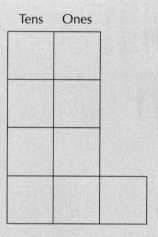

Tens   Ones

2. Explain to students they'll roll two different-colored dice, one color for the number of tens and the other for the number of ones. Roll the dice and model how to record on the first row of the chart.

3. Choose a student to play a game with you at the board. Ask the student to draw a recording chart on the board.

4. Play the game according to the rules.

Finding Differences

You need:
> a partner
> 2 dice, each a different color
> a recording sheet

Rules

1. Before you begin to play, decide with your partner which color die will tell how many tens and which will tell how many ones.

2. Player 1 rolls both dice, figures out what number the dice show, and then records the number on the recording sheet. For example:

3. Player 2 repeats Step 2.

4. Players work together to figure the difference between their numbers and record next to the chart on their recording sheets. For example:

> Jillian had 36.
> Mrs. Wickett had 64.
> 64 is 28 larger than 36.
> 64 − 36 = 28

5. Players repeat Steps 2, 3, and 4 two more times for a total of three rounds of play.

6. Each player finds the total number of tens and ones he or she rolled and records on the bottom row of the chart. Then each player combines the total tens and the total ones to figure their total for the game. For example:

7. Players work together to figure the difference between their totals and record on their recording sheets. For example:

> Jillian had 117.
> Mrs. Wickett had 163.
> 163 is 46 larger than 117.
> 163 − 117 = 46

5. To reinforce the experience, choose two different students to play a second model game, guiding them as needed.

6. To support students' efforts to write about the game, create sentence frames. Use the students' sentences from the second model game (Step 5). In one of the student's sentences, erase the names and numbers and replace them with blank lines. In the other student's sentences, underline the names and numbers to remind the class how to fill in the blanks.

_____ had __ .	Sam had 41.
_____ had __ .	Tina had 45.
__ is __ larger than __ .	45 is 34 larger than 11.
__ − __ = __	45 − 11 = 34

As an alternative, make copies of the recording sheet for students to use (see Blackline Masters).

7. Assign partners and distribute materials.

8. Observe as students play, stopping to ask and answer questions as appropriate. When students finish, ask them to play another game, this time with five rounds.

9. Lead a class discussion for students to share their thoughts, strategies, and experiences with the game.

Teaching Notes

The students in the following vignette used a variety of strategies for finding differences between two numbers. Some students used the traditional subtraction algorithm. Others counted on beginning with the smaller number, keeping track of how many it took to reach the larger number. Usually students who used this counting-on strategy added on tens first and then ones; however, a few students counted on by first adding ones to get to a friendly number and then counting on by tens until they reached the larger number.

During the lesson, a common misconception was revealed. When explaining how to subtract $64 - 36$, Rachel began by saying, "Four minus six is two." If Rachel were adding the two numbers, since addition is commutative, it would have been fine for her to think of the problem as either $4 + 6$ or $6 + 4$, since both would produce the same answer. However, subtraction isn't commutative, so reversing the numbers in the problem doesn't work. It may be that Rachel saw subtraction as commutative (even without being familiar with this terminology) and merely thought that $6 - 4$ produces the same result as $4 - 6$. Or it might be that Rachel learned that we don't take larger numbers from smaller numbers, so she did what made sense to her in this instance. This erroneous concept is common among students in the early grades who haven't yet learned about negative numbers and therefore don't understand that $4 - 6 = {}^-2$. Or it might be that when Rachel saw the problem, she took the easy route of subtracting 4 from 6. In the vignette, you'll read about how I addressed the issue when it occurred during our class discussion.

It is important that the students have the support needed to do the writing involved. The vignette describes how I provided support to my students. Another way to lend support for the writing is to use the recording sheet provided in the Blackline Masters section. The Blackline Master recording sheet has the sentence frames already written for the students so that they have to write only the correct information in the blanks. I chose not to provide my students with duplicated copies of the recording sheet because they had the skills necessary in mathematics, language, and writing to accomplish the task independently in a timely, accurate manner.

This activity provides multiple ways to help students develop and reinforce understanding and skills. For example, some students benefit from the use of base ten blocks when finding differences between numbers or combining the total number of tens and ones to figure their total score. Others can be helped through mental or paper-and-pencil computation.

The Lesson

▲▲▲

As the children settled, Ben noticed I was holding a bag of dice and commented, "I bet we're going to play a game today!"

I nodded and said to the students when they were quiet, "Ben is right. Today you'll learn a new game. The dice will be an important part of the game. You'll play with a partner and each of you will make your own recording sheet." I paused and drew the following on the board:

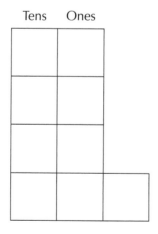

I continued, "To play, you'll roll two dice, a green one and a white one. The green die will determine the number of tens, and the white will tell you how many ones you get for your turn. On your record-

ing chart, you'll record the number of tens in the left column and the number of ones in the right column." I turned to the board and labeled the columns:

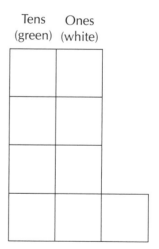

At this point, I asked for a volunteer to play the game with me. I selected Jillian because she was confident, was able to follow directions accurately and easily, and had a good command of the basic computation skills reinforced by this game. These attributes would help us model the game clearly and quickly. Before starting the game, I asked Jillian to draw on the board a copy of my recording form.

To begin the game, I rolled the two dice. The green die showed a 6 while the white die showed a 4. To reinforce the rule for using the numbers on the dice, I asked the class, "What does the green die tell me?"

Most hands were up instantly. Kassidee explained, "The green die tells you how many tens."

I said, "The green die says six. That means I get six tens, so I'll record a six in the first box under the Tens column." I turned to the board and recorded a 6 in the correct place.

I continued, "If the green die tells me how many tens I get, what does the white die tell me?"

"The white die tells you how many ones," Arin explained.

"I rolled a four on the white die, so that means I get four ones," I explained as I recorded the 4 as follows:

Tens   Ones
(green)   (white)

6	4	

"I got six tens and four ones. How much is that worth altogether?" I asked the students.

Instantly hands were waving in the air, indicating that this was an easy question for the students. I said to the class, "Tell me in a whisper voice."

"Sixty-four!" the students whispered.

Jillian's turn was next. She rolled a 3 on the green die and a 6 on the white die. She correctly recorded the numbers on her recording form and commented that she got only thirty-six.

I said to the class, "Round One of the game is over. Now Jillian and I must do some writing about what happened. Jillian had thirty-six and I had sixty-four." I recorded this on the board under my chart and instructed Jillian to do the same:

Jillian had 36.
Mrs. Wickett had 64.

I asked the students, "How much larger is sixty-four than thirty-six?" The students were quiet for a moment as they thought about my question. Then they began to talk among themselves as hands began to go up. When most of the students had raised their hands, I called on Connor.

Connor explained, "I think sixty-four is twenty-eight larger. I know because I added three tens to thirty-six, which is sixty-six. Three tens is thirty. Sixty-six is two bigger than sixty-four, so I subtracted two from thirty, and that made twenty-eight."

I recorded Connor's thinking on the board:

Connor $36 + 30 = 66$
$66 - 64 = 2$
$30 - 2 = 28$

I said to the class, "Raise your hand if you got twenty-eight." Most students raised their hands. Next I asked, "Who got a different answer and would like to share your thinking?"

Rachel raised her hand. She said, "I got thirty-two. I thought in my head sixty-four minus thirty-six. Four minus six is two. Sixty minus thirty is thirty. Thirty and two equals thirty-two." Rachel's error is a common one. She treated subtraction as if it were commutative, that is, as if the order of the numbers could be reversed, as in addition and multiplication, without affecting the result. As an example, when adding, $4 + 2 = 2 + 4 = 6$, and when multiplying, $4 \times 2 = 2 \times 4 = 8$. That's not the case with subtraction: $4 - 6 = {}^-2$ while $6 - 4 = 2$.

Finding Differences   99

I recorded Rachel's thinking on the board:

Rachel   64 − 36 = 32
4 − 6 = 2
60 − 30 = 30
30 + 2 = 32

I said to Rachel, "I agree with part of your thinking and disagree with part of it. I agree that sixty minus thirty equals thirty. But I don't agree that four minus six equals two. "

This class was familiar with number lines and fascinated with the idea of negative numbers. With this in mind, I drew a number line on the board with eleven marks. I labeled the middle mark 0. With the help of the students, I finished numbering the number line from $^-5$ through $^+5$. Then I had Rachel come to the board. I asked her to begin at $^+4$ and count to the left six as a concrete way of representing $4 - 6$.

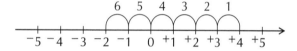

Rachel exclaimed, "Oh yeah! It's really negative two. That means I have to subtract two from the thirty I got when I subtracted sixty minus thirty. So it should be twenty-eight, not thirty-two."

I revised Rachel's initial thinking on the board:

Rachel   64 − 36 = 32
4 − 6 = −2
60 − 30 = 30
30 − 2 = 28

The class agreed the difference between thirty-six and sixty-four is twenty-eight. Jillian and I completed our writing about Round 1 as follows:

Jillian had 36.
Mrs. Wickett had 64.
64 is 28 larger than 36.
64 − 36 = 28

Jillian and I played two more rounds for a total of three rounds, completing the game:

Mrs. Wickett		Jillian	
Tens (green)	Ones (white)	Tens (green)	Ones (white)
6	4	3	6
4	4	6	5
5	5	1	6

round 1: Jillian had 36. Mrs. Wickett had 64. 64 is 28 larger than 36. 64 − 36 = 28

round 1: Jillian had 36. Mrs. Wickett had 64. 64 is 28 larger than 36. 64 − 36 = 28

round 2: Jillian had 65. Mrs. Wickett had 44. 65 is 21 larger than 44. 65 − 44 = 21

round 2: Jillian had 65. Mrs. Wickett had 44. 65 is 21 larger than 44. 65 − 44 = 21

round 3: Jillian had 16. Mrs. Wickett had 55. 55 is 39 larger than 16. 55 − 16 = 39

round 3: Jillian had 16. Mrs. Wickett had 55. 55 is 39 larger than 16. 55 − 16 = 39

Next I explained to the class, "The bottom row of boxes is to figure the total number of tens, the total number of ones and how much each of us got altogether. How many tens did I have?"

The students chorused, "Fifteen." I recorded *15* in the bottom box of the column labeled Tens.

I asked, "How many ones did I get?"

"Thirteen," the students responded.

I recorded *13* in the bottom box of the column labeled Ones.

I said, "I have fifteen tens and thirteen ones. How much is that altogether?" I paused a moment to give the students time to consider my question. I was interested to know if they would remember that fifteen was the number of tens and not the number of ones and if they also could figure the value of fifteen tens.

I said, "Talk with your neighbor. First one of you talks for thirty seconds while the other listens. After thirty seconds I'll remind you to change roles so that the first

100   Lessons for Extending Place Value

talker listens and the first listener talks." As the students shared their ideas with their partners, I listened carefully to determine what ideas students understood and misunderstood. Most students realized that fifteen tens equals 150. At the end of thirty seconds, I reminded the students to switch roles. At the end of the second thirty seconds, I asked for the students' attention.

I called on Vinay to explain how he figured my total. Vinay said, "I know that fifteen tens is the same as one hundred fifty. Thirteen ones is one ten and three ones. I put the one ten with the other fifteen and that's sixteen tens, or one hundred sixty. Then I added three more and got one hundred sixty-three."

I recorded Vinay's thinking on the board:

Vinay   15 tens = 150
        13 = 1 ten and 3 ones
        15 tens + 1 ten = 16 tens = 160
        160 + 3 = 163

Halley explained, "My way is a lot like Vinay's. I know that fifteen tens equals one hundred fifty. Then I counted by tens from one hundred fifty to one hundred sixty for the one in the thirteen ones, and then I added three more to make one hundred sixty-three."

I recorded on the board:

Halley   15 tens = 150
        150, 160
        160 + 3 = 163

Sam shared, "You could start with thirteen and count up by tens fifteen times. Thirteen, twenty-three, thirty-three, until you've done it fifteen times, and that will equal one hundred sixty-three."

Olina was skeptical. She asked, "Does that really work?" If Olina hadn't questioned Sam's idea, I would have suggested to the class that we try it to verify that it worked.

I replied, "Let's try it. We'll count together by tens fifteen times beginning with thirteen and see if we stop on one hundred sixty-three." I asked Olina to keep

track on the board of our counting with a tally mark each time we counted up by ten. Together we counted until Olina made fifteen tally marks. We stopped on 163. I then completed my chart:

Tens (green)	Ones (white)	
6	4	
4	4	
5	5	
Total 15	13	163

Next we completed Jillian's chart and we each wrote the following to summarize the game:

Jillian had 117.
Mrs. Wickett had 163.
163 is 46 larger than 117.
163 − 117 = 46

PLAYING A SECOND GAME AND CREATING SENTENCE FRAMES

To reinforce the rules for playing and how to record and write about the game, I asked two students to play another game to model for the class. I chose Sam and Tina. Sam and Tina recorded their game on the board as Jillian and I had done. As they played I offered guidance only as needed, mostly with the writing portion. The game went quickly, taking about ten minutes or so.

When they finished I took a few moments to develop sentence frames for the students to use when they played. To do this, I used the sentences on Sam's recording chart, erasing the names and numbers and replacing each of them with a

Finding Differences   101

line to indicate a blank to be filled in. As a reminder to the students about what went in the blanks, I left Tina's recording intact but underlined the same information I'd erased in Sam's work.

_____ had __ .	<u>Sam</u> had <u>41</u>.
_____ had __ .	<u>Tina</u> had <u>45</u>.
__ is __ larger than __ .	<u>45</u> is <u>34</u> larger than <u>11</u>.
__ − __ = __	<u>45</u> − <u>11</u> = <u>34</u>

The students were eager to play. I put the dice and paper for recording on a counter and reminded the students that each player needed a sheet of paper and each pair needed a white die and a green die. I assigned partners. The students were quick to gather their materials and begin playing.

OBSERVING THE STUDENTS

As the students settled in various parts of the room, they immediately got to work copying the recording chart from the board and determining which partner would roll first. While this wasn't a problem for most students, it was for Kito and his partner, Halley. I stood back, observing and listening for a few moments in hopes the two could resolve the problem on their own. Cooperation was difficult at times for both of these students. It was evident they were making no progress, so I stepped in.

I said to the pair, "I notice that you seem upset with each other. What seems to be the problem?" Although I knew from watching what the problem was, I asked them to give them a chance to verbalize their difficulties.

Halley said, "We can't decide who goes first because we both want to go first."

Kito added, "I told Halley I should go first in the first game and then she could go first."

Halley explained, "I said we should roll a die and the one with the highest roll should go first. That's fair, but Kito didn't want to do that." Kito shrugged and gave no response.

I said to Kito, "Halley has suggested a way she thinks is fair to determine who goes first. Do you have another way?"

Kito replied, "I wanted to have the person who's older go first because I know I'm older than Halley."

I responded, "If you already know you're older, does that seem like a fair way to determine who goes first?" Kito shook his head "no."

"What if we roll the die and the person with the lower number goes first?" Kito suggested. Halley nodded her agreement and handed the die to Kito. Kito rolled a 6, gave a slight smile to Halley, and said, "It looks like you'll go first unless you roll a six, too." Halley rolled a 4, and the two finally got started playing the game.

I checked on Rachel and her partner to be sure that when Rachel compared numbers, her work was accurate. I didn't want her repeating, and thus reinforcing, the same error she'd made earlier during the class discussion. As I approached, I listened as her partner, Keara, patiently explained how to compare numbers by counting on. The girls were comparing forty-six and twenty-three.

Keara explained, "It's really easy to just start with the smaller number and count until you get to the bigger number. You start with twenty-three. Add ten and that's thirty-three; ten more is forty-three. That's twenty so far. Then add three more to forty-three to get to forty-six, and you know the difference is twenty-three." Rachel looked skeptical. I decided to intervene and build on what Keara had explained. I grabbed a few base ten blocks and sat down with the girls.

I said, "Keara has a great idea, but I can tell that it doesn't make much sense to you, Rachel. I thought using the blocks might help you see what Keara is trying to explain." Rachel nodded her agreement that she was confused as I laid out two tens and three ones blocks. I asked Rachel, "What is the total value of these blocks?" She quickly indicated the value of the blocks was twenty-three.

I explained, "Keara's idea was to start with twenty-three, the smaller of the two numbers rolled, and see how many tens and ones you have to add to get to forty-six." Rachel nodded as I explained. "How much do I have if I add another ten to the twenty-three?" I laid a tens block in a second pile near the twenty-three.

"Thirty-three," Rachel replied quickly and then she counted the blocks to reassure herself that thirty-three was correct. I nodded my agreement.

I placed a second tens block beside the previous block. I asked, "How much now?"

Rachel lit up. "Both piles of blocks put together make forty-three. You've added two tens to twenty-three to make forty-three."

Next I asked, "How many more do I need to add to make a total of forty-six?"

Rachel reached for the blocks. She added three ones cubes, counting on from forty-three as she did so.

"What you did with the blocks is like what I said," Keara commented.

Rachel summarized by saying, "So the difference between twenty-three and forty-six is twenty-three. I don't have to subtract because I can just start adding on to the smaller number." Rachel smiled, pleased with herself. I moved on, leaving the girls to continue their game. When I checked back a while later, Rachel was successfully using the strategy of adding on to compare numbers.

Arin was having difficulty figuring her total. She had nine tens and sixteen ones, and as I walked past, she asked, "Is my total twenty-five?" Arin was ignoring the value of the tens.

To draw her attention to the meaning of the 9, I asked her, "In which column is the nine?"

Arin replied, "It's in the tens."

Next I asked, "How much are nine tens worth?"

"Oh, the nine isn't really a nine. It's ninety," she replied. I wrote *90* beneath the Tens column on her chart.

Next I asked, "What is the total number of ones you got?"

"Sixteen," Arin said. I wrote *16* beneath the Ones column of her chart.

Finally, I asked, "What is ninety plus sixteen?"

After a moment she replied, "One hundred six."

I suggested that Arin and her partner play another game and complete their charts with the additional information about the number of tens and ones. (See Figure 8–1.)

As Tobias wrote about his game with James, he chose to vary his sentences slightly from the sentence frames posted on the board. (See Figure 8–2.) His recording was accurate, as was his partner's. I suggested that James and Tobias play a

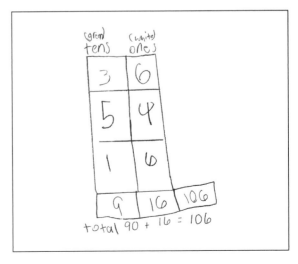

▲▲▲▲▲**Figure 8–1** *Writing the value of each column below it helped Arin.*

Finding Differences   103

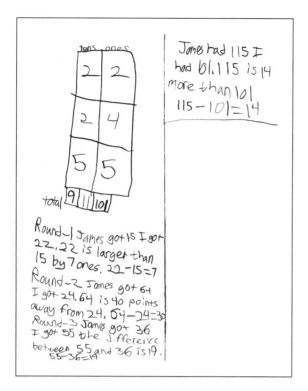

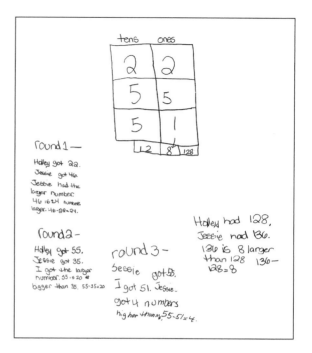

new game, this time playing for five rounds rather than three. The boys were eager to try it.

Like Tobias, Halley varied from the sentence frames. She included statements telling which number rolled for each round was larger. Her partner, Jessie, used the sentence frames provided on the board. (See Figures 8–3 and 8–4.)

Tina and Vinay had a typical game and they recorded the results correctly. (See Figure 8–5.)

As students finished, I checked their work for accuracy and also asked them how they figured their totals and how they compared their totals. Then I asked them to play another game, this time playing for five rounds. Having them play the initial short version allowed me the opportunity to clear up misunderstandings and provide guidance before the students became engaged in a longer game. The longer game provides increased practice with

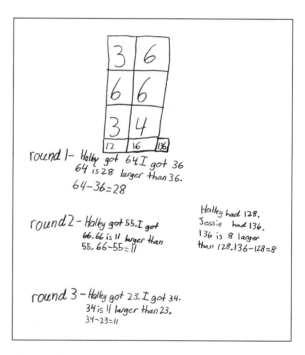

finding differences and ultimately provides larger totals to compare.

When most students had finished their first game, I gave a two-minute warning.

104   Lessons for Extending Place Value

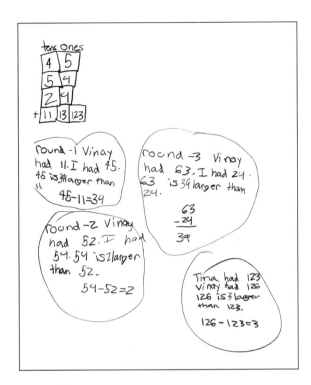

▲▲▲▲▲Figure 8–5 *Tina and Vinay's game was typical.*

After two minutes, I called the class together, collecting the students' papers as they settled on the floor. I was interested in their perceptions of the game. I asked, "How did you like the game?" All the students gave it a thumbs-up.

Olina said, "It wasn't too hard and it wasn't too easy. I didn't get bored and I didn't get frustrated. It was just right."

Ben shared, "The numbers we rolled were good because we could find the differences mostly in our heads. I just counted on from the smaller number to the bigger number."

Kassidee commented, "Something I just thought of and we didn't think about when we were playing—who wins? It was really nice not to worry about winning." I commented that it wasn't a win-lose kind of game, but rather an activity that helped them think about differences between numbers. With that, I ended the lesson.

EXTENSIONS

1. To make the game easier for students, have them play only two rounds and then compare.

2. For more of a challenge, add a column for hundreds to the recording sheet and have players use three dice to generate numbers in the hundreds. This could result in totals in the thousands, depending on the numbers rolled and the number of rounds played in a game.

Questions and Discussion

▲▲▲

▲ *What are ways other than dice to generate random numbers for children to compare?*

If you don't have dice in two colors, or you prefer not to use dice, here are a couple of alternatives: Students can use spinners numbered 1 to 6. The first spin determines the number of tens and the second spin tells the number of ones. Or write the numbers from 1 to 6 on two different colors of small paper squares. Sort them by color into two containers. Players then draw one number from each container, replacing each number in the appropriate container at the end of the turn.

▲ *When pairing students, how would you handle an odd number of students?*

With this particular activity, I would get the other students started and become a partner so that all games were played in pairs. Because subtraction is a key component of this game,

Finding Differences   105

finding differences between more than two numbers per round doesn't make sense. For other activities, it's fine for a group to have three students.

▲ *What are some methods you use to assign partners?*

Sometimes I pair students randomly by drawing names. Sometimes I ask students to work with the person sitting beside them or across from them. At times I assign partners with particular combinations in mind. For example, I might assign two strong students to work together so they will challenge each other, or I might assign a stronger student and a weaker student to work together so that the stronger student can reinforce his or her knowledge while explaining his or her thinking and helping the weaker student. There are times when I allow students to select their partners, although before doing this I spend some time with the students, helping them learn appropriate ways of asking someone to work with them and ways of accepting or declining an invitation to be a partner. From the first day of school, we talk about how these sorts of responses can affect others in good ways as well as in bad ways, working toward developing a supportive classroom culture for learning and growing together.

▲ *Why did you choose to have the children make their own recording sheets rather than use the Blackline Master provided?*

I feel it's important to give students many opportunities to organize and record their work without the structure of a worksheet. Presenting work in a written form comprehensible to others is an important skill. To encourage students' success, as I did in the lesson, I begin by modeling for the students one way to record. In addition, I often provide sentence frames to help them write about their experiences, especially for less experienced children. The students in the vignette had previous experience making their own recording sheets and had the needed skills in organization, writing, and math, so making their recording sheets was not an ordeal that got in the way of their learning. Also, in our school, as in many others, we can make only a limited number of copies of worksheets.

When time is an issue or if students don't have the needed skills to make their own recording sheets, a worksheet for recording is useful.

▲ *I notice that you write the minus sign higher in front of negative numbers. Is this necessary?*

You're right to notice that the sign indicating that a number is negative is written higher than a minus sign. This is one of those mathematical conventions that isn't always followed but that I find useful to differentiate the two symbols. The minus sign is an operation sign; that is, it indicates the operation of subtraction and tells the child that some mathematical action is called for. The negative sign, however, indicates that a number is less than zero. In students' later mathematical studies, they'll encounter expressions that include both a minus sign and a negative sign; for example, eight minus negative five. We record this symbolically as $8 - {}^-5$. This expression can also be written by using parentheses with two minus signs: $8 - (-8)$, but I think that the convention of a raised negative sign helps with clarity, and it's easy to introduce to third graders.

CHAPTER NINE
BALANCING NUMBER PUZZLES

Overview

In this lesson, students use their knowledge of ones, tens, and hundreds to solve balancing number puzzles. They strengthen their number sense as they apply their computation skills in addition and subtraction to find missing addends. The idea of balance is represented using drawings that show both sides in balance, similar to a pan balance, thus indicating the sides are equivalent. Students solve balancing number puzzles as a whole group and in pairs and later go on to create their own balancing number puzzles for others to solve along with possible solutions.

Materials

▲ overhead base ten blocks, 1 flat, 10 longs, 10 ones cubes
▲ optional: transparencies of 100 flat, 1–2
▲ optional: base ten blocks, 1–2 flats, 10–12 longs, and 10–15 ones cubes per student

Time

▲ two class periods plus additional time for extensions

Teaching Directions

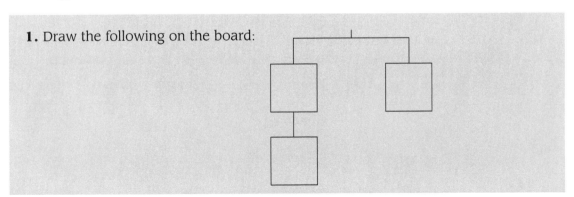

1. Draw the following on the board:

2. Referring to the board, ask students: "What does this remind you of?" As students share their ideas, guide them as needed to make connections between the drawing and things in their world that balance.

3. Write *64* and *100* as shown.

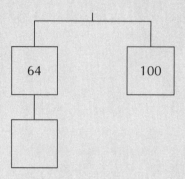

Ask students: "Now that I've added some numbers to my picture, what do you know?" Have students share their ideas with their partners and then with the whole group.

4. Divide the empty box in the drawing into two halves and label as shown.

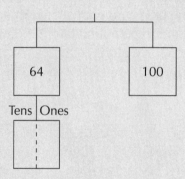

5. Ask students: "How many more tens do I need to add to sixty-four to get to one hundred?" Share and discuss students' ideas.

6. Check using base ten blocks the number of tens needed. Using an overhead projector, project an overhead flat. To show sixty-four, lay on top of the flat six tens and four ones. Together figure the number of tens and ones needed to completely cover the flat. Complete the puzzle. Lead a discussion about why the solution makes sense.

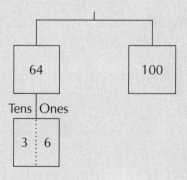

7. Introduce the second problem by drawing the following on the board:

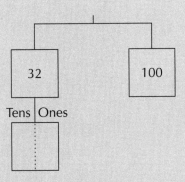

Repeat Steps 5 and 6.

8. To introduce the third problem, draw the following on the board:

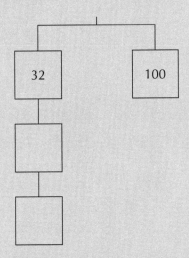

Ask students to share their ideas about this new problem. Record their ideas on the board.

9. Draw the following on the board:

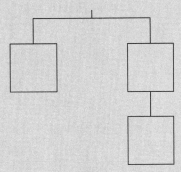

Repeat Step 8. Then draw the following on the board and repeat Step 8 again. For these problems, have students work in pairs to find possible solutions to fill in the empty boxes. Lead a class discussion for volunteers to share their ideas.

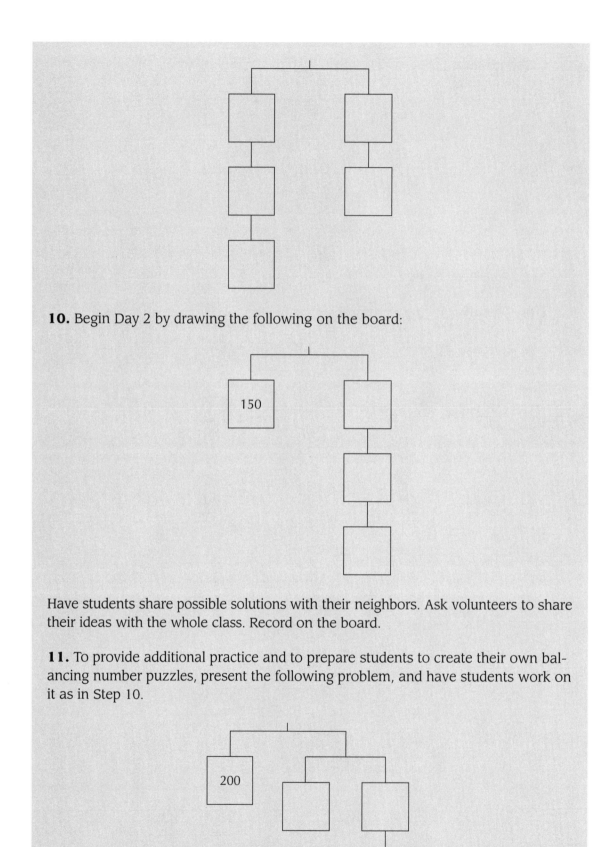

10. Begin Day 2 by drawing the following on the board:

Have students share possible solutions with their neighbors. Ask volunteers to share their ideas with the whole class. Record on the board.

11. To provide additional practice and to prepare students to create their own balancing number puzzles, present the following problem, and have students work on it as in Step 10.

Draw the following on the board and repeat Step 10.

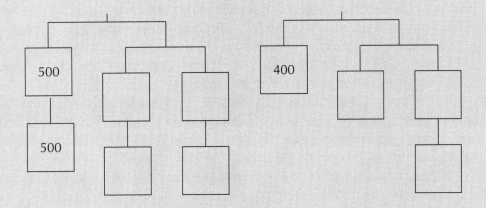

12. To model for students how to create their own balancing number puzzles, draw the following on the board:

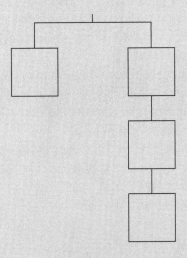

Have students share and discuss ways to complete the puzzle. Record on the board.

13. Choose one student idea from Step 12. Ask students: "For someone to solve this puzzle, what information should I give?" Make sure students understand how to give clues so others can solve their puzzles.

14. Tell students to draw a puzzle and solve it in two or three ways on one side of their paper. Then on the other side, they should draw the puzzle with clues for someone else to solve. Students may work in pairs or alone to create their balancing number puzzles.

15. As students work, circulate through the class, observing and answering and asking questions as needed. If time allows, ask a volunteer to share a puzzle with the class.

Teaching Notes

Balancing Number Puzzles is a challenging, enjoyable activity. To ensure access and success for all my students in the following vignette, I spent time carefully guiding the discussion and the students' thinking on the first balancing numbers puzzle, thus laying a solid foundation for the rest of the lesson. As a result, the children were successful throughout the remainder of the lesson.

To support second language learners or any other children who need additional help to understand the idea of two sides balancing, you may want to introduce the lesson by showing students a pan balance or a mobile to help them to grasp the idea of balance as represented in this lesson.

During the early part of Day 1, I used overhead base ten blocks to help students visualize what the numbers represented and to verify for the class the correctness of solutions. While it was not necessary for this class, you may find it helpful to make available base ten blocks to some or all of your students so they can verify for themselves whether or not solutions are correct. I stopped using the base ten blocks early in the lesson. You may find it helpful to use them for a longer period of time. While it might seem unnecessary for you to use base ten blocks at all, I encourage you to do so initially because it will cement students' understanding and make the rest of the lesson more accessible and enjoyable.

If you do not have access to overhead base ten blocks, use transparencies of a flat, and with an overhead pen, color in the tens and ones needed to solve the problems. If you do not have base ten blocks for your students to use, see the Base Ten Blocks Blackline Master in the back of this book.

Because this lesson is intended for third graders, the majority of the discussion centers on positive whole numbers, with a few ideas involving negative numbers. The problems presented have additional solutions including fractions and other numbers not typically accessible to third graders.

The Lesson

DAY 1

As the children settled, I drew the following on the board:

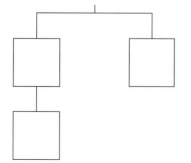

The students were interested in what I was drawing and became quiet. I turned from the board and asked as I pointed to my completed drawing, "What does this remind you of?"

I paused a few moments to give students time to think. I was hoping students would see that the drawing balanced and make a connection between my drawing and something in their world that balanced. If the students didn't make this connection, I planned on asking them questions that would help them make it. Hands began to go up. After several moments, I called on Roberto.

"It reminds me of the mobile over my baby brother's crib. It balances and there are little animals hanging from each side," Roberto explained. Several children nodded their agreement with Roberto and started sharing with their neighbors about their younger brothers and sisters. I called the class back to order.

To refocus the students, I said, "Roberto mentioned the idea of balance. What is it about my picture that makes you think balance is involved? Turn and talk with your neighbor." The students began chatting among themselves about their ideas. Soon many hands were up, indicating students were eager to share their ideas with the class. I called on Tina.

Tina came to the board, pointed to the top horizontal line of my drawing, and explained, "The top line goes straight across and not up and down. I think that means what is on each side is the same so it balances."

To be certain I understood Tina's idea and to restate her thinking for a few who looked uncertain, I asked, "Are you saying that this horizontal line tells you both sides are the same amount?" Tina nodded.

Next I pointed to the top horizontal line and asked Tina and the others, "What would this line look like if one side were heavier, or more, than the other?" The students were eager to share. I called on Olina to come to the board and draw her idea. She drew the following:

She then explained, "The low side is more and the high side is less. It's like a teeter-totter."

I asked, "Who has another idea about how the line could look?"

Tobias shared, "It could go the other way from Olina's way. The low side would be the high side and the high side would be the low side." Tobias came to the board and drew his idea beneath Olina's.

I called on Abel and he posed the following question: "If one side is a lot more than the other, would the line be more up and down? And if the sides are almost the same, would the line be almost straight?"

I appreciated Abel's thinking and wanted to encourage the children to investigate his ideas along with other ideas that affect balance in the physical world; however, I also wanted to remain focused on the lesson. I replied to Abel, "You asked two interesting questions that we can investigate later. For this lesson, when a line is horizontal, we'll assume the amounts on each side are equivalent, or equal."

As the students sat quietly, I wrote *64* in the upper box on the left side of my drawing and *100* in the box on the right.

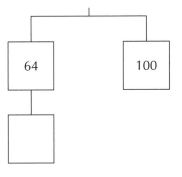

I said, "Now that I've added some numbers to my picture, what do you know?" Almost all hands were up. I asked the students to share their ideas with their neighbors. I wanted to give as many children as possible the opportunity to express their thoughts. As they shared I listened, satisfied that most were grasping the idea that both sides had to be equivalent. I wasn't too worried about the few who weren't grasping the idea yet because I knew the base ten blocks I planned to use

Balancing Number Puzzles   113

along with the class discussion would give these children additional support, allowing their understanding to develop. After a few moments I called the class to order.

Vinay shared first. He explained, "I think both sides have to equal one hundred."

"Why do you think both sides have to equal one hundred?" I asked Vinay.

Vinay paused a moment to gather his thoughts and then said, "There's only one box on the right, and it has one hundred in it. Whatever is in that one box is all that side can equal. Both sides have to be the same, so the other side has to equal one hundred, too."

Keara added, "The side with sixty-four has to have something added to sixty-four to equal one hundred, and that's what goes in the empty box."

"Who has another way of explaining what Keara and Vinay just shared?"

James explained, "Sixty-four plus something is equal to one hundred. It has to be that way for both sides to be equal." The others showed their agreement with James by showing thumbs up.

I divided the empty box below the 64 into two parts with a vertical dotted line, labeling the left side *Tens* and the right side *Ones*.

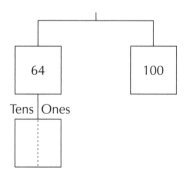

I asked the students, "How many more tens do I need to add to sixty-four to get to one hundred?" I paused a moment and then asked the children to respond using a whisper voice. Some students said three tens were needed while a few stated that four tens were needed.

I said, "I heard two answers, three tens and four tens. Who would like to explain your thinking?" I called on Jael.

Jael explained, "I think four tens. If you start with sixty and count on by tens to one hundred, it's four tens. Sixty, then one ten is seventy, two tens is eighty, three tens is ninety, and four tens is one hundred."

I recorded on the board:

60
70 (+ 1 ten)
80 (+ 2 tens)
90 (+ 3 tens)
100 (+ 4 tens)

"Raise your hand if Jael's thinking makes sense to you," I said. A few hands went up. "Who has a different idea?"

Sam shared, "If we only had sixty instead of sixty-four, Jael would be right. But we actually have four more than sixty, so it can't be four tens; it has to be three tens and some ones because sixty-four and forty, or four tens, is one hundred four. That's too much. Sixty-four and three tens is ninety-four. I think three tens are needed."

"Oh yeah!" Christopher muttered. "I see now."

"Who has another way of thinking about this?" I asked.

Halley said, "In my head, I started at sixty and I counted on forty and landed on one hundred. Then I took off four because sixty-four is four bigger than sixty. When I did that, I got thirty-six. So three tens are needed."

Kassidee had a different idea. She explained, "I went backwards. I started at one hundred and went back six tens for the six tens in sixty. That leaves four tens. But I still had to take out the four ones. That would leave only three tens and six ones."

I recorded on the board:

Kassidee   100 − 6 tens = 4 tens
4 tens − 4 ones = 3 tens and
6 ones

The students were quiet. I said, "Show me with your fingers how many tens are needed." Almost all students put up three fingers.

I said, "Let's check another way. We can use base ten blocks." Using an overhead projector, I projected an overhead flat (a hundreds block). I said, "The hundreds flat can represent the one hundred on the right side of my drawing." I laid six tens and four ones on top of the flat. I continued, "My blocks show that I have covered up sixty-four on the flat. Many of you said you thought we needed three more tens. I'll add three more tens to the flat and see if that is close to one hundred." I did so. This left six spaces on the flat uncovered. I asked the class, "Are there enough uncovered spaces left to add another ten?"

The students chorused, "No!"

"So how many tens did I need to add?" I asked.

"Three," they responded.

I wrote a *3* in the tens side of the empty box. "How many ones?" I asked.

"Six," the class chorused. I wrote in the *6* so my drawing looked as follows:

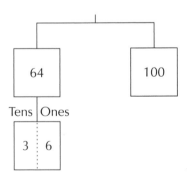

"Who can explain why our solution makes sense?" I asked.

Rachel explained, "It's right because both sides are the same amount. I know because when I add sixty-four and thirty-six, I get one hundred. The four and six make ten. Six tens and three tens are nine tens, plus the other ten, which is ten tens, and that's the same as one hundred."

I recorded on the board:

Rachel   64 + 36 = 100
4 + 6 = 10

6 tens + 3 tens = 9 tens
9 tens + 1 ten = 10 tens = 100

"Who would like to explain it another way?" I asked.

Paul said, "My way is a lot like Rachel's way, except that I started with the tens. Six tens and three tens equals nine tens. Then I added four and six, and that makes another ten. Nine tens and the ten I just got make ten tens, and that's one hundred, so it balances."

I recorded on the board:

Paul   6 tens + 3 tens = 9 tens
4 + 6 = 10
9 tens + 1 ten = 10 tens = 100

Jessie explained, "Both sides must equal one hundred. I just counted on from sixty-four. I counted on three tens and then six ones. Sixty-four, seventy-four, eighty-four, ninety-four, ninety-five, ninety-six, ninety-seven, ninety-eight, ninety-nine, one hundred." Jessie used her fingers to help her keep track as she counted.

I recorded her idea as follows:

Jessie 64, 74, 84, 94, 95, 96, 97, 98, 99, 100
3 tens = 30   6 ones = 6

Introducing a Second Problem

The students were quiet. I drew a new picture on the board beside the one we'd just finished, filling two boxes with numbers.

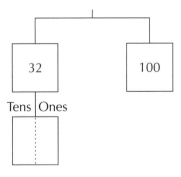

I asked the students, "Is the drawing supposed to balance?" The children responded with their thumbs up. Next I asked, "How do you know?"

"The line on the top goes straight across like the first one," Adama explained. I nodded.

Ben added, "Both sides have to equal one hundred like the last one."

I asked, "Why do both sides have to equal one hundred?"

Ben clarified, "The box on the right side says how much that side is worth. It's worth one hundred. The other side has to be the same amount."

I said to the class, "If both sides have to equal one hundred, what has to be in the empty box on the left side? Please think about this quietly for a few moments." After a few minutes I asked for volunteers to share their ideas.

Karlee said, "You need seven tens and eight ones." I filled in the empty box according to Karlee's suggestion.

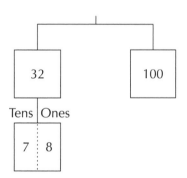

I responded, "Put your thumb up if seventy-eight makes sense to you, put it down if it doesn't, or put your thumb sideways if you're not sure." About one-fourth of the students agreed with Karlee's answer, about one-fourth were uncertain, and about half disagreed.

Christopher, who'd had trouble earlier, explained, "I disagree. Seventy-eight is too much. If I add the three tens from the thirty-two to seventy-eight, that's one hundred eight. Too big!"

Karlee considered what Christopher was saying. She used her fingers to help her keep track as she added thirty to seventy-eight. I paused for a moment, giving Karlee time to sort through the information before her. I hoped that she would see her error.

She finally said, "I know something is too big, but I don't really know what to do."

To help Karlee and others who were uncertain, I said, "We have to change a number. What number can we change?"

A bit bewildered, Karlee shrugged.

To support Karlee, I once again projected a base ten flat and covered it this time with three tens and two ones. I asked her, "Since we already know thirty-two and one hundred are part of the problem, can we change either of those numbers?" She shook her head. Then her face lit up with understanding.

"Oh, yeah! I see now. The seventy-eight is too big. I can tell by looking at the blocks that there isn't enough room for seven more tens! I think maybe sixty-eight would work."

I erased the 78 and replaced it with *68*. I said to the students, "What do you think about sixty-eight?" The students talked among themselves, and after a few moments, I called the class to order.

Sam said, "I think sixty-eight is right. If you add sixty-eight and thirty-two, that will be one hundred. If you add the ones together it's ten because eight and two equal ten. Then put the tens together, three tens and six tens, and that's nine tens. Then put the one ten from adding the ones together with the nine tens, and that's ten tens, which is one hundred."

I recorded on the board:

Sam   *68 + 32 = 100*
            2 + 8 = 10
      6 tens + 3 tens = 9 tens
      1 ten + 9 tens = 10 tens = 100

The students showed their agreement with Sam's thinking by putting their thumbs up. To confirm that sixty-eight was correct, I laid six more tens and eight ones on the flat. These blocks combined with the thirty-two already there covered the flat completely, showing that sixty-eight was correct.

A Balancing Number Puzzle with More than One Solution

The students were clear in their understanding of how to solve balancing number puzzles so far. I decided to add an additional challenge. In the next puzzle, I left two boxes empty, creating a situation for multiple solutions. I drew the following on the board:

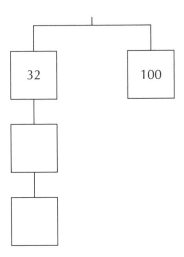

As I completed the drawing, I overheard students discussing several possible solutions. Some were surprised that there might be more than one way to make the numbers balance. I asked for the students' attention. "Who would like to share what you are thinking?" I asked. Hands waved in the air.

Abel said, "There's more than one way! I had one way and Adama and I were talking, and she had a different way. Both were right!"

"What were your ways?" I asked Abel and Adama.

Adama said, "You can put sixty in the top empty box and eight in the bottom empty box. Then it's like the last problem. If you add sixty to thirty-two, it equals ninety-two, and then eight more make one hundred." I wrote *60* and *8* as suggested by Adama:

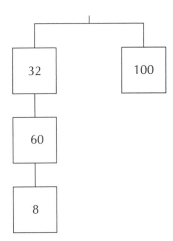

Abel then shared his solution. "I think eighteen and fifty would work. I added eight to thirty-two to get forty; then ten more makes fifty. That's where I got the eighteen. Then add fifty to fifty, and that's one hundred."

I recorded on the board:

Abel   *32 + 8 = 40*
       40 + 10 = 50
        10 + 8 = 18
       32 + 18 = 50
       50 + 50 = 100

I also wrote *18* and *50* beside the boxes where I'd written 60 and 8, reinforcing the idea that there was more than one way to solve the problem.

Tina shared next. "I think seventy should go in one box . . ." She paused a moment and then continued, "That's too much. I'm stuck. Can I call on someone to help me?" I nodded.

Vinay waved his hand excitedly. He often thought in creative ways and had a gleam in his eyes. Tina called on Vinay. He explained, "The seventy Tina said will work. The other number has to be negative two. Then it's sixty-eight, and we already know that thirty-two and sixty-eight equal one hundred."

"Oh yeah!" several students responded.

I added Vinay's idea to the list. I asked the students, "What number sentence could we write to tell about Vinay and Tina's idea?"

Sam volunteered, "You can write thirty-two plus seventy minus two equals one hundred."

I recorded on the board:

Sam   32 + 70 − 2 = 100

Two More Problems

I presented the children with the first of two more balancing number problems, leaving all the boxes blank. The students worked in pairs to figure solutions; then volunteers shared their ideas in a whole-class discussion.

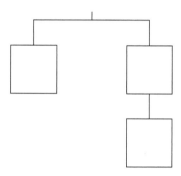

Ana suggested that the left side could be 400 while the two boxes on the right could be 200 and 200.

Sam shared that 200 on the left and 240 and ⁻40 on the right would work.

Tobias wanted 10 on the left and 5 and 5 on the right.

Jade liked 120 on the left and 90 and 30 on the right.

When all who wanted to had shared, I drew the second problem, again leaving all boxes blank. Again students worked in pairs to find solutions.

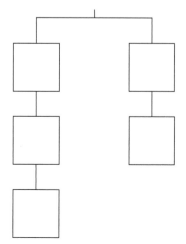

Keara suggested that all boxes be filled in with 0s. This amused the rest of the students.

Paul explained, "My way is really cool. I discovered that you could put three threes on one side and a four and five on the other. Both sides equal nine."

Halley got very excited and waved her hand. "I just had a really good idea. Paul made me think of it. You could change the three threes to three thirties and the four to forty and the five to fifty and it will still work. I just multiplied everything by ten. Three thirties is ninety and forty plus fifty is ninety!"

The others were impressed with Halley's thinking.

James built on Halley's thinking and shared, "The left side could be one, four, and five. That equals ten. The right side could be two fives. That is ten, too. Then do like Halley did and multiply everything by ten and it still works. Ten plus forty plus fifty equals one hundred and so does fifty plus fifty."

Ben had a different idea. "Put three fives on the left side and a sixteen and a minus one on the right side. Three fives is fifteen and sixteen minus one is fifteen."

I gave all students who wanted to the opportunity to share their ideas. They were enjoying the activity and getting a lot of practice with computation. I ended the lesson there, promising to return to it the following day, when they would be able to solve more balancing numbers puzzles and then make up their own.

DAY 2

To begin the next part of the lesson, I drew the following on the board:

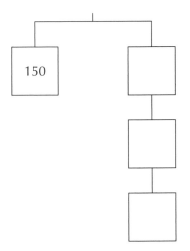

The students were eager to share their ides. I asked them to turn and talk with their neighbors. After a few moments, I asked for their attention and for volunteers to share.

James shared, "One hundred fifty is equal to fifty plus fifty plus fifty."

I recorded on the board beneath my drawing:

James   150 = 50 + 50 + 50

Karena said, "You could do one hundred fifty with forty, ten, and one hundred."

Tobias suggested, "Ninety, ten, and fifty equal one hundred fifty."

I added Karena's and Tobias's ideas to the list:

James   150 = 50 + 50 + 50
Karena 150 = 40 + 10 + 100
Tobias   150 = 90 + 10 + 50

Sam, who enjoyed thinking in unusual ways, had the following idea; "One hundred fifty equals one hundred plus ninety minus forty." I included his idea on the list.

I noticed Jillian, who seemed to be deep in thought. Jillian loved to learn and explore ideas. I asked her what she was thinking.

Jillian explained, "I was wondering something. If you use three of the same numbers to make one hundred fifty, like fifty, fifty, and fifty, instead of making the boxes go down, could you make them go across, since they are all the same amount?" Most of the other students sat

with questioning looks on their faces and I wasn't sure I understood Jillian's thinking, so I asked her to come to the board to draw her idea. She drew the following:

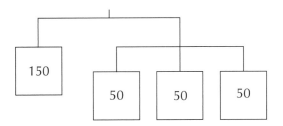

The students started talking among themselves about Jillian's idea. I called the class back to order.

I said, "Jillian has an interesting idea. What do you think? Does it make sense that she can arrange the same numbers as she did?"

The students agreed that she could. Connor summed it up. He said, "On the line with the three fifties, the first and last one balance each other, so that works, and the middle one helps the other two fifties to balance with the one hundred fifty without making one side of the line heavier than the other."

I was glad Jillian had brought this idea up. I had deliberately chosen this problem with the intent of introducing this idea to the students once someone had suggested that three 50s equal 150. The children were engaged and excited.

The next problem I presented caused some struggle.

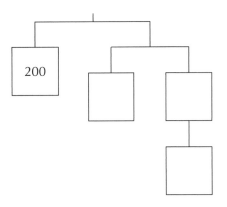

Balancing Number Puzzles   119

Initially, the children were quick to see that both sets of boxes on the right side had to equal one hundred. Ben explained, "Both sides on the right side have to be one hundred because the horizontal line connecting the boxes is straight. That means both sides have to be the same amount. And then the left side is two hundred, so the total amount on the right side has to be two hundred."

Tanya then suggested that the boxes could be completed as follows:

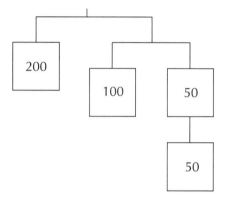

I asked the students, "Is there another way to fill in the boxes?" This question met with confused expressions. I paused to give students time to consider my question. I continued, "Talk with your partner about this. First one of you talks for thirty seconds; then when I give the signal, the first listener talks and the first talker listens." After thirty seconds I reminded the students to change roles, and after the second thirty seconds, I asked for the students' attention. About half the students raised their hands.

Halley shared first. "I think I figured this out. The hundred has to stay the same, or the sides won't balance. But I think you could put in the other two boxes forty-nine and fifty-one. That equals one hundred, so it balances with the hundred, and one hundred plus one hundred equals two hundred, so the whole thing balances."

Halley's explanation triggered excitement, especially from those who weren't too certain. If Halley hadn't shared her insight, I would have guided the students to this understanding through questions about what could be changed and what had to remain the same.

I recorded Halley's solution numerically under the drawing:

Halley   200 = 100 + 49 + 51

All who wanted to shared their ideas and I recorded them on the board. Sam shared an idea involving fractions rather than negative numbers as he had done previously in this lesson. He suggested the following:

Sam   200 = 100 + 49\frac{1}{2} + 50\frac{1}{2}

Together we worked on two other problems in the same way.

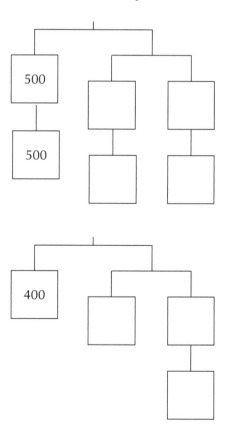

Creating Balancing Number Puzzles
To model for the children how to create a balancing numbers puzzle, I drew the following on the board:

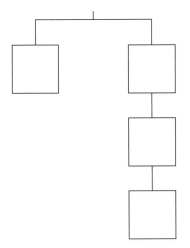

I said to the students, "Today, you'll create your own puzzles. But first, let's create a balancing numbers puzzle together. Where would it make sense to start?"

Tanya shared, "You could put three numbers on the right. Then add them up and that will tell you what number to put on the left."

"Who can say it a different way?" I asked.

Keara restated, "Write one number in each box on the right. Add them up. Put the total in the box on the left."

I returned to Tanya and asked, "Can you give us an example to show how your idea works?"

Tanya nodded and said, "Write one, two, and three in the boxes on the right. Then write six on the left because one plus two plus three equals six."

I wrote the following on the board:

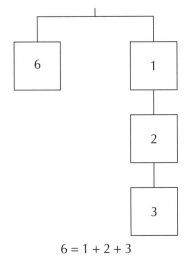

$$6 = 1 + 2 + 3$$

Other students were eager to share their ideas.

Roberto said, "You could do it the other way around from Tanya's way. You could think of one number and write it on the left and then think of three numbers that add up to it."

"Tell me more," I encouraged.

Roberto continued, "You could write twenty on the left side. That means the three numbers on the right side have to equal twenty. Ten plus five plus five equal twenty. Another way to make twenty is fifteen plus three plus two. There are a bunch more ways than that."

I commented to the class, "Roberto has shown us that the puzzles you make may have more than one solution." I turned and recorded Roberto's suggestions on the board next to Tanya's.

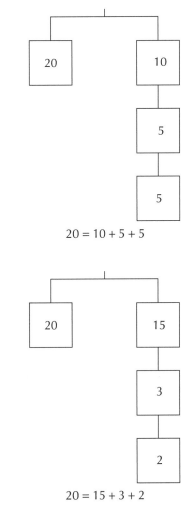

$$20 = 10 + 5 + 5$$

$$20 = 15 + 3 + 2$$

I turned to the class and said, "Suppose I wanted someone else to solve Roberto's last balancing numbers puzzle. What information should I give him or her?" I paused a moment as the children thought about this and then talked quietly among themselves. When about half the students had their hands up, I called on Olina.

Olina said, "You should draw the puzzle with no numbers first. Then I think you have to write in the number on the left so the person knows how much the other numbers have to equal." Several students nodded their agreement.

I asked, "What if I gave only one of the numbers on the right? Would that be enough information to figure out Roberto's solution?" The students shook their heads, indicating that it wouldn't work.

Sam explained, "If you did that then the person could just write two more numbers on the right, add them up, and write the total on the left, and that probably wouldn't be what Roberto had. I think you'd have to write the number on the left side of Roberto's puzzle."

The students had had enough experience with the puzzles that they seemed clear about what to do. I said, "In just a few moments you will create your own balancing numbers puzzles. You may work alone or with a partner. If you work with a partner, you each need to record your puzzle on your own sheet of paper. On one side of the paper, draw your puzzle and then solve your puzzle in two or three ways. On the other side, draw the puzzle for someone else to solve. Are there any questions?"

Jillian asked, "Can we do more than one puzzle?"

I replied, "When you finish with your first, let me look at it. Then you may create a second one."

Karlee had another question. "Can we share them with the class when we're finished?"

"That's a great idea and just what I had in mind," I responded.

There were no more questions. A few students chose to work in pairs, but most were eager to create puzzles on their own. I handed the students paper and then circulated through the class, peering over shoulders. Although most students were working on their own puzzles, there was much animated discussion as students shared ideas and even tried to solve each other's puzzles.

Jenae was delighted with her effort. "I figured out two ways to do my puzzle! The first way is one thousand plus one thousand equals two thousand and the second way is one hundred plus one hundred equals two hundred." She beamed as I looked over her paper. I was thrilled with Jenae's success, as she struggled with math and was showing confidence in herself. I told her many other students would want to try her puzzle, so she needed to draw it on the other side of her paper for someone else to solve. (See Figure 9–1.)

A wonderful aspect of this lesson is that it allows different children to grapple with the same idea at their own level of understanding. (See Figures 9–2 through 9–6.)

When most students had completed at least one puzzle, I gave a two-minute warning for the students to finish what they were doing. At the end of two minutes, I asked for the students' attention. About seven minutes remained of class. I asked for a volunteer to share his or her puzzle with the class.

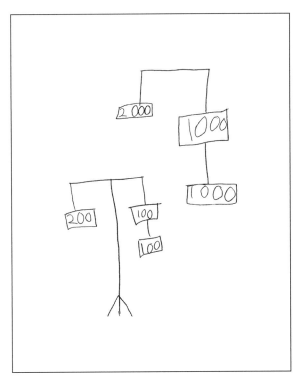

▲▲▲▲▲▲Figure 9–1   *Jenae successfully completed the task.*

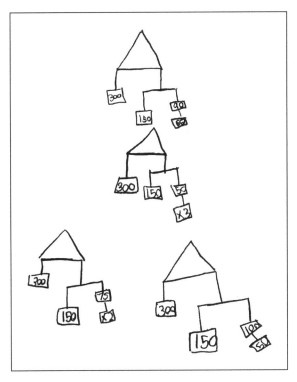

▲▲▲▲▲▲Figure 9–2   *Sam used multiplication in his balancing number puzzles.*

▲▲▲▲▲▲Figure 9–3   *James showed some complexity in his work.*

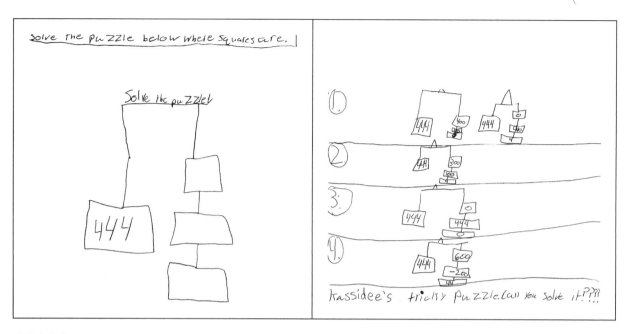

▲▲▲▲▲▲Figure 9–4   *Kassidee created one puzzle and several solutions.*

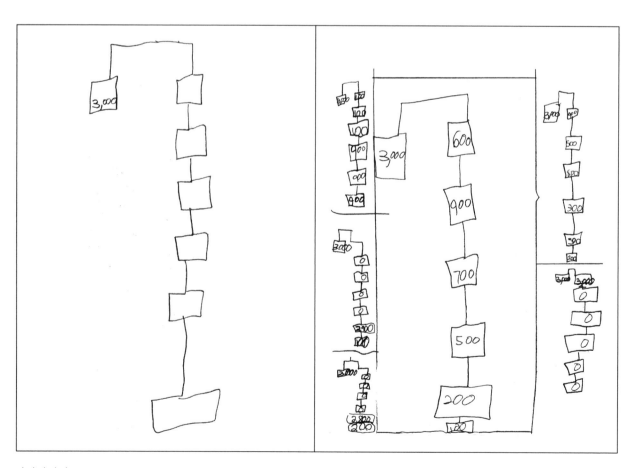

▲▲▲▲▲▲Figure 9–5   *Like Kassidee, Tobias created a puzzle and showed multiple solutions.*

124   Lessons for Extending Place Value

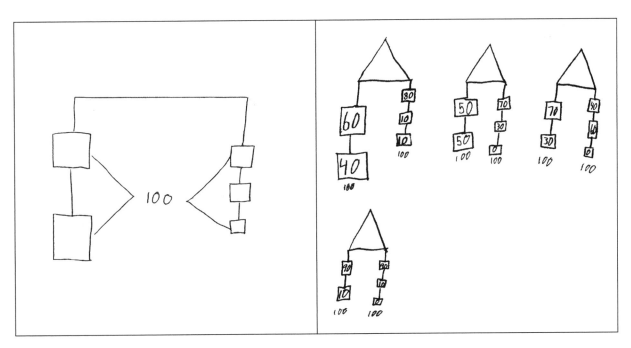

Figure 9–6 *Jessie used a slightly different format for her puzzle.*

Hands leaped into the air. I called on Tina. She came to the board and drew the following:

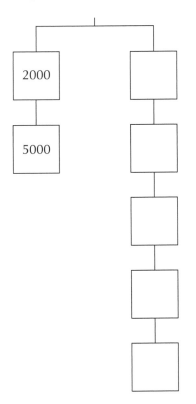

I said to the students, "Think quietly in your head for a few moments about what

solutions Tina might have thought about for this puzzle. In a few minutes she'll call on some of you to share your ideas." The students sat thinking quietly. After a few moments, I asked Tina to call on students to share solutions for her puzzle. As the students shared, I recorded their ideas on the board; then we verified as a class if each idea was a solution to Tina's puzzle; then Tina verified if the solution was one of hers or a different one. (See Figure 9–7.)

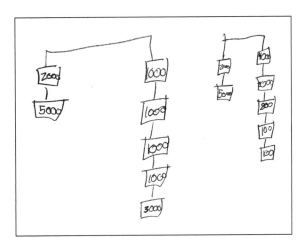

Figure 9–7 *Tina solved her puzzle in two ways.*

Balancing Number Puzzles   **125**

The students were fully engaged and disappointed when I ended math class for the day. I explained that we'd share other puzzles on other days and they were pleased. I collected their papers to look at and for safekeeping.

EXTENSIONS

On other days, have students solve other puzzles as the class solved Tina's is in the vignette. Another way for students to share puzzles is to put the puzzles together in several books. Students can solve a puzzle on a separate sheet of paper and then look on the back of the puzzle to see if their solution is the same as the puzzle maker's. Placing the puzzles in several books helps keep them from getting lost and allows several students to work on puzzles at the same time. Also, you can copy a few puzzles onto a worksheet or an overhead transparency for students to solve in their spare time or as a warm-up for class.

Questions and Discussion

▲ *Why did you begin this lesson with the numbers sixty-four and one hundred?*

There is nothing special about these numbers. I chose them because the students had previous experience and a degree of comfort with them. The numbers were not too big and not too small. This familiarity gave the students access while the size kept them interested. Any numbers with which students are familiar yet find interesting can be used to begin the lesson.

▲ *When students worked in pairs, why did you have each record on a separate sheet of paper?*

I asked that partners make their own recording sheets because this tends to keep both children involved and on task. This increases learning for both students. Also, when both students must record, they typically collaborate instead of having one child do all the work while the other watches.

CHAPTER TEN
1,001 THINGS TO SPOT REVISITED

Overview

1001 Animals to Spot, by Ruth Brocklehurst, provides an enjoyable context for students to apply their understanding of place value to solve addition and subtraction problems. Similar to *1001 Things to Spot in the Sea* (see Chapter 6), this children's book presents a variety of animal scenes, each showing illustrations in the borders of the animals to spot with a number of how many there are in the scene. For practice and to introduce the investigation, the whole class searches the cover for the animals listed and then adds to find the total of how many it has spotted. As a class, students search for animals in the first two scenes, figure out how many they've spotted together, and figure how many more they need to spot to reach 1,001. For the remaining scenes in the book, they calculate the totals in pairs. Finally, they figure the total number of animals they've spotted in the entire book.

Materials

▲ *1001 Animals to Spot,* by Ruth Brocklehurst (Tulsa, OK: EDC, 2002)
▲ chart paper for class chart (see "Teaching Notes"), 1 piece
▲ 6 12-by-18-inch sheets of construction paper for the animal lists (see "Teaching Notes")

Time

▲ four class periods plus additional time for extension

Teaching Directions

1. Gather the students so that they can see the cover of *1001 Animals to Spot,* by Ruth Brocklehurst. Allow students a few moments to explore and discuss the

127

cover; then lead a brief discussion about the number of animals there are to spot on the cover.

2. Read aloud the introductory information on page 3, "Things to spot."

3. Show the students the first scene, "On the farm." Give them a few moments to explore the scene and spot and count the animals shown in the borders.

4. Focus on the left-hand page of the scene and ask students: "How many animals did we count on page four?" Write on the board an addition expression to represent the number of animals to be counted on page 4:

$3 + 5 + 9 + 8 + 10$

Lead a discussion for students to share how they figured the number of animals to spot and count on page 4. Record their strategies on the board.

5. Repeat Step 4 to figure the number of animals to spot and count on page 5.

6. Have students figure the total number of animals to spot and count for the entire scene (pages 4 and 5).

7. On a piece of chart paper, start a class recording sheet to record the total for each scene.

1,001 Animals to Spot
On the farm   71

8. Share with the students the second scene, "On safari." Discuss addition strategies that could be used to figure the total animals to spot in the scene. Ask students to use a strategy that makes sense to them to figure mentally the sum of the animals to spot in the scene. Lead a class discussion for students to share their totals and how they figured them. Record their thinking on the board.

9. Ask students to figure mentally the sum of the first two scenes (143). Then ask them how many more they have to spot in order to find all 1,001 animals (858), and ask for number sentences that represent the problem. Discuss their ideas.

10. On the class chart, record the total for "On safari."

1,001 Animals to Spot
On the farm   71
On safari   72
In the desert
In the Arctic
In the woods
In the ocean

In the rainforest
In the garden
In the outback
In the swamp
In the mountain
By the sea
Children's farm
Leo's pictures

11. Read the rest of the book with the students, having them search for some of the things in each scene.

12. Engage the students in figuring the number of things to spot in each of the other scenes. Post the charts listing the animals to spot and count (see the "Teaching Notes" section) and organize students into pairs. Together, each pair selects a scene from the charts, figures the total with paper and pencil, checks with a calculator, and reports the total to you to record on the class chart. Then as a check on the accuracy of the totals on the chart, each pair selects a second scene and figures the total.

13. Ask students to work individually or in pairs to figure the grand total of the animals to spot in the book, using the completed class chart with the total from each scene. As students finish, have them do the problem again, this time using a calculator.

Teaching Notes

1001 Animals to Spot, by Ruth Brocklehurst, is a delightful picture book in the same series as *1001 Things to Spot in the Sea* (see Chapter 6). The lesson described here is appropriate for students nearer the end of the school year, while the lesson based on *1001 Things to Spot in the Sea* is appropriate for students nearer the beginning of the school year. The main difference is that at this time in the year, the children should be more comfortable mentally combining the numbers for the animals to spot on each page, rather than relying on cubes or base ten blocks. For experience with subtraction, students keep running totals for the scenes and figure how many more animals they need to spot to reach 1,001.

The book shows animals from around the world in thirteen different scenes. It begins with an instruction page that explains to the reader that in each scene there are animals to find and count and also introduces Leo, the artist, who appears in each scene. Small pictures of the animals to be found and counted are shown in the scenes' borders, along with a number for each that tells how many can be spotted. After the thirteenth scene, a page lists other animals and how many of them Leo, the artist, drew. According to the instruction page, there are 1,001 animals to spot altogether. Adding the animals from the thirteen scenes (909) and the animals that Leo drew (92) gives a total of 1,001 animals in all.

A note of caution: We discovered a discrepancy in different editions of *1001 Animals to Spot*. In some books, the scene titled "In the garden" indicates that the reader should find seven spiders; other books indicate that there are eight spiders to find. In books where the scene says that there are eight spiders to find, the total number of animals to spot in the entire book is 1,002. (It seems that the error was discovered and corrected in later printings. However, there still are eight spiders in the illustration!) Talk about this discrepancy with your students, and tell them that making mistakes is one of life's realities that we all try to avoid. And if your book asks the reader to find eight spiders, know in advance that your grand total will be one too many—an error by the publisher, not a result of incorrect figuring by the children.

There are five books in this series. As a class, we investigated *1001 Animals to Spot*, but four students wanted to check out the other books (*1001 Things to Spot in the Sea*, *1001 Things to Spot in the Town*, *1001 Things to Spot on the Farm*, and *1001 Things to Spot Long Ago*). As it turns out, of these four books, only *1001 Things to Spot in the Sea* has exactly 1,001 things to spot! While only four students were involved in this extension, the other students were interested and listened as the four shared what they had found out. (For additional information about this, see the "Extension" section at the end of this chapter.)

The students in the following vignette were at the end of their third-grade year. They hadn't had experience with any other book in the series, as suggested in Chapter 6; therefore, this lesson begins with a short introductory activity of spotting animals in each scene. However, they had experienced all of the other lessons in this book and were gaining proficiency with applying place value ideas when computing. Also, their number sense was developing well. The students used calculators near the end of the lesson. They had previous experience with calculators, so I didn't spend any time teaching them how to use them. If your students are not familiar with using calculators, however, you will need to provide additional support.

Before teaching Day 2 of this lesson, you will need to list all of the scenes on a class chart to record the total number of animals spotted in each:

1,001 Animals to Spot

On the farm   71
On safari
In the desert
In the Arctic
In the woods
In the ocean
In the rainforest
In the garden
In the outback
In the swamp
In the mountains
By the sea
Children's farm
Leo's pictures

Also before teaching Day 2, make a set of charts for each of the scenes after the first two, listing the numbers and types of animals to be spotted. Using six pieces of 12-by-18-inch construction paper folded in half lengthwise works well; you can write one list on each half.

130   Lessons for Extending Place Value

In the desert

10 black ants
4 rattlesnakes
8 scorpions
10 tarantulas
9 painted grasshoppers
6 woodpeckers
4 jack rabbits
5 tortoises
7 gila monsters
3 coyotes

In the woods

10 blue butterflies
7 rabbits
9 blackbirds
2 badgers
10 squirrels
8 wood pigeons
7 deer
10 hedgehogs
5 foxes
10 shrews

In the garden

7 moths
10 mice
6 green caterpillars
8 spiders
8 sparrows
10 bees
9 snails
2 kittens
8 starlings
6 worms

In the mountains

9 mountain goats
5 eagles
10 butterflies
9 pikas
10 geese
7 marmots
3 vultures
1 snow leopard
3 black bears
5 yaks

In the arctic

10 caribou
4 polar bears
10 seals
6 snowy owls
9 lemmings
1 humpback whale
6 Arctic foxes
4 killer whales
8 baby seals
5 narwhals

In the ocean

8 cuttlefish
9 seahorses
10 barracudas
10 clownfish
3 sharks
8 shrimps
3 manta rays
10 snappers
6 dolphins
7 parrotfish

In the outback

5 goanna lizards
8 hopping mice
6 spiny anteaters
9 galahs
6 wombats
8 kangaroos
5 joeys
4 dingoes
10 emus
10 parakeets

By the sea

5 oystercatchers
10 mussels
6 crabs
8 seagulls
6 sea urchins
6 seals
5 squat lobsters
10 winkles
10 limpets
7 sea anemones

In the rainforest

5 sloths
7 arrow-poison frogs
8 toucans
3 coral snakes
1 jaguar
9 parrots
7 spider monkeys
10 egrets
5 armadillos
8 boas

In the swamp

1 alligator
7 herons
10 bullfrogs
1 manatee
5 woodpeckers
8 newts
10 apple snails
10 dragonflies
9 turtles
9 grasshoppers

Children's farm

5 peacocks
9 doves
6 llamas
8 hens
7 goats
10 ducks
5 Shetland ponies
10 guinea pigs
3 camels
10 rabbits

Leo's pictures

6 otters
10 wildebeests
10 hairy caterpillars
10 wallcreepers
9 scarlet ibises
7 blue-tongued skinks
3 giant clams
4 turkeys
5 magpies
9 puffins
9 red ants
10 walruses

The Lesson

DAY 1

As the students gathered on the rug, I held up the book *1001 Animals to Count,* by Ruth Brocklehurst, and asked them to sit so they could see the cover. This was the first book in this series the students had seen. (They hadn't done the lesson on *1001 Things to Spot in the Sea* in Chapter 6.) As they settled, the students discussed the animals on the cover among themselves. Several focused on the small pictures of animals with numbers beside them—1 jaguar, 8 frogs, 5 monkeys, 3 caimans, 2 toucans, and 6 red birds. They began to search for those animals, counting them as they found them. Soon all the students were involved in searching for and counting animals. After several moments, I asked for their attention.

I asked the class, "How many animals do you think we're supposed to spot on the cover?" I gave them time to think about this. Some pointed and counted while others seemed to be adding the numbers. After a few moments, I asked them to check their answers with their neighbors. A few moments later, I asked for their attention.

"Who would like to share how you figured the total for the cover?" I asked.

Several students reported how they had arrived at twenty-five. Karlee, for example, pointed to the numbers on the cover and explained, "I know it's twenty-five because three plus two is five. Five and five is ten. Add the six and eight and that's fourteen. Put the fourteen and ten together and that's twenty-four. Add the one to twenty-four and it's twenty-five." I pointed out to the students that Karlee had put two, three, and five together to make ten. Several others indicated that they had also used this strategy of making a ten.

I then opened the book to page 3 and read aloud the introductory information. On this page, readers are introduced to Leo, an artist, and challenged to find him in each of the scenes in the book. After I read the sentence, "There are one thousand one animals to spot altogether," Kassidee raised her hand.

She asked, "Does the one thousand one include the animals on the cover we just counted?"

I replied, "That's a good question. No, the cover was just for practice. There are supposed to be one thousand one animals inside the book." She nodded.

I showed the students the first scene, "On the farm." They immediately spotted Leo, the artist, and began searching the scene to find and count the number of each of the animals shown on the borders. I gave them a few minutes to accomplish this. When most students were finished finding and counting the animals, I asked for their attention. We discussed what a duckling and a foal are, and then I asked for individual students to point out and count each of the types of animals listed.

I asked the students, "Are there any animals shown that weren't counted?" The students studied the scene quietly for a moment and then began to put their hands up. Turkeys, horses, sheep, and butterflies were some of the animals students noticed that weren't pictured in the borders.

I settled the class, pointed to the left-hand page of the spread, and asked, "How many animals did we count from the list on page four?" To help students think about my question, I wrote on the board an addition expression using the numbers of animals to be counted:

$$3 + 5 + 9 + 8 + 10$$

When most students had their hands up, I called on James. He explained, "I think it's thirty-five animals. I made eights and tens. There's already one eight listed and three plus five equals eight. There's one ten listed. I got another ten by thinking of nine as one less than ten. Then I added it all up—eight plus eight plus ten plus ten minus one. Eight plus eight is sixteen; ten plus ten is twenty; sixteen and twenty equal thirty-six. I have to subtract one from thirty-six because there was really a nine, not a ten, so that makes thirty-five." I recorded on the board:

$James \quad 3 + 5 + 9 + 8 + 10$

$$8$$
$$9 = 10 - 1$$
$$8 + 8 + 10 + 10 - 1 = 35$$

Kito had another way of thinking about how to find the sum of the animals on page 4. He explained, "I split the three into a two and a one. Then I put the two with the eight to get a ten. I put the one with the nine to make a ten. That made three groups of ten and one group of five." I recorded:

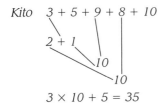

$$3 \times 10 + 5 = 35$$

Next I asked the students to figure the total number of animals listed to find on page 5. As I did for page 4, I wrote an addition expression on the board:

$$6 + 4 + 10 + 6 + 10$$

Adama shared first. She explained, "I made groups of ten. There were already two tens. I put the first six and four together to make another group of ten; that makes three groups of ten. Three times ten equals thirty, and that leaves one group of six. Thirty plus six equals thirty-six."
I recorded on the board:

$Adama \quad 6 + 4 + 10 + 6 + 10$

$$10$$
$$3 \times 10 = 30$$
$$30 + 6 = 36$$

I asked the students, "How many animals did we spot altogether in the scene?"

Jenae explained, "That's easy. It's thirty-five plus thirty-six. Three tens plus three tens makes six tens, or sixty. Five ones and six ones equals eleven. Eleven is one ten and one one. Put the one ten with the other six tens, and that's seven tens, or seventy. Add the one one to the seventy and it equals seventy-one." Jenae's explanation showed her growing understanding of how to apply her knowledge of place value to compute accurately. She beamed with pleasure as I recorded her thinking on the board:

$Jenae \qquad\qquad 35 = 3 \ tens + 5 \ ones$
$$36 = 3 \ tens + 6 \ ones$$
$$3 \ tens + 3 \ tens = 6 \ tens$$
$$5 \ ones + 6 \ ones = 11 \ ones$$
$$11 \ ones = 1 \ ten + 1 \ one$$
$$6 \ tens + 1 \ ten = 7 \ tens$$
$$7 \ tens = 70$$
$$70 + 1 = 71$$

Tina thought of the problem differently. She explained, "I thought of thirty-five as twenty-five plus ten. I thought of thirty-six as twenty-five plus eleven. Twenty-five plus twenty-five equals fifty. Ten plus eleven equals twenty-one. Fifty plus twenty-one equals seventy-one." I recorded on the board:

$Tina \qquad\qquad 35 = 25 + 10$
$$36 = 25 + 11$$
$$25 + 25 = 50$$
$$10 + 11 = 21$$
$$50 + 21 = 71$$

Before ending the day's lesson, I posted a piece of chart paper, titled it *1,001 Animals to Spot*, labeled two columns, and recorded our result:

1,001 Animals to Spot

On the farm   71

After class, I added the titles of the other scenes in the book and posted the chart.

DAY 2

The next day, I again gathered the students so all could see the book. I opened to the

1,001 Things to Spot Revisited   **133**

second scene, "On safari," and the children immediately started to find and count the animals. After several minutes, I asked for their attention and said, "Who would like to show us where the ten ostriches are in the scene?" All hands were up. I called on Karena, who came up and carefully pointed out the ten ostriches.

I continued in this way, asking students to show the location of the other animals on the page. When Reggie came up to show the four elephants, he got stuck after quickly pointing out three of them. Karlee suggested that he look by the mountains for the last one. He did so and quickly found the fourth elephant.

After we found and counted all the animals, I asked the students, "What strategy could you use to figure the number of animals altogether?" Hands went up quickly. I called on Aubrey.

Aubrey explained, "I'm going to find groups of ten like we did the last time. I can put the four and six together to make ten." Several students nodded their agreement with Aubrey's idea.

Adama added, "You could just start with the first number and add to it the second number, then the third. But sometimes that's hard and I get mixed up."

"I see how to put numbers together to make two groups of ten," Rachel said. "There are two fours and two sixes. Put a six and a four together, and that's ten; then put the other six and four together, and that's another ten."

The students were quiet. I pointed to the chart I had made that listed the scenes in the book. I said, "We figured out that there were seventy-one animals to spot on the farm. Now use one of the strategies just mentioned, or another one that makes sense to you, to figure out in your head how many animals are on safari. Raise your hand when you have the answer." I paused to give the students time to calculate. When most hands were up, I called on Kassidee.

Kassidee said, "I see three tens. That's thirty. Then put the two fours with the two sixes like Rachel said. That's two more tens, so now there are five tens, and that's fifty. That leaves the eight, nine, and five. Eight and nine are seventeen. Fifty and seventeen equals sixty-seven. Add the last five to sixty-seven and it equals seventy-two."

I recorded on the board:

$$\begin{aligned} \textit{Kassidee} \qquad 3 \textit{ tens} &= 30 \\ 6 + 4 + 6 + 4 &= 2 \textit{ tens or } 20 \\ 30 + 20 &= 5 \textit{ tens or } 50 \\ 8 + 9 &= 17 \\ 50 + 17 &= 67 \\ 67 + 5 &= 72 \end{aligned}$$

Kito said, "You could make two more groups of ten if you took the five apart. You could make the five into two, two, and one. Put one of the twos with the eight and that's another ten. Put the one together with the nine and that's a ten. That's five tens and two tens, which is seven tens, plus the two left over, which comes out to seventy-two."

I recorded Kito's idea on the board:

$$\begin{aligned} \textit{Kito} \qquad 5 &= 2 + 2 + 1 \\ 8 + 2 &= 10 \\ 9 + 1 &= 10 \\ 5 \textit{ tens} + 2 \textit{ tens} &= 7 \textit{ tens} \\ 7 \textit{ tens} + 2 &= 72 \end{aligned}$$

I continued recording for all who wanted to share and recorded 72 on the chart of scenes next to On safari. Then I asked the students, "How many animals have we spotted altogether so far?" As the students mentally figured the answer to my question, I recorded the problem on the board:

$$71 + 72 = \square$$

When all hands were up, I called on Rachel. "We've found one hundred forty-three animals so far," Rachel shared.

I said to the other students, "Put your thumb up if you agree with one hundred forty-three, put your thumb down if you disagree, or put your thumb sideways if you're not sure." Aubrey, Jael, and Reggie put their thumbs sideways, indicating uncertainty; the other students had their thumbs up. I said to Rachel, "Please share with us how you figured your answer."

Rachel explained, "I multiplied two times seven tens. I got that because there is a seventy-one and a seventy-two and they each have seven tens. Two times seven tens equals one hundred forty. Then I added the ones. Two plus one is three. One hundred forty plus three equals one hundred forty-three."

Many students indicated their agreement with and understanding of Rachel's explanation by nodding their heads. Reggie, one of the students whose thumbs were sideways, commented, "At first I got one hundred forty. I forgot to add the two from seventy-two and the one from seventy-one. Now I agree with Rachel."

The students were quiet. I recorded the answer on the board:

$71 + 72 = 143$

Then I said, "So far we've spotted one hundred forty-three animals in the first two scenes. How many more do we have to spot in order to find all one thousand one animals? First think about this by yourself, and then in a few moments, I'll ask you to share your thinking with your partner." The students were quiet, and after thirty seconds or so, I asked them to turn to their partners and share. Initially the room came alive with conversations. After a few minutes, the students got quieter, indicating to me that they were ready to go on. I asked for their attention and for volunteers to share their thinking. I called on Halley.

Halley said, "Roberto and I think there are eight hundred fifty-seven more animals to spot."

Paul's hand shot into the air. "I disagree with Halley. At first Tobias and I thought the same thing as Halley and Roberto. But

we figured out we were wrong. We only figured out the answer for one thousand animals to spot. There are really one thousand one. So we think there are really eight hundred fifty-*eight* more animals to spot."

"Oh yeah!" responded Halley and several others.

Olina said, "We got eight hundred fifty-eight, too. Can we tell how we got it?" I nodded and Olina continued. "We counted on. We started with one hundred forty-three and went by tens to get close to two hundred—one hundred fifty-three, one hundred sixty-three, one hundred seventy-three, one hundred eighty-three, one hundred ninety-three. That was fifty. So then we needed seven more ones to get to two hundred. And then we needed eight hundreds to get to one thousand and one more one to get to one thousand one. So it was . . ." Olina stumbled for a moment and then continued, "So we added on fifty, and seven, and eight hundred, and one more, and that's eight hundred fifty-eight."

Keara shared, "Our way is sort of like Olina's, but different. We started in the middle. We knew that from two hundred to one thousand was eight hundred. Then we knew that from one hundred fifty to two hundred was fifty. We put that with the eight hundred, so now it's eight hundred fifty. Then we added seven for one hundred forty-three to one hundred fifty, and one more for one thousand to one thousand one. We got eight hundred fifty-eight."

No one had other ideas to share. To connect the students' figuring to mathematical notation, I asked the students, "What number sentence could we write to represent the problem we just solved?"

Ben said, "You could do it with subtraction. But in my head I did it with addition. I thought one hundred forty-three plus a number equals one thousand one. So my partner and I counted up from one hundred forty-three until we got to one thousand one like Olina and Roberto did."

I wrote on the board:

$143 + \square = 1,001$

Jessie shared next. She said, "If you want to write it as a subtraction problem, it would be one thousand one minus one hundred forty-three. The answer would also be the same thing that goes in the box for Ben's idea. I didn't do subtraction because it's too hard to do it in my head. Addition is easier."

I wrote on the board:

$1,001 - 143 = \square$

Connor made an interesting observation. He said, "If the problem were written down and I had paper and pencil, I probably would do subtraction. But when it's said out loud and I only have my brain, I used addition."

To end the lesson, I added the new information we had found to the class chart:

1,001 Animals to Spot

On the farm	*71*
On safari	*72*
In the desert	
In the Arctic	
In the woods	
In the ocean	
In the rainforest	
In the garden	
In the outback	
In the swamp	
In the mountains	
By the sea	
Children's farm	
Leo's pictures	

DAY 3

The students in this class were comfortable calculating both in their heads and with paper and pencil. They also were familiar with working in pairs. Because of this, rather than continue with the remaining scenes one by one, working with the whole class on each, I read the rest of the book

with the class and then organized the children into pairs to figure the totals.

I gathered the students together once again, reminding them to sit where they could see the book. When the students were settled, I opened the book to the next scene, titled "In the desert." As before, the children quickly found Leo and then chatted among themselves as they searched for the animals listed. I chose two of the animals for us to count together—the ten tarantulas and the seven gila monsters. Next we moved to the scene "In the Arctic." After giving them a moment to search the page, I had them find and count the six Arctic foxes and the eight baby seals. We continued in this way to the last scene, "Children's farm."

I then posted the set of charts I had prepared with the lists of animals to spot for the remaining twelve scenes. I explained to the students, "Today you'll work in pairs to find the number of animals to spot in each scene. Each pair will take a different scene. Work with your partner to show on your paper how you figure the total number of animals to spot. When you both agree you have correctly figured the sum of the animals to spot for your scene, let me know and I'll record the total you got. Then you can pick another scene. This will help us check that the answers for the scenes are correct."

"Do we have to figure out how many to get to one thousand one?" Vinay asked.

"Not at this time," I responded. "Let's just get the totals for each scene posted."

I assigned partners by pairing students sitting beside each other. As I did so, I asked each pair which scene it would like to do and then checked it off on the chart with all the scenes listed to indicate that it was taken. Then I handed the students a sheet of paper and dismissed them to begin working. Because there were only twelve choices and thirty children in the class, in some cases there were two pairs of students working on the same scene. I put a second check mark next to these.

Observing the Students

As the students worked, I circulated, observing how the students approached the task and the computation strategies they used. I have found that with students this age, their verbal explanations during class discussions are often more sophisticated than their written work. Ideas expressed during discussions are often complex, making them difficult to write down on paper, especially for younger, less experienced children. However, I hoped to see students make use of strategies shared during the class discussion, in particular, grouping numbers together to make tens. Most students did this to some extent. Jessie and Reggie's paper was typical. (See Figure 10–1.)

Like Jessie and Reggie, Halley and Karena found one group of ten by combining two smaller groups. I asked them how they decided to pair the other numbers. Halley

explained, "We put the numbers together because of the addition facts we know. Like we know that eight plus eight equals sixteen and seven and six equals thirteen."

Karena added, "It seemed easy that way. We checked our work twice and got the same answer both times, so we think it's right." (See Figure 10–2.)

As students finished, I asked them to check their work with a calculator. I explained, "One of you should slowly read each number while the other carefully enters it into the calculator. Both of you should check each number entered in the calculator to be sure it is correct. When you've entered all of the numbers, press the equals button to get the total. If the calculator gives the same number you got before, there's probably no mistake. If the calculator gives a different number, there's a mistake somewhere. It might be that you incorrectly entered a number on the calculator, or you may have made an error in your earlier work. Either way, you need to check your calculations again."

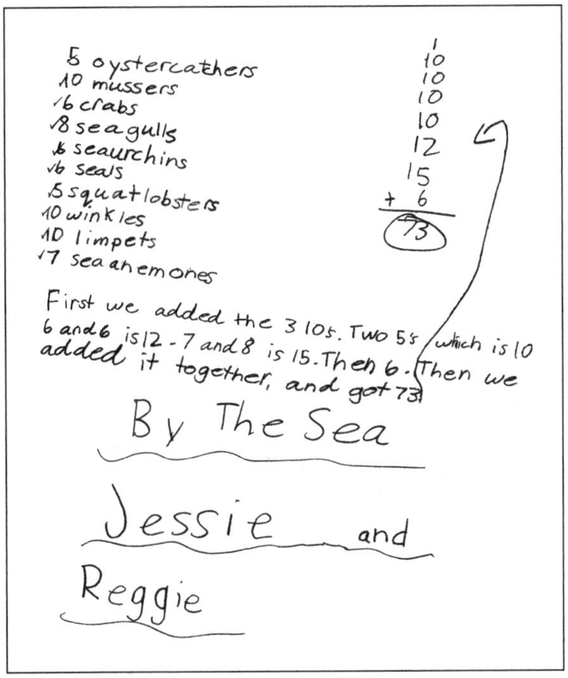

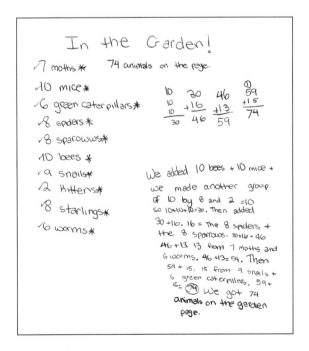

▲▲▲▲▲▲Figure 10–1 *Jessie and Reggie's paper was typical.*

▲▲▲▲▲▲Figure 10–2 *Halley and Karena found groups of ten and used their knowledge of basic addition facts.*

When a pair had verified its total, I had it choose another scene and figure the number of animals to spot. When I'd recorded the total number of animals to be spotted for each scene, I gave a two-minute warning and then called the class to order. The completed chart of scenes looked as follows:

1,001 Animals to Spot

On the farm	71
On safari	72
In the desert	66
In the Arctic	63
In the woods	78
In the ocean	74
In the rainforest	63
In the garden	74
In the outback	71
In the swamp	70
In the mountains	62
By the sea	73
Children's farm	73
Leo's pictures	92

"Wow! That's a lot of animals!" Christopher commented. There were several other comments. Some children wondered about whether or not the numbers would add up to 1,001.

I said to the students, "Tomorrow, we'll see if there are actually one thousand one animals to spot in the book." I collected their papers and ended class.

DAY 4

"Today we'll try to find out if there are actually one thousand one animals to spot in our book," I said to the students. I pointed to the class chart of scenes and continued, "Use the numbers on our class chart of scenes to help you figure. Each of you will need to use your own sheet of paper to show how you figure the total. You may work individually or with a partner. If you'd like to work with a partner, please stand up. If you work with a partner, you still need to complete your own paper." Several

students stood up. I quickly paired them and handed each student a sheet of paper. Then I gave each of the students wishing to work independently a sheet of paper. All students quickly got involved in figuring the total and soon the classroom came alive with conversation and intense thinking. As they worked, I circulated throughout the room.

As students finished, I suggested that they do the problem again using a calculator. They had already done the calculating, and this gave them additional practice using this tool. As I suspected, many children got an incorrect answer with the calculator! It's easy for children (and for me, too) to make errors when they enter numbers on a calculator, and it was a good lesson to reinforce for the children that it helps to rely on more than one approach when solving problems.

Figure 10–3 shows how one pair calculated the grand total.

EXTENSION

Four students were particularly interested in exploring the other books in the series. Together they searched each of the other books, counting the items shown in the borders of each scene, figuring first the total of each scene and then the grand total of the book to see if there were indeed 1,001 things to spot. Your students will likely find, as we did, that there are discrepancies. The students found that there were 988 things to spot in the book *1001 Things to Spot Long Ago,* 975 things to spot in *1001 Things to Spot in Town,* and only 773 things to spot in *1001 Things to Spot on the Farm.* After students find the discrepancies, encourage the children to write to the publisher to point out the errors and how they found them. (See Figure 10–4.)

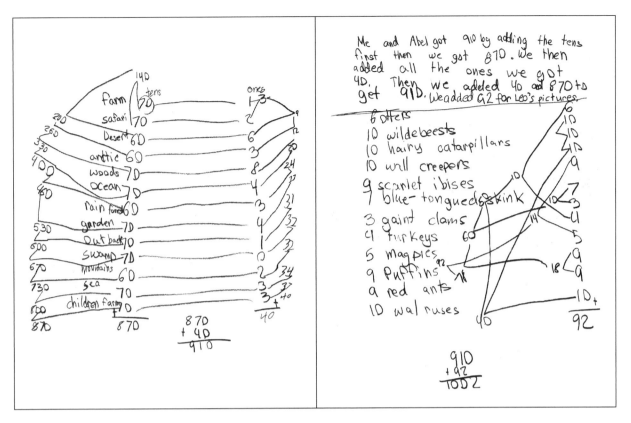

Figure 10–3 *Sam and Abel used their knowledge of place value to figure the grand total.*

Usborne\EDC Publishing
10302 E. 55th Place
Tulsa, Oklahoma 74146

Dear USBORNE,
We are students from Carrillo School. We have worked on your 1001 books to figure out if there really are 1001 things. The books just weren't right except for 1001 Things to Spot in the Sea. We checked all books 4 or 5 times, and it didn't come out to 1001. Here's what it comes out to. 1001 Things to Spot in the Sea is 1001. 1001 Things to spot long ago is 988.

1001 Things to spot on the Farm is 773. 1001 Animals to Spot is 1002. 1001 Things to Spot in the Town is 975. It says on page three in every book "There are 1001 things to spot altogether." We think you should make sure it's 1001 exactly. We still like your books. Thanks for letting us write you a letter. Go to back

Sicerely,
Halley
Jessie
Vinay

P.S. The numbers we gave you do not include the pictures on the cover. When we included the pictures on the cover we still didn't get 1001. For On the Farm we got 809 In the Town we got 999. Long ago was 1,014. 1001 Animals to spot is 1027.

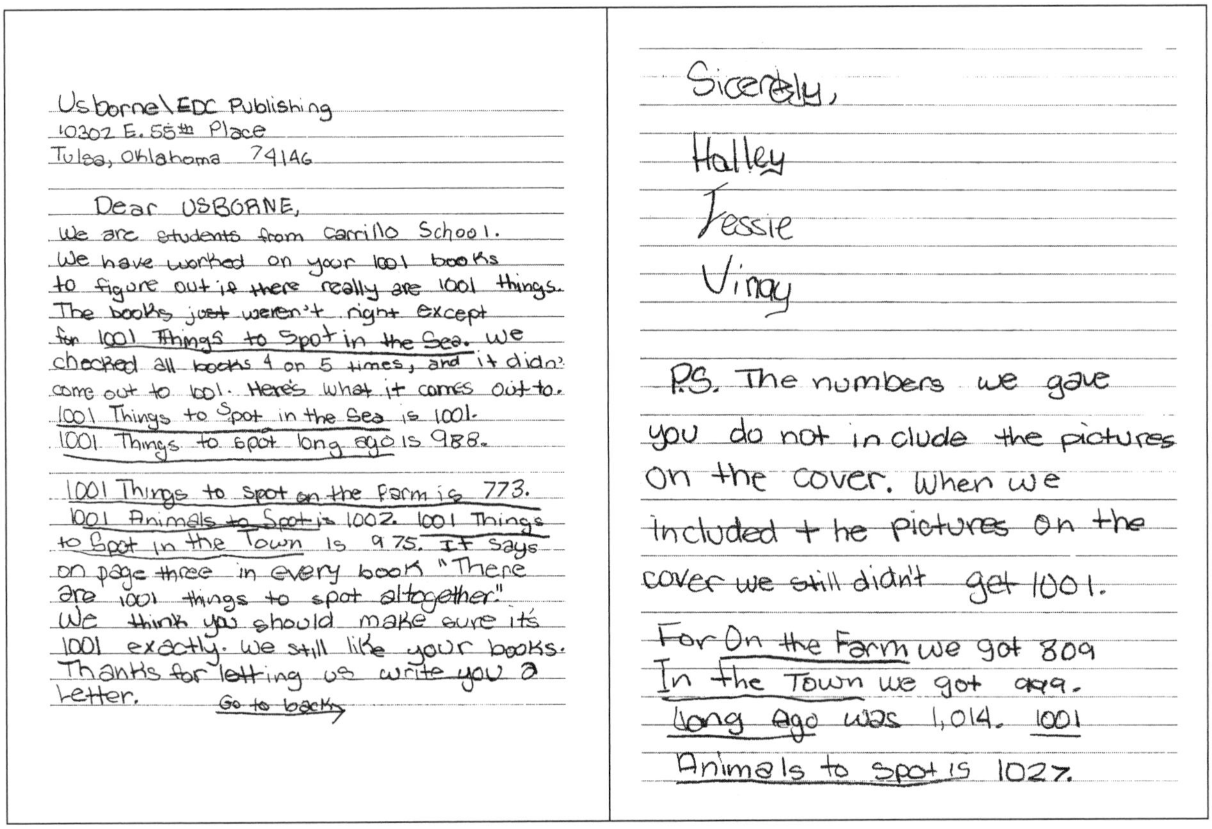

Figure 10–4 *Halley, Jessie, and Vinay wrote to the publisher to point out the discrepancies they found.*

CHAPTER ELEVEN
RACE TO 200

Overview

In this lesson, partners play the game *Race to 200,* using their understanding of tens and ones to try to become the player whose score is closer to 200. The game provides support for students to develop their number sense and their computation skills with multiplication and addition. Two versions of the game are presented; the first uses one die for smaller, more manageable numbers and the second uses two dice, creating a more challenging game with larger numbers.

Materials

▲ base ten blocks in zip-top baggies, each with 30 ones cubes, 25 longs, and 4 flats, 1 per pair of students

▲ dice, 1 per pair of students for Day 1; then 2 per pair of students

▲ optional: Base Ten Blocks sheets cut out and placed in zip-top baggies, 1 per pair of students (see Blackline Masters)

▲ optional: rules for *Race to 200,* 1 per pair of students (see Blackline Masters)

Time

▲ three class periods

Teaching Directions

1. Tell students they're going to learn a new game, *Race to 200.* Explain they'll use base ten blocks and play with a partner. The goal is to be the player with a score closer to 200 after six rolls of a die. Emphasize that it's OK to go over 200; what's important is who's closer to 200.

140

Race to 200

Object: Be the player with the score closer to 200.

Rules

1. Each player must take six turns.

2. On your turn, roll the die. You may take ones or tens. The die tells you how many.

3. Both players record the turn. Add the total for each turn to the previous score. For example:

4. After each player has taken six turns, compare scores to see whose score is closer to 200 and record underneath the chart. (It's OK to go over 200.)

_____ has _____ points.
_____ is _____ points from 200.
_____ has _____ points.
_____ is _____ points from 200.
_____ wins.

2. On the board, write the object and the first three rules. Explain them to the class.

3. Choose a student and model how to play and record the game. On the board, draw two large rectangles to represent sheets of paper. Divide one in half and label it as shown. Have your partner do the same in the other rectangle.

Race to 200	
Mrs. Wickett	Jillian

4. To model a turn, roll the die. Model how students might think about their choices by thinking aloud about whether to take ones or tens. Record your turn.

Race to 200	
Mrs. Wickett	Jillian
$6 \times 10 = 60$	

5. Have your partner also record your turn, then hand the die to your partner.

6. Repeat Steps 4 and 5, alternating turns and keeping a running total until you and your partner have taken six turns each.

Race to 200	
Mrs. Wickett	Jillian
$6 \times 10 = 60$	$3 \times 10 = 30$
$6 \times 10 = 60$	$6 \times 10 = 60$
$\overline{120}$	$\overline{90}$
$5 \times 10 = 50$	$2 \times 10 = 20$
$\overline{170}$	$\overline{110}$
$4 \times 1 = 4$	$6 \times 10 = 60$
$\overline{174}$	$\overline{170}$
$6 \times 1 = 6$	$1 \times 10 = 10$
$\overline{180}$	$\overline{180}$
$1 \times 10 = 10$	$3 \times 10 = 30$
$\overline{190}$	$\overline{210}$

7. At the end of the game, model how to compare scores and write about them beneath your scoring charts, as shown in Step 4 of the rules. Finish writing the rules on the board.

8. Have students play the game in pairs for the rest of the period. Circulate, giving guidance as needed and answering questions. When necessary, refer students to the board for the rules or model game scoring.

9. The issue of a tie game is likely to arise as students play. When it does, stop the students to lead a brief discussion so they know that tie games are possible and OK.

10. On Day 2, have students play again, this time using two dice and using the sum of the dice to determine the number of ones or tens to take. Circulate again. As students finish a game, ask them what they have learned, what their strategy was, or how they will change their strategy the next time they play. Many students will have enough time to play two games.

11. At the end of class, collect the recording sheets so you can look at them, and tell students they'll play again the next day. Explain that they should think about their strategies—what's good about a strategy, what works, what doesn't work, and how they can improve it.

12. On Day 3, have students play again, this time paying attention to their strategies. Lead a class discussion for students to share their strategies. Record their ideas on the board.

Teaching Notes

Prior to this lesson, the students in the vignette had had several experiences with base ten blocks, as described in earlier chapters. As a result of these experiences, they were comfortable using base ten blocks and with multiplying by ones and tens.

If you do not have access to base ten blocks, use the Base Ten Blocks Blackline Master at the back of this book. Duplicate at least one sheet per child on tagboard and ask a parent volunteer, an older student, or your own students to carefully cut out the blocks. They can then be placed in quart-sized zip-top baggies for safekeeping.

When students initially learn the game, they use only one die. This results in smaller numbers and keeps the game more manageable, allowing students more easily to focus on learning the rules and how to record. On Day 2, they use two dice.

The recording can be challenging for third graders; therefore, I recommend modeling how to record for a complete game, as explained in the vignette. You'll most likely still need to provide follow-up support when circulating among the students as they play. Also, recording numbers beyond one hundred and adding sums from each turn can be tricky for some third graders. *Race to 200* offers a context to develop these skills.

The Lesson

▲▲▲

DAY 1

"Today we are going to learn to play a new game," I said to the students. This news met with great excitement. After settling the students, I continued, "The name of the game is *Race to Two Hundred.* You'll be playing with a partner. The object is to be the player with a score closer to two hundred after six rolls of the die." Excited murmurs passed among the students. I held up a zip-top baggie containing the needed base ten blocks, catching the students' attention once again. "You must take six turns, no fewer and no more." I wrote on the board:

Race to 200

Object: Be the player with the score closer to 200.

Rules:

1. Each player must take six turns.

I continued, "When it's your turn, you roll the die. You may take ones or tens blocks. The number on the die tells you how many. For example, if I roll a six, I can take either six ones or six tens." I added this to the information on the board:

Race to 200

Object: Be the player with the score closer to 200.

Rules:

1. Each player must take six turns.

2. On your turn, roll the die. You may take ones or tens. The die tells you how many.

3. Both players record the turns. Add the total for the turn to the previous score.

Sam piped up, "No matter what, I'd always take tens. That's how to get the most."

"What would be the most you could get in six rolls if you always took tens?" I asked Sam and the others. The children thought quietly for a few moments and then hands began to go up. When about half the students had raised their hands, I called on Olina.

Olina shared, "I know the most you could get on one turn is sixty. The biggest number on the die is six, and six times ten is sixty. But I don't think I know how many you could get in six turns." Several students nodded their agreement with Olina's thinking as she shared. Hands shot up once again when she stopped. I called on Abel.

Abel explained, "I counted up by sixties; well, I actually counted up by sixes. I just dropped off the zero and remembered to put it back again when I was done. I counted by sixes six times because of taking six turns. That's thirty-six. Then I put back the zero, so it's three hundred sixty."

Vinay intervened, "I know why what Abel said works. It's because you could think of it as taking six longs each turn, so that's thirty-six longs. Each long is worth ten ones cubes, so multiply thirty-six times ten, and that's three hundred sixty, just like Abel said. Can I show with the blocks?" I nodded. Vinay made six piles of six longs. He counted the piles by sixes to show there were thirty-six longs. Then he recounted, this time counting each long as ten. He concluded, "Thirty-six tens is the same amount as three hundred sixty."

Halley announced, "I know what the littlest amount you can get is. It's six. You would just have to get six ones on the dice and take one ones cube each time. That's how you could get six. You can't get any less; in fact, I don't think it would be very easy to actually get six because I think it would be really, really hard to roll six ones in a row without cheating or something like that."

I said to the students to redirect the conversation, "I agree with you that six is the least you could get and three hundred sixty is the most. What is the amount you want to get?"

"Two hundred," the students chorused.

Isaac said, "I think we aren't supposed to get the biggest amount, so I think we'll have to think about whether we should take tens or ones."

"Oh yeah!" several students agreed.

Modeling the Game

To model the game for the students, I asked for a volunteer to play with me. I chose Jillian because I knew that she was strong mathematically and could follow directions well. These traits would keep the game moving and there wouldn't be much chance that she'd make errors or get stuck.

I said to Jillian and the others, "I'll go first to show you what to do. I know I have to take six turns and I want to be closer to two hundred than you. We'll each keep track of our scores." I drew two rectangles on the board to represent sheets of paper. I said to Jillian, "One will be for you and one will be for me. We'll divide our papers in half." To show the students, in the first rectangle I drew a line from the top to the bottom to divide it in half. Next I wrote the title, *Race for 200*, and then I wrote both our names.

Race to 200	
Mrs. Wickett	Jillian

Jillian did the same with the second rectangle. I continued, "I'll go first to show what to do. I have to take six turns and I want to get as close as I can to two hundred." I rolled a 6. "Hmm, I rolled a six. If I take six tens, that will be sixty, and if I take six ones, that will be six. I think I'll take six tens. Six groups of ten is sixty." I took six longs from the collection of base ten blocks. "To record my turn, I'll write six, then a times sign, which means groups of,

144   Lessons for Extending Place Value

then a ten, and finally, equals sixty since six groups of ten is sixty." I turned to the board and recorded as follows:

Race to 200	
Mrs. Wickett	Jillian
$6 \times 10 = 60$	

Jillian nodded her agreement with what I wrote and then I reminded her to record my turn. I handed her the die and reminded the students they should wait for their partner to hand them the die rather than grab it. This slows down the game, helps children pay attention to their partners' turns, and prevents later arguments.

Jillian rolled a 3. She took three longs and we both recorded her turn. She handed me the die.

I rolled another 6. I thought aloud to model for the children points they should consider. "If I take six longs again, I'll have one hundred twenty. That's only eighty away from two hundred. I have four more turns, and I don't want to get too many, but it's early in the game and I can always take ones for the rest of my turns. I think I'll take six tens for this turn." I took six longs and added them to my pile of longs. I said to the students, "Now I have twelve longs, or one hundred twenty. I can trade ten of the longs in for one hundreds flat." I counted out ten longs, returned them to the collection of base ten blocks, and took one flat. I asked Jillian, "Do you agree with what I just did?" She nodded. I continued, "Now I have to record my turn and then add both turns together to show my total of one hundred twenty." Jillian also recorded my turn and I handed her the die.

Race to 200	
Mrs. Wickett	Jillian
$6 \times 10 = 60$	$3 \times 10 = 30$
$6 \times 10 = \underline{60}$	
120	

Jillian rolled a 6 and took six longs. We each recorded her turn and she handed me the die.

I rolled a 5, took five longs, and we each recorded my turn. I handed the die to Jillian.

She rolled a 2 and took two longs. Jillian had eleven longs and decided to trade ten of them for a hundreds flat. We recorded her turn and she handed me the die.

Race to 200	
Mrs. Wickett	Jillian
$6 \times 10 = 60$	$3 \times 10 = 30$
$6 \times 10 = \underline{60}$	$6 \times 10 = \underline{60}$
120	90
$5 \times 10 = \underline{50}$	$2 \times 10 = \underline{20}$
170	110

This time I rolled a 4. I said, "I have one hundred seventy and two more turns after this one. I rolled a four. If I take four longs, that's four tens, or forty. Then I would have two hundred ten. If I take four ones, that would be four, and my total would be one hundred seventy-four. Jillian has one hundred ten, so right now I'm closer, and even if she rolls a six and takes six tens, she can't catch up to me on her next turn. I think I'll take four ones." I recorded my turn, reinforcing for the children as I did so the need to write the 4 under the 0 in 170. Jillian also recorded my turn and I handed her the die.

Jillian rolled a 6. She and the other students were thrilled. She quickly took six

Race to 200   145

longs and we both recorded her turn. She was now only four points behind me. She handed me the die.

Race to 200	
Mrs. Wickett	Jillian
$6 \times 10 = 60$	$3 \times 10 = 30$
$6 \times 10 = \underline{60}$	$6 \times 10 = \underline{60}$
120	90
$5 \times 10 = \underline{50}$	$2 \times 10 = \underline{20}$
170	110
$4 \times 1 = \underline{\quad 4}$	$6 \times 10 = \underline{60}$
174	170

I rolled a 6. Thinking aloud, I said, "If I take six longs, I'll have two hundred thirty four. That's farther away from two hundred than I am now! I think my only choice is to take six ones. That gives me a total of one hundred eighty." I took six ones and added them to my pile. Christopher reminded me that I had ten ones and could exchange them for one long. I took Christopher's advice. Jillian and I recorded my turn and I handed her the die.

The students were completely involved and cheering Jillian on. She carefully rolled the die and got a 1. The room erupted in excitement. Jillian took one ten and we recorded her turn. She handed me the die. Now we both had 180.

The room was silent with anticipation. I rolled for my final turn and got a 1. I took one ten for a final total of 190 and we recorded my turn. I handed Jillian the die.

Jillian rolled a 3. She said, "If I take three ones, you win because I would only have one hundred eighty-three. But if I take three tens, I'll have two hundred ten, and you'd win because I went over two hundred." Several students immediately raised their hands.

Sam said, "You can go over two hundred. You just have to be closer to two hundred." I nodded my agreement with

Sam and the students began to discuss the situation among themselves. Jillian looked baffled. I asked for the students' attention.

I asked, "Jillian, would you like to call on someone for advice?" She shook her head "no."

Jillian replied, "I have a question. If I take three longs, that's thirty, so I'll have two hundred ten. That's ten away from two hundred. You have one hundred ninety. That's ten away from two hundred, too. Who wins?" I had chosen Jillian as my partner because she was good at explaining her thinking, didn't get rattled, and could analyze situations well.

I said to the rest of the class, "Who do you think would win?" Again discussions erupted among the students. I paused a few moments to give students a chance to share and listen to one another's ideas. Most seemed to feel the game would be a tie. I asked for the students' attention. The students were eager to share their ideas, and I called on Jael.

Jael said, "I think you should win because Jillian went over two hundred."

Tobias argued, "That's OK. It doesn't matter if someone goes over two hundred. What matters is who is closer. They're the same. Both are ten points away. I think it's a tie."

Jessie shared, "At first I thought like Jael, but then I thought more and even though one hundred ninety seems closer to two hundred than two hundred ten, it's not. I thought that was weird. I guess it seems closer because when you count, you go past one hundred ninety first, then two hundred, and two hundred ten is last."

I confirmed Tobias's and Jessie's thinking and said to the students, "According to the rules, if Jillian takes three longs, the game is a tie game. Each of us will be ten points from two hundred."

Jillian took three longs and we each recorded her turn.

Race to 200	
Mrs. Wickett	Jillian
$6 \times 10 = 60$	$3 \times 10 = 30$
$6 \times 10 = \underline{60}$ 120	$6 \times 10 = \underline{60}$ 90
$5 \times 10 = \underline{50}$ 170	$2 \times 10 = \underline{20}$ 110
$4 \times 1 = \underline{\quad 4}$ 174	$6 \times 10 = \underline{60}$ 170
$6 \times 1 = \underline{\quad 6}$ 180	$1 \times 10 = \underline{10}$ 180
$1 \times 10 = \underline{10}$ 190	$3 \times 10 = \underline{30}$ 210

I said, "When the game is over, you need to summarize what happened. I had one hundred ninety points; Jillian had two hundred ten. We were each ten points from two hundred. The game was a tie game." I completed my recording as follows:

Race to 200	
Mrs. Wickett	Jillian
$6 \times 10 = 60$	$3 \times 10 = 30$
$6 \times 10 = \underline{60}$ 120	$6 \times 10 = \underline{60}$ 90
$5 \times 10 = \underline{50}$ 170	$2 \times 10 = \underline{20}$ 110
$4 \times 1 = \underline{\quad 4}$ 174	$6 \times 10 = \underline{60}$ 170
$6 \times 1 = \underline{\quad 6}$ 180	$1 \times 10 = \underline{10}$ 180
$1 \times 10 = \underline{10}$ 190	$3 \times 10 = \underline{30}$ 210

Mrs. Wickett had <u>190</u> points.
She was <u>10</u> points from 200.
Jillian had <u>210</u> points.
She was <u>10</u> points from 200.
It was a tie.

I completed writing the rules for *Race to 200* on the board.

Race to 200

Object: Be the player with the score closer to 200.
Rules:
1. *Each player must take six turns.*
2. *On your turn, roll the die. You may take ones or tens. The die tells you how many.*
3. *Both players record the turn. Add the total for each turn to the previous score.*
4. *After each player has taken six turns, compare scores to see whose score is closer to 200 and record underneath the chart. (It's OK to go over 200.)*
     _____ *has* _____ *points.*
     _____ *is* _____ *points from 200.*
     _____ *has* _____ *points.*
     _____ *is* _____ *points from 200.*
     _____ *wins.*

There were no questions, and the students were eager to get started. I showed them where the zip-top baggies of materials and paper were located, and then I assigned partners. The students were quickly engaged in the game. I was surprised that no one asked about how to decide who should go first, but this didn't seem to be a problem. Some pairs simply chose one person to go first while others rolled the die to determine the first player. A few decided in other ways, such as according to whose name was first alphabetically or whose birthday was first chronologically.

As I circulated through the class observing, I had to remind several students to figure the running total. I pointed out where this was on Jillian's and my recording sheets, which remained posted on the board. Before too long, Abel and his partner, James, ran out of longs. The boys were upset with one another. I asked the boys, "Do either of you have ten or more longs?" They both nodded. I continued, "When you get ten longs, what can you do?"

Abel and James were both strong math students and both boys knew they could exchange ten longs for a hundreds flat. The real issue in this case was a lack of cooperation. They said together, "We can change in ten longs for a hundreds flat." I nodded. James quickly put ten longs into the pile of base ten blocks and took a hundreds flat.

Abel was less willing. He said, "James always acts like he's the boss of me."

I replied, "In this case, because you two couldn't cooperate, you reached a point in your game when you couldn't go any further."

Abel replied reluctantly, "OK, I like this game. I'll cooperate." He also exchanged ten of his longs for a hundreds flat. It was James's turn. Abel handed him the die. I watched them for a few moments to be sure the boys were back on track.

Tobias had volunteered to be Jenae's partner. Jenae often struggled and Tobias was very patient with her. Their effort was a tribute to cooperation. As I walked by, Tobias blurted out, "Jenae is a genius! She is really good at playing this game." Jenae beamed and showed me her paper. (See Figure 11-1.)

Karena and Halley made a common error when figuring how far Halley's score was from two hundred. Her score was 164, and the girls concluded that Halley's total was 46 rather than 36 points away from 200. (See Figure 11-2.)

As students completed their games, I asked them to collect and put away their materials and read quietly. I collected their recording sheets and ended math for the day. Figure 11-3 shows another pair's completed game.

Note: It's rare that the model game played with a student results in a tie. Usually the question of a tie occurs when the children are playing. When that happens, I interrupt the children, ask for their attention, and we discuss tie games. Having this discussion related to an actual tie game provides a concrete example that leads to understanding more effectively than if you discuss ties when you introduce the rules. (See Figure 11-4.)

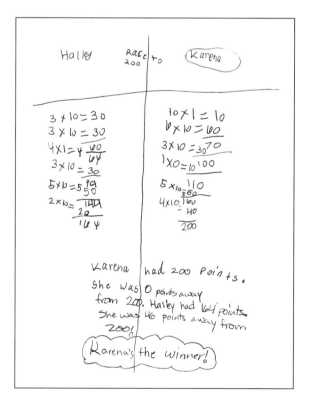

▲▲▲▲▲▲Figure 11-2 *Halley and Karena made a common error when figuring Halley's total.*

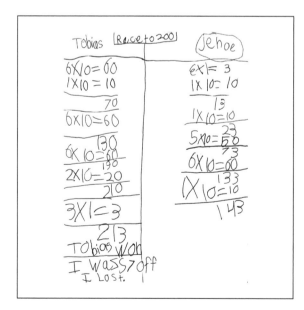

▲▲▲▲▲▲Figure 11-1 *An example of excellent cooperation between students.*

148   Lessons for Extending Place Value

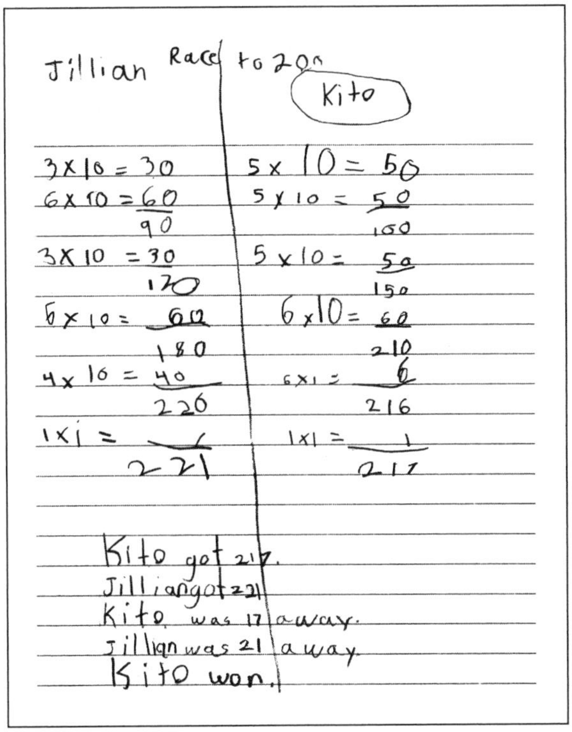

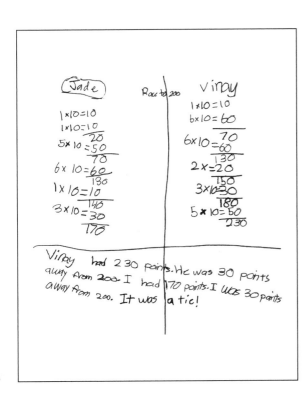

▲▲▲▲▲▲Figure 11–3　*Jillian and Kito used both tens and ones to play their game.*

▲▲▲▲▲▲Figure 11–4　*Jade and Vinay were surprised at their results. Even though they were both fairly far away from 200, they had a tie game.*

DAY 2

My announcement that we were going to play *Race to 200* once again met with enthusiastic cheers. One student who had been absent the previous day was back, so I asked Christopher to explain the game. He quickly explained that the object was to be the player closer to 200. He also reminded the class that each player had to take six turns and the number rolled each turn determined the number of ones or tens a player could take.

I said to the students, "One thing that will be different about the way you play today is you'll use two dice rather than one, as we did yesterday. You'll find the sum of the dice and use that to determine how many ones or tens to take." Because a few students had had difficulty with recording the day before, I again modeled how to do so. I rolled two dice and found the sum, 9. I said, "I've rolled nine. I want to be the player closer to two hundred. I think I'll take nine longs, or tens." I took nine longs and then recorded on the board:

Race to 200	
Mrs. Wickett	Harvey
9 × 10 = 90	

I reminded the students that both players needed to record each turn and to keep a running total during the game. I showed the students where to get materials and then assigned partners.

Most students were quickly engaged in the game. The directions had not been clear, however, to Karena and her partner, Jael. Karena thought she was supposed to multiply the two numbers rolled, but Jael added her two numbers. (See Figure 11–5.)

Race to 200　149

Both girls often needed additional support and time to better understand the task at hand. Because the rest of the students were engaged in the game, I was able to sit with the girls and give them help and guidance until they better understood what to do. When I checked back a short time later, they had made progress. (See Figure 11–6.)

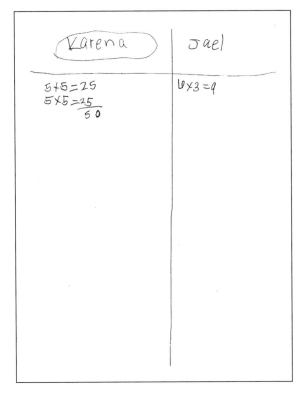

▲▲▲▲▲▲Figure 11–5   *Jael and Karena were confused.*

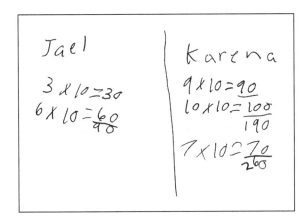

▲▲▲▲▲▲Figure 11–6   *After additional help, Jael and Karena were successful.*

Some students got carried away and were trying to reach the highest score possible, 720. Earlier we had discussed that the greatest score possible when playing with two dice is 720 (when 12 is rolled on all six turns and the player takes twelve longs, or tens, each time) and the smallest score possible is 12 (when 2 is rolled on all six turns and the player takes two ones each time). The students who were trying to get as high a score as possible found they quickly ran out of blocks and had to spend time discussing how to deal with the situation. Paul was one such student. He and his partner, Vinay, used centimeter grid paper and quickly cut out additional longs and flats. Paul's final score was 335. Vinay had remembered the goal of the game, and his final score was 218. (See Figure 11–7.) I asked Paul if he would change his strategy the next time he played. He grinned and said he would remember to take ones rather than tens earlier in the game. He reflected that he could have made a big difference in his score if on his fourth turn he had taken nine ones rather than nine tens. He lamented, "I would have had a final

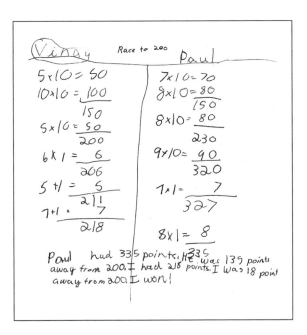

▲▲▲▲▲▲Figure 11–7   *Paul forgot the object of the game, to be closest to 200, and got a score of 335.*

150   Lessons for Extending Place Value

score of two hundred fifty-four instead of three hundred thirty-five!" He paused a moment and then shared his thinking: "Three hundred thirty-five minus ninety is two hundred forty-five, but then I have to add in nine ones because that's what I would have taken instead of nine tens, so that's two hundred fifty-four."

As students finished their first game, I checked their work for accuracy. I also asked the children what strategy they had used and if they would change it for the next game. When most students were finished, I asked for everyone's attention. I said, "I'm going to collect your recording sheets so that I can look them over this evening. Tomorrow you'll have the opportunity to play again. Between now and tomorrow, think about your strategy. Is your strategy the best strategy, or can it be improved? What would you do the same as you did today? What would you do differently? After you have the chance to play

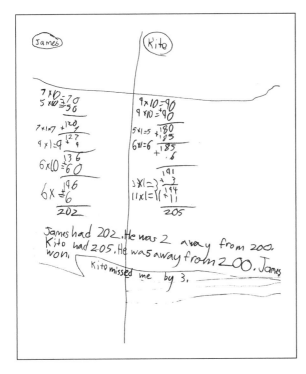

▲▲▲▲▲Figure 11–8 *James and Kito kept the goal of the game in mind and played a close game. Their final scores were only three points apart.*

tomorrow, we'll have a class discussion to share your ideas." I collected their papers and ended math class on that note.

Figure 11–8 shows a close game between James and Kito.

DAY 3

When class began the next day, the students started by playing *Race to 200* with their partners. I reminded them to be thinking about good strategies for being the player closest to 200. As I circulated, I questioned some students about their ideas. I was careful not to interrupt too many of their games, as this can lead to frustration, but having a sense of how they were thinking would help me prepare for the class discussion.

I checked in early with Abel, James, and Sam. Sam's partner had to leave class for a bit, so the boys agreed to be a trio. I was concerned that they might not be focused on their game. While they were a bit wild, they were playing and recording their turns as they should. Each boy had taken two turns. Abel had 97 points, James had 120, and Sam's total was 200. I asked each boy what they were thinking as they decided whether to take tens or ones for their second turn.

Abel explained, "If I took seven tens that would be seventy. I had ninety from before. Seventy and ninety is one hundred sixty. It's only my second turn and one hundred sixty seemed a big number for my second turn, so I took ones instead of tens. I have ninety-seven instead of one hundred sixty."

James said, "I was behind Sam and Abel. I rolled a five and that isn't such a big number. If I took five ones, I'd have seventy-five, and that seemed really small. So I took five tens and I have one hundred twenty. I'm still pretty far from two hundred, and if I get too close, I can always take ones."

Sam explained, "I think it's good to get close to two hundred early. Then all you have to do is take ones and you won't get too far away from two hundred."

The boys had different ideas, but all seemed to be using their understanding of tens and ones and their number sense. (See Figure 11–9.)

Jillian and Keara were having a serious discussion about their strategies. Jillian finally convinced Keara that they should start out with big numbers by taking longs. When I checked back later, both girls had final scores less than 200 and had written about their strategies on the back of their papers. Jillian won and stated that she felt sorry for Keara. Keara stated that even though she lost, she still had fun playing the game. (See Figures 11–10 and 11–11.)

After twenty minutes or so, most students had completed at least one game. I asked the students to bring their papers and gather on the rug.

A Class Discussion

When the students were settled, I began the discussion. I asked, "What strategy did you find helpful so you could be closer to two hundred?" Hands shot into the air. I called on Tina.

Tina said confidently, "One thing for certain is on your first turn, it's important to take tens!"

I recorded on the board:

Tina   On your first turn, take tens.

I turned to the others and asked, "How many of you agree with Tina's strategy for the first turn?" Everyone raised a hand.

Paul shared, "I agree with what Tina said, but about your third turn, you should start to think about if you should takes ones

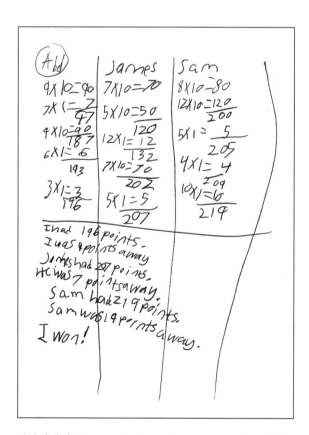

▲▲▲▲▲▲Figure 11–9   *Time ran out for Abel, Sam, and James. They each took five turns rather than six. Abel won.*

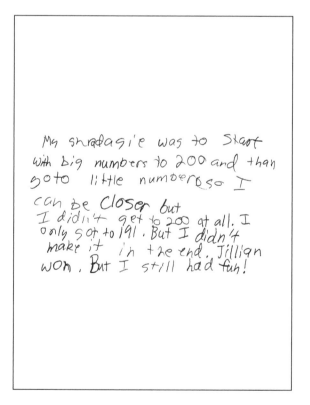

▲▲▲▲▲▲Figure 11–10   *Keara's thoughts about her game with Jillian.*

instead of tens. If you just keep on taking tens, you might get too big of a score." I added Paul's idea to the list with Tina's.

Jillian said, "You should start with big numbers by taking tens; then you should be sure to take small numbers like ones as you get close to two hundred or you'll go way over two hundred." I recorded Jillian's idea.

Tina On your first turn, take tens.

Paul About your third turn, you should start to think about whether it's better to take ones instead of tens. If you keep taking tens, you might get too big a score.

Jillian Start with big numbers by taking tens; then take ones as you get closer to 200 so you don't go way over 200.

As I recorded Jillian's strategy, I wondered what she considered to be close to 200. "What is a number you consider to be closer to two hundred?" I asked her.

Jillian paused and thought for a moment and then said, "Maybe one hundred sixty." Several hands popped up, indicating students had other ideas about what scores were close to 200.

Kassidee said, "I think maybe one hundred fifty is getting close."

Tanya added, "Maybe even one hundred ten or one hundred twenty."

Olina said thoughtfully, "I don't agree with any of those ideas. I think you can actually get much closer to two hundred than that because all you would do is take ones. I think maybe one hundred eighty would be a good time to start taking ones."

Jenae commented, "I think it depends on how many turns you have left, but I don't exactly know why."

Halley added, "I think Jenae's right. I do think you have to think about how many turns you have left. If you have one hundred eighty and it's your second turn, you'd better take ones, especially if you

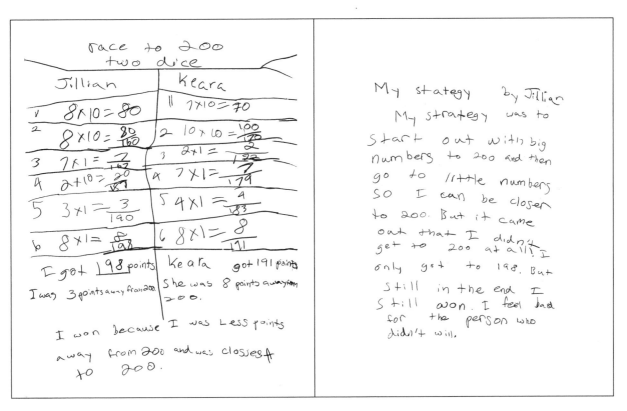

▲▲▲▲▲Figure 11–11 *Jillian's recording sheet.*

Race to 200   153

roll a big number. But if you have one hundred eighty and it's your last turn, well that's different."

Sam built on what Halley said. "You do have to think about what turn you're on and how big the number is that you roll."

The students sat quietly. I asked if anyone had any other strategies. Tanya raised her hand.

"Well," she explained, "I think when you get to one hundred, you should stop automatically using tens and go back and forth from tens to ones to get close to two hundred."

I added Tanya's strategy to the others.

Tina   On your first turn, take tens.

Paul   About your third turn, you should start to think about whether it's better to take ones instead of tens. If you keep taking tens, you might get too big a score.

Jillian   Start with big numbers by taking tens; then take ones as you get closer to 200 so you don't go way over 200.

Tanya   At about 100, stop using tens and go back and forth from tens to ones to get close to 200.

Kassidee had one last idea to share. She explained, "I think you could actually do it the other way—start out with ones

for the first turn, or maybe even two turns, and then start taking tens. I didn't do it that way, but it seems like it could work." As I added Kassidee's suggestion to the list on the board, several students nodded their agreement with her idea.

The students sat quietly thinking and I ended the lesson for the day.

EXTENSIONS

1. Have students play *Race to $2.00*. The game is played exactly the same as *Race to 200* except that instead of using base ten blocks, players use pennies, dimes, and dollars.

2. Change the game to *Race to 100* to make it easier. The rules remain the same as *Race to 200*.

3. As students become more comfortable and proficient, change the game to *Race to 600*.

4. Students can play *Race to 200* as described in the vignette, playing according to one of the strategies shared during the class discussion. After students have played several games using a selected strategy, lead a class discussion to determine if some strategies seem to be more effective than others.

Questions and Discussion

▲▲

▲ *Multiplication by ten seems difficult for my students. What do you suggest?*

Rather than representing a turn with a multiplication sentence, students can use repeated addition to show what they did. For example, if a 6 was rolled, rather than write $6 \times 10 = 60$, a student could write $10 + 10 + 10 + 10 + 10 + 10 = 60$. As your students seem ready, you can then suggest that a shorter way of writing repeated addition is to use multiplication.

▲ *In the vignette, James and Abel argued because they ran out of tens. Why not provide more tens so students don't have this problem?*

There are two important reasons for providing the numbers of blocks I do. One reason is mathematical. Students must exchange ones for tens and tens for hundreds or they run out of blocks. This helps strengthen their understanding of equivalence and the base ten number system. The second reason is social. Students have to cooperate. Cooperation is an important life skill. When students don't cooperate, they run out of materials as Abel and James did. If they want to keep playing, they have to find a way to work together.

CHAPTER TWELVE
TEN TIMES BETTER

Overview

Ten Times Better, written by Richard Michelson, uses poetry and watercolor illustrations to provide a context for this lesson. A poem for each number from one to ten presents a particular attribute of an animal, and immediately following each is a second poem that presents a different animal with an attribute that is ten times better. The book helps reinforce for children the connection between how many tens are in a number and how much those tens represent. Also, the lesson helps students generalize about the result of multiplying a number by ten. After being introduced to the book, students write their own "ten times better" sentences and multiplication equations to represent their sentences, and finally they illustrate and share their work.

Materials

▲ *Ten Times Better*, by Richard Michelson (New York: Marshall Cavendish, 2000)

Time

▲ two class periods

Teaching Directions

1. Begin by reading the text accompanying the illustrations in the first two spreads of the book *Ten Times Better*, about the elephant and the squid. Discuss so that children understand the relationship that compares the elephant's one trunk and the squid's ten tentacles.

2. Continue with the next two animals—the camel with two humps and the sage grouse with twenty feathers.

156

3. For the next spread, read about the three-toed sloth. Then ask students to predict what is ten times better (thirty). To encourage children to look for patterns, write the following on the board:

1   10
2   20
3   30

Read about the centipede's legs to confirm that thirty is correct.

4. Ask students to predict the pair of numbers that comes next. They should explain why their predictions make sense. Then continue by reading about the boar's four tusks and the frog's forty warts. Add *4* and *40* to the list of numbers from Step 3.

5. Point to the first pair of numbers you recorded on the board in Step 3 and ask: "What multiplication sentence could I write to represent what happened at the beginning of the book?" Record.

1   10   1 × 10 = 10   10 × 1 = 10
2   20
3   30
4   40

Repeat for the other three pairs of numbers. Ask students what patterns they notice.

6. Continue reading the rest of the book, recording on the board, and discussing patterns the students notice.

7. After reading the text about the bees on pages 32 and 33, ask students to figure the number of bees shown on these two pages (34 bees + 35 bees = ?). Record on the board as students explain how they figured. Next, ask students how many more bees are needed to make one hundred. Again have students share how they figured and record on the board. Show students the fold-out part of page 33 to confirm that thirty-one more bees were needed to make one hundred.

8. To begin Day 2, review the book if necessary, especially if students were absent the day before.

9. Write the following sentence frame on the board to model for students how to write a "ten times better" sentence:

_____ *are really fine, but ten times better, or __, is divine.*

10. Fill in the blanks:

Four paws on a kitten are really fine, but ten times better, or 40, is divine.

11. Ask for another idea to complete the sentence frame with a different number. For this "ten times better" sentence, also write a multiplication equation that represents it and then illustrate it.

12. Have students each write their own "ten times better" sentence, record a multiplication equation, and draw an illustration. As students work, circulate through the class, observing and assisting as needed.

13. Encourage students who correctly complete one "ten times better" sentence, multiplication equation, and illustration to do a second one.

After all students have completed at least one "ten times better" sentence, multiplication equation, and illustration, lead a class discussion and allow those who wish to share their work to do so.

Teaching Notes

Ten Times Better, by Richard Michelson, is a collection of poems illustrated with watercolor paintings of animals. The situations presented in this book lead children to think about what is ten times better, or larger, in an enjoyable, fun context. The animals and accompanying text are presented in pairs. The poem that describes the first animal in each pair presents a characteristic of the animal that relates to its number, while the second poem insists that ten times better is more desirable. For example, to present his case, the ant states,

> Who goes outside without their pants
> and has six legs? You guessed it: ants.
> We've never learned arithmetic,
> but six is better. That's our pick.

The croc retorts,

> Fiddlesticks! Six, the best? Poppycock!
> You want TEN TIMES BETTER? Dial a croc.
> I have SIXTY teeth. I'm a great masticator.
> (That means I chew first, and ask questions later.)

Nine other pairs of poems such as these represent multiplying the numbers one through ten by ten. Included at the back is an additional section that presents information about each of the animals in the book. The information includes a question that children can answer by applying what they've learned about multiplying by ten. See the extension suggested at the end of this chapter.

While the animals in the book consistently make the case for ten times more being ten times better, it's arguable whether more necessarily means better. However, that's the premise of the book. At the same time, the mathematical concept is better described as "ten times larger," and you'll see in the lesson that I used *larger* and *better* interchangeably.

Prior to this lesson, the students in the vignette were involved in a unit of study focused on developing their understanding of the concept of multiplication. The students understood that multiplication is about combining equal groups. *Ten Times Better* provided them an opportunity to apply this understanding when multiplying by ten.

The students in the vignette, as part of their study of multiplication, had brainstormed and generated charts of things that come in groups from two to twelve. See *Teaching Arithmetic: Lessons for Introducing Multiplication, Grade 3,* by Marilyn Burns (Sausalito, CA: Math Solutions Publications, 2001), for additional information. During Day 2 of the lesson, the students referred to these charts for ideas. If your students have not done this activity, it would be helpful to take a day to do it prior to starting Day 2 of this lesson.

Initially, the students in the following vignette had difficulty understanding the poems and determining what parts of the animals were being compared. It was helpful to work through the first few pages slowly with much discussion about how to interpret and understand the author's language and his poetry.

The Lesson

DAY 1

The students gathered quickly on the rug in anticipation of enjoying a new book. I held the book *Ten Times Better,* by Richard Michelson, so the students could see the cover.

"*Ten Times Better,*" Connor read aloud. "I bet this has something to do with multiplication!"

I said to the class, "Connor thinks my book has something to do with multiplication. How many of you agree?" Several hands went up immediately.

Halley explained, "It has something to do with times because of the words *ten times.*"

Kito added, "Ten times better' sounds like you're thinking about two things and one of them is better . . . ten times better!"

Jenae observed, "There are ten fingers on the cover, but I'm not too sure what that has to do with it."

Jillian said, "This isn't about ten times better, but there is a starfish on the cover and it has five arms. Ten fingers is two times five, or two times better, so maybe it's about ten times better and two times better, too."

When all who wanted to share had done so, I began to read the book. After

reading about the first two animals, the elephant and the squid, I asked the students why the squid, in the second illustration, thought that it was ten times better than the elephant, in the first illustration. As they talked among themselves, their initial ideas indicated this was not an easy question for the students. I guided the discussion to focus carefully on these first two spreads, both the pictures and the words, so the children could better analyze the rest of the book. After giving the students a few moments to share their thoughts with those around them, I asked for their attention. When the students were settled, I asked for volunteers to share their ideas.

Jael said with hesitation, "Maybe the author likes squids better than elephants."

James added, "Maybe squids are smarter or something like that."

After listening to a few more students share, I could tell they were confused and unable to see clearly what the author was trying to get across. To help them gain better understanding, I redirected their attention to the first illustration, asking them what stood out. The students noticed that the trunk of the elephant was easy to see. Next I asked the students to listen as I reread the passage that accompanies the

Ten Times Better   159

picture of the elephant and refers to its trunk as a schnoz.

I said to the students, "The elephant's trunk stands out clearly in the illustration. Is the word *trunk* actually used in the poem about the elephant?" They quickly responded by shaking their heads "no." "Is there a word used in the poem that means nose or trunk?" I paused as a few hands went up. I called on Ana.

Ana explained, "The way you said it, it didn't sound right, but I think the word that means trunk is *schnoz'll*. But I don't think I ever heard that word before." Several others nodded their agreement. Halley was waving her hand excitedly.

Halley said, "I think I get it! I think the word is really *schnoz,* but to make it rhyme with *nozzle,* they made it a contraction, so it's *schnoz'll!* I think that's funny!" Several students giggled along with Halley while others played with the word *schnoz'll* by repeating it to themselves several times. After a few moments I called the students back to order, this time refocusing their attention on the text of the second spread. I read aloud, "Big nose? Big deal." To reinforce the focus on the elephant's trunk or nose, I asked the children again, "What was the important thing about the elephant?"

"The schnoz!" they replied, giggling.

I finished reading the text for the second spread and then asked the students, "What is it about the squid that is ten times better than the elephant's schnoz, or nose?"

"The tentacles," they chorused.

Tobias shared, "I get it now. It's like if there is one trunk, then the squid has ten tentacles, so ten times means that whatever is bigger is ten of the other thing bigger." I appreciated Tobias's effort to make sense and to restate his understanding using his own words. I nodded my encouragement. The others were quiet. I continued sharing the book by showing the next spread, with the Bactrian camel.

I said, "What stands out about this camel is that it has two humps. What number do you suppose is ten times better than two?"

The class stated in unison, "Twenty."

Ana explained, "It has to be twenty of something because if you count by twos ten times, then that would be twenty." To prove her point, Ana counted aloud by twos ten times, using her fingers to keep track of how many twos she'd counted.

I asked the students, "How would you write a multiplication sentence for Ana's idea?"

Paul suggested, "I think it would be two times ten because the times sign means groups of. No, wait, it would be ten times two because it would be two camel humps on ten camels and each camel is a group of humps. So ten times two."

Halley disagreed. "I know the times sign can mean groups of, but I think it could also be two times ten because then it could mean two ten times. Two humps on ten camels; each camel would be like a 'time.'"

I recorded on the board:

$$10 \times 2 \qquad 2 \times 10$$

I commented, "Halley's way and Paul's way are both correct. What's important is that you can explain how the numbers in the multiplication sentence fit the situation you are representing. Both Halley and Paul could explain how their number sentences matched the problem."

I read the spread about the Bactrian camel and the sage grouse, once again asking the students what was ten times better about the second animal than the first. This time, the question was much easier for the students, and most quickly recognized that twenty grouse feathers were ten times better, or more, than two camel humps.

I read the poem about the three-toed sloth, then showed the students the illustration, asking them what number would

160   Lessons for Extending Place Value

be ten times better than three. They immediately responded that thirty was ten times better. To help the students see patterns, I recorded on the board:

$$1 \quad 10$$
$$2 \quad 20$$
$$3 \quad 30$$

I read the poem about the centipede with thirty legs and confirmed that thirty was indeed ten times better. (A common misunderstanding is that centipedes all have one hundred legs. A common centipede is the house centipede, *Scutigera forceps*, which is about 2 inches long and has fifteen pairs of legs.)

I pointed to what I'd written on the board and asked, "Here's what we know so far. What do you think the next number will be, and what do you think will be ten times better?" I paused as the students shared with their neighbors. After a couple of moments, I asked for their attention. Most students had raised their hands. I called on Jessie.

Jessie said, "The next number will be four because it's going in order, one, two, three. Ten times four is forty. And besides that, the second column is counting by tens—ten, twenty, thirty. Forty's next." The students showed their agreement with Jessie with thumbs up. I verified the students' prediction by reading the next spread, about the wild boar's four tusks and the frog's forty warts.

I pointed to the 1 and 10 recorded on the board and asked, "What multiplication sentence could I write to represent what happened in the beginning of the book?"

"One times ten equals ten," Karlee said. I recorded on the board:

$$1 \quad 10 \quad\quad 1 \times 10 = 10$$
$$2 \quad 20$$
$$3 \quad 30$$
$$4 \quad 40$$

"Why does Karlee's idea make sense?" I asked the class.

"It means one ten times is ten," Tanya said.

"Tell me more about what you're thinking," I encouraged Tanya.

"Well, there was one trunk and ten tentacles," Tanya explained.

Jillian added, "One plus one plus one plus one plus one plus one plus one plus one plus one plus one equals ten is another way to think of it, and that means the same as one ten times."

The students were quiet so I asked next, "What is a multiplication sentence for the second pair of numbers, two and twenty?"

Adama said, "It means two was added ten times to make twenty, so two times ten equals twenty." I recorded on the board:

$$1 \quad 10 \quad\quad 1 \times 10 = 10$$
$$2 \quad 20 \quad\quad 2 \times 10 = 20$$
$$3 \quad 30$$
$$4 \quad 40$$

Tina said, "I think it could also be ten times one or ten times two because you could think of it as ten groups of one or ten groups of two."

Jade observed, "Either way, it's the same amount."

Paul said, "I notice a pattern. Whenever you multiply by ten, it's like putting a zero in the ones place of the number you want to make ten times better." If Paul or another student hadn't shared this pattern, I would have asked the children what patterns they noticed in order to draw this idea out.

"Oh yeah!" "Hey, I see what he means!" were some of the responses. Although the students had explored this idea before, their rediscovery and delight reminded me of the importance of giving students multiple opportunities to explore the same idea in different contexts. I added Tina's thinking to the information on the board:

$$1 \quad 10 \quad\quad 1 \times 10 = 10 \quad\quad 10 \times 1 = 10$$
$$2 \quad 20 \quad\quad 2 \times 10 = 20 \quad\quad 10 \times 2 = 20$$
$$3 \quad 30$$
$$4 \quad 40$$

I continued sharing the book, discussing ideas, counting the objects in the illustrations to confirm something was ten times "better," and finally recording on the board as I had been doing. When I got to the spread using bees to illustrate ten times ten, I noticed several students had skeptical expressions on their faces. I pointed to the illustration of the bees and said, "Some of you seem troubled. What's bothering you?"

James explained, "That really doesn't look like one hundred bees." Several others voiced their agreement with him. I knew that this last spread had an extra page that folded out, so James's observation was right. I was pleased that James and others had a strong enough sense of number to question this illustration. Together we counted the bees. On the page on the left side of the spread, we counted thirty-four bees. On the right-hand page, we counted thirty-five bees.

"Hey!" Jade burst out. "There are little parts of bees going off the page. I bet there are more on the back!"

Sam said, "I think she's right. There has to be more bees. Thirty-four and thirty-five only equals sixty-nine."

I asked Sam, "How do you know that?"

Sam explained, "Thirty-five plus thirty-five is seventy. That's one too many because one of the numbers is really thirty-four, not thirty-five. So subtract one, out and that's sixty-nine." I recorded on the board:

$$Sam \quad 35 + 35 = 70$$
$$70 - 1 = 69$$

Kassidee explained it differently. "I added the tens. Three tens plus three tens is six tens, or sixty. Then I added the ones. Four ones plus five ones is nine ones. Sixty plus nine is sixty-nine." I recorded:

$$Kassidee \quad 3\ tens + 3\ tens = 6\ tens\ or\ 60$$
$$4 + 5 = 9$$
$$60 + 9 = 69$$

"I know another way," Vinay began. "You could take the three from the thirty-five and think of it as three times ten. Then do the same thing for the three from the thirty-four. So it would be three times ten plus three times ten. That's six times ten or thirty plus thirty, but either way, it's sixty. Then add the four and the five, and that's nine ones. Put it together and it's sixty-nine." I recorded:

$$Vinay \quad (3 \times 10) + (3 \times 10) = 6 \times 10 = 30 + 30 = 60$$
$$4 + 5 = 9$$
$$60 + 9 = 69$$

Jade was persistent about her idea that more bees were on another page. She said, "Please, can you show us the next page? I really think there are more bees on it." The other children joined in asking to see the next page.

"Ten times ten is one hundred. The illustrator drew sixty-nine. How many would have to be on another page to make one hundred?" I asked. The room came alive as the students shared their thinking with neighbors. After a few moments, hands began to go up. When most students had raised their hands, I called on Olina.

Olina shared, "I think forty-one."

"Why do you think it's forty-one?" I asked.

"Well, because you add one to the sixty-nine to make seventy and then thirty more to get to one hundred . . . hey, wait. The answer is only thirty-one and I said forty-one. I'm confused."

Olina's error is one commonly made by third graders. I said, "The way you explained it made sense. I agree that if you start with sixty-nine and add one you have seventy, and then you need thirty more to make one hundred, for a total of thirty-one. For the answer to be forty-one I think you'd have to start with fifty-nine. If you add one to fifty-nine, that equals sixty, and then you'd need four more tens, or forty, to reach one hundred. Forty plus one equals forty-one."

162   Lessons for Extending Place Value

Olina's look of confusion cleared and she responded, "I get it now!" I recorded on the board:

$$Olina \qquad 69 + 1 = 70$$
$$70 + 10 + 10 + 10 = 100$$
$$30 + 1 = 31$$

"Did anyone think of it differently?" I asked the others.

Roberto said, "I thought at first it was forty-one, too, because it's forty from sixty to one hundred and I added one more. I'm not exactly sure why I thought that. But then I remembered that sixty-nine is nine bigger than sixty, so forty is too much. Then I counted back nine from forty and got thirty-one."

I recorded Roberto's idea beneath Olina's:

$$Roberto \quad 40 + 60 = 100$$
$$40, 39, 38, 37, 36, 35, 34, 33,$$
$$32, 31$$

Kassidee shared, "I started at one hundred and counted back by tens to seventy and that was three tens, or thirty. Then I needed one more to get to sixty-nine, so thirty and one more makes thirty-one."

Jillian said, "I did it like Kassidee, except I looked at the hundred chart. Even though the numbers are mostly turned so we can't see them, I knew where one hundred could go, down on the bottom in the right corner. Then I counted up the chart three tens, which is where seventy would be. I know that because all the numbers in the column above one hundred have to end in zero. It's a pattern. That's thirty and then one more to get to sixty-nine makes thirty-one altogether." I added Kassidee's and Jillian's ideas to the board.

Halley shared last. She explained, "I did it with multiplication." Halley's comment surprised me even though Halley thought in unexpected, creative ways as she worked to connect new ideas with previous learning. I encouraged her to continue. "Well, this is what I think. You want to get to one hundred bees. You've got sixty-nine bees so far. The question is sixty-nine and how many more make one hundred. It takes one to get to seventy, then three groups of ten to get to one hundred. So I think you could solve it by one plus three times ten. You'd have to put those things that look like sideways smiles around the three times ten part." I wrote the following on the board under the other four ideas:

$$Halley \quad 100 = 69 + ?$$
$$100 = 69 + 1 + (3 \times 10)$$

"Is this what you mean?" I asked Halley, pointing to what I'd written on the board. She studied the board a moment, grinned, and then nodded.

I commented, "The sideways smiles are called *parentheses.*"

Halley made one additional comment: "You could use y instead of a question mark."

The students had had some previous experience using y as a variable. I erased the question mark and replaced it with y.

Finally, I unfolded the page to reveal that Jade and the others were right. Together we counted the rest of the bees and found there were indeed thirty-one more bees, making a total of one hundred.

DAY 2

To begin the next part of the lesson, I reminded the students, "Yesterday, we read the book *Ten Times Better*. Who remembers what the point of the book was?" I asked this question as a way to review for a few students who had seemed uncertain and for the two students who had been absent. Most students immediately raised their hands. I called on Adama.

Adama explained, "The book would show something on one page and then show something else that was ten times bigger, or better. Like it showed two camel humps and then ten times bigger was a bird, I forget the kind of bird, with a bunch of feathers, twenty to be exact. Twenty is ten times better than two." A few other students gave additional examples.

When no one had anything additional to add, I said, "Today we are going to write our own 'ten times better' sentences. You may choose animals, as shown in the book, or you can choose something from the Things That Come in Groups lists, or you could even think up something that wasn't in the book or on the lists. Here's a sentence frame that might help you think about this." I wrote on the board a sentence frame that was simple so the students would remain focused on the mathematics.

_____ are really fine, but ten times better, or __, is divine.

I looked over at the Things That Come in Groups charts and said to the class, "I'm thinking of kitten paws. One kitten has how many paws?"

"Four," the students answered.

I continued, "In the first blank space, I'm going to write 'Four kitten paws.'"

I did so and the sentence frame looked as follows:

Four kitten paws are really fine, but ten times better, or __, is divine.

Karena said, "I know what comes next. Can I tell?" I nodded. She continued, "It's forty. Ten kittens would have forty paws!" Karena was pleased with herself. I nodded my agreement and filled in the second blank.

Four kitten paws are really fine, but ten times better, or 40, is divine.

"Before you write your own 'ten times better' sentence, let's do one more together. Someone make a suggestion for our sentence. Remember, you can choose something from the Things That Come in Groups lists." As the students thought, I rewrote the sentence frame on the board under the first one.

"Corners on a hexagon," someone suggested.

"How should the sentence begin?" I asked.

"Six corners on a hexagon are really fine," Ben said. I asked Ben to come to the board and fill in the blank. He did so correctly.

"How should the sentence end?" I asked.

Jessie said, "The second blank should have a sixty because six ten times would be sixty. Six, twelve, eighteen, twenty-four, thirty, thirty-six, forty-two, forty-eight, fifty-four, sixty." Jessie gave a sigh of relief and then came to the board to complete the sentence.

I used this second example to model for the students what else to do with the sentences they would write. I asked the students, "What number sentence could we use to represent our word sentence?"

Tobias said, "I think six times ten equals sixty, because you have six corners ten times and that makes sixty."

I wrote on the board beneath the word sentence, $6 \times 10 = 60$.

Tina reminded us, "You could do ten times six equals sixty and think of it as ten groups, or hexagons, with six corners on every one."

I recorded Tina's number sentence below Tobias's.

Six corners on a hexagon are really fine, but ten times better, or 60, is divine.
$6 \times 10 = 60$
$10 \times 6 = 60$

I asked, "How could I illustrate our 'ten times better' sentence?"

Hands flew into the air immediately. I called on Arin.

Arin said, "Draw one hexagon to show the six corners. Maybe you could use numbers and count the corners. Then draw ten more hexagons to show ten times more corners. And maybe you

164   Lessons for Extending Place Value

should number all those corners to show that sixty is ten times bigger than six. That's a lot of numbers!"

I quickly drew one hexagon and then ten more, as Arin had suggested. Rather than number all the corners, I wrote a 6 beneath each hexagon, explaining that that was a quicker way to show there were six corners per hexagon. Then I skip-counted by sixes ten times to reach sixty.

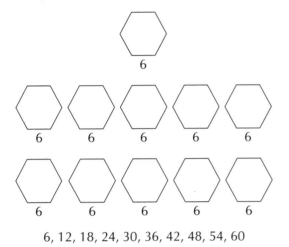

6, 12, 18, 24, 30, 36, 42, 48, 54, 60

I said, "Now it's your turn to write your own 'ten times better' sentences. You may use the sentence frame on the board, or you may use your own sentence. Remember to write a number sentence to go with your

word sentence. Don't forget your illustration." To reinforce these points, I pointed to the example on the board. The children showed their excitement by sharing ideas with nearby neighbors. After settling the class, I asked if there were any questions.

Vinay asked, "Can I do more than one?"

I said to Vinay and the others, "When you finish one 'ten times better' sentence, raise your hand so I can come and read it. Then, after I read it, you can do a second." I also reminded the students to refer to the board if they needed a reminder about what to do. Then I handed each student a sheet of paper and they got to work.

The room buzzed as children shared their ideas and settled into the task. Many giggled as students shared their pictures and ideas with members of their table groups. Some students used the sentence frame on the board while others wrote their own. (See Figures 12–1 through 12–7.)

After most students were finished with their first problem and working on their second, I gave them a three-minute warning. After three minutes, I gathered the students on the rug and gave those who wanted to do so the opportunity to share their work with the rest of the class.

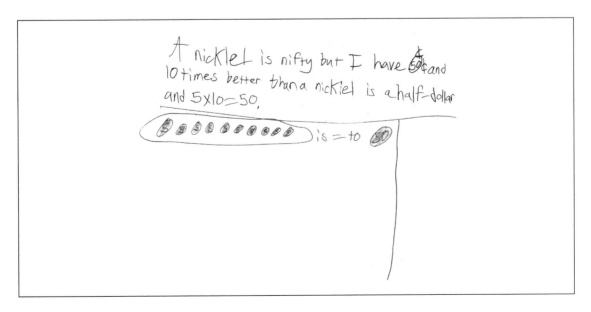

▲▲▲▲▲▲Figure 12–1   *Tobias used money and rhymed* **nifty** *with* **fifty** *(cents).*

Ten Times Better   **165**

Figure 12–2   *Paul, a skateboard enthusiast, changed his sentence slightly.*

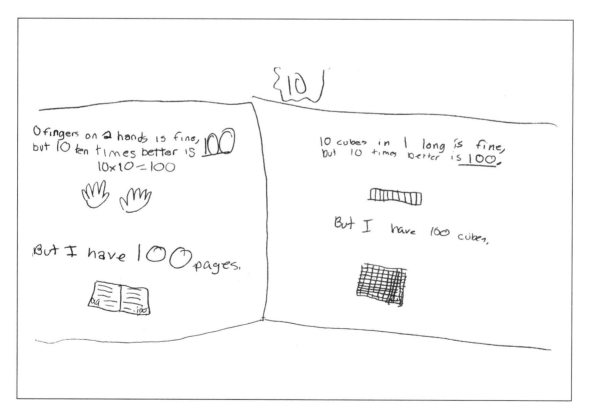

Figure 12–3   *For her first problem, Olina used two different objects, fingers and book pages. In her second problem, she used base ten blocks.*

166   Lessons for Extending Place Value

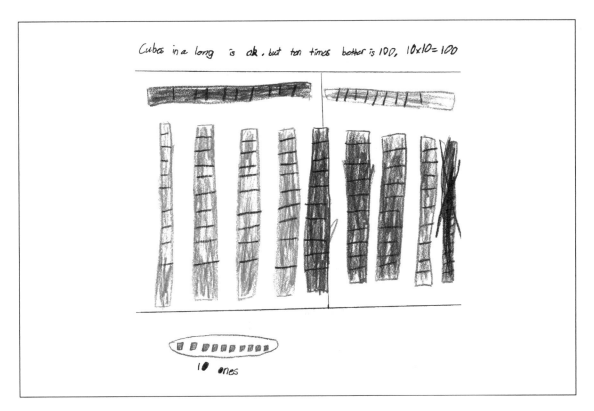

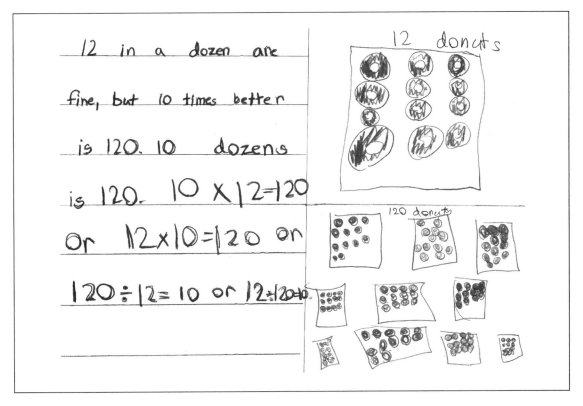

Figure 12–4 *Jessie used base ten blocks for her "ten times better" problem.*

Figure 12–5 *Sam used a larger number, twelve, in his sentence. He commented that he wanted to show on his paper that he understood that multiplication and division are related. However, he made an error in writing the last division problem.*

▲▲▲▲▲▲Figure 12–6 *Arin struggled but successfully completed the assignment using fingers.*

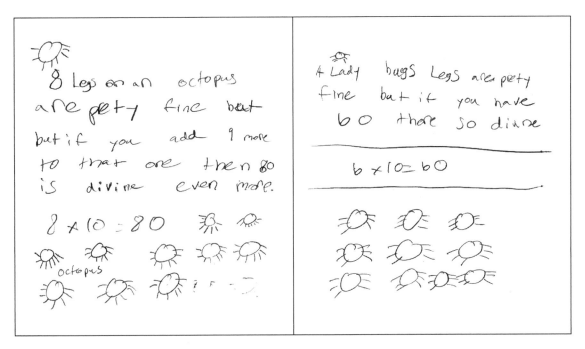

▲▲▲▲▲▲Figure 12–7 *Initially Jillian's work showed slight confusion. After I talked with her, she was able to complete the assignment successfully.*

EXTENSION

At the end of *Ten Times Better* is a section with additional information and a question about each of the animals in the poems. For example:

> If a starfish loses an arm, it may grow a new one. The missing arm, meanwhile, may grow a new body. Now there are two starfish where there used to be only one.
>
> Most starfish have five arms, but some have TEN TIMES MORE. How many arms would a starfish like this have?

Each of the questions can be solved by applying knowledge of multiplication by ten, providing students the opportunity to use and reinforce this knowledge. From time to time, select information about one of the animals from this section. Present it to the children and pose the accompanying question for them to solve. (See Figures 12–8 through 12–12.)

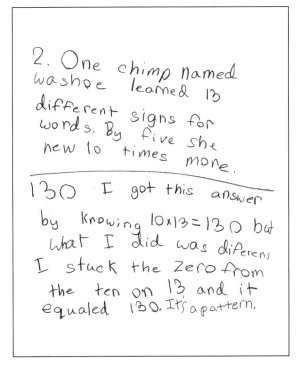

▲▲▲▲▲▲Figure 12–8 *Sam correctly figured the number of words the chimp learned in five years. He noticed a pattern when numbers are multiplied by ten.*

Ten Times Better 169

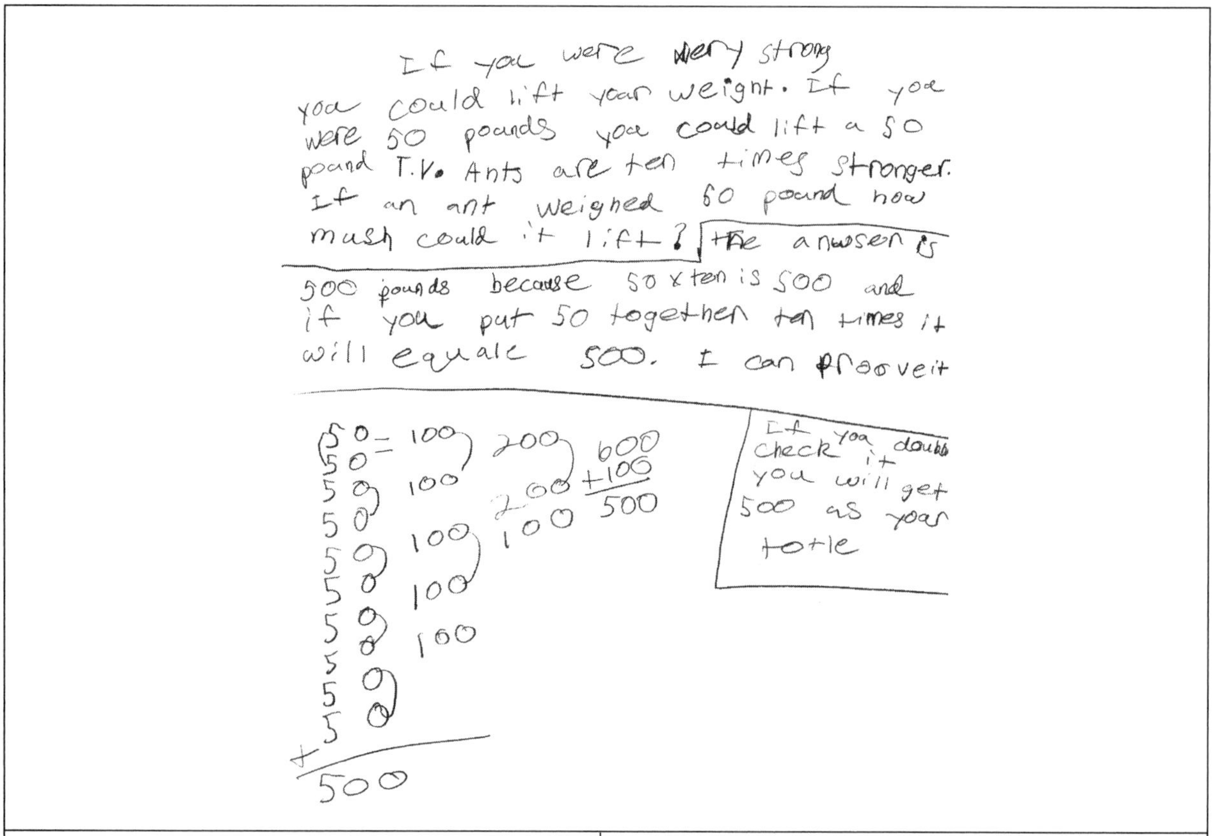

▲▲▲▲▲▲Figures 12–9, 12–10, 12–11   *Jillian, Sam, and Tina show how they figured the amount an ant can lift.*

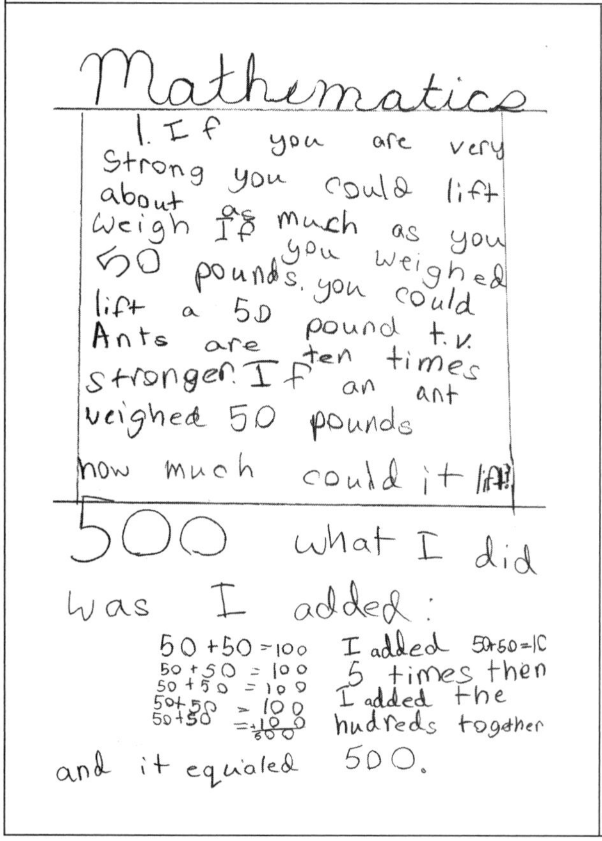

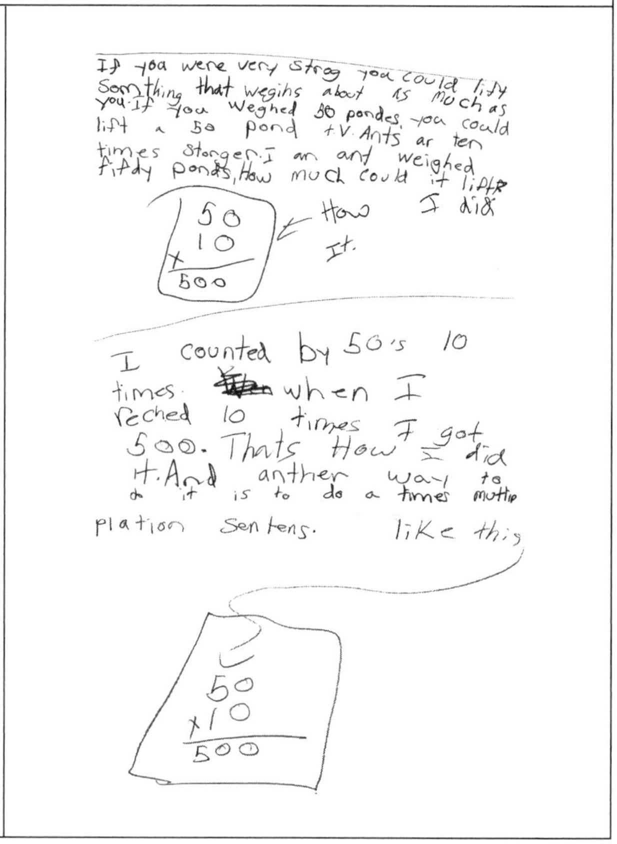

170   Lessons for Extending Place Value

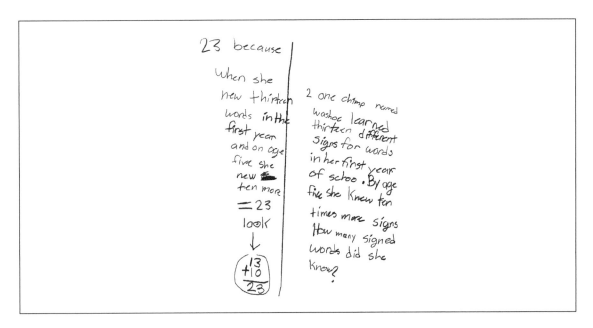

▲▲▲▲▲Figure 12–12   *Jade added rather than multiplied to find how many words one chimp learned in five years. She needed additional experience to understand the difference between additive and multiplicative situations.*

Questions and Discussion

▲▲

▲ *In addition to careful discussion, what are other ways I can support my students' understanding of the poetry, illustrations, and mathematics?*

Careful discussion and prior experience were enough to support the class in the vignette. However, this may not be the case for your class. One way to make the experience more concrete is to represent each situation with manipulative materials. For example, using the first two spreads, have students use one tile to represent the elephant's trunk, and then ask them to show you with tiles what would be ten times "better," or more. Help students connect the representation of the tiles to the one trunk and ten tentacles in the illustrations. Continue as appropriate for your students.

Another way to make the experience more concrete is to draw pictures on the board. For example, draw one elephant trunk and then ask a student to come to the board to draw ten times as many. Refocus the students' attention on the illustrations, helping them see that ten times better, or ten, is represented in the book by squid tentacles.

As students use concrete materials or draw pictures, it's important to help them make the connection to the numerical representation by using multiplication equations to show what they're doing. Also, recording as suggested in Steps 3 and 5 of the teaching directions helps students more easily see important patterns that emerge when multiplying by ten.

▲ *Why do you include students' names when you record their ideas on the board?*

I include students' names when recording on the board because it honors their thinking and contribution to the class discussion. Seeing their words recorded in writing with their names attached gives a sense of pride and accomplishment and encourages some children who might otherwise remain silent to participate.

Ten Times Better   **171**

CHAPTER THIRTEEN
MULTIPLICATION BY TEN AND ONE HUNDRED

Overview

In this lesson, students apply their knowledge of place value to multiplying whole numbers by ten and one hundred. To begin, children play a game called *Guess My Rule,* using a T-chart to keep track of pairs of numbers. The students study the pairs of numbers on the T-chart, searching for patterns to help them discover the rule used— multiplying the first number of the pair, recorded in the left column of the T-chart, by ten to get the number recorded in the right column. Later in the lesson, students work in pairs to investigate the following question: When multiplied by ten, will all whole numbers have a product with a zero in the ones place? Finally, students play *Guess My Rule* again to investigate the results of multiplying whole numbers by one hundred.

Materials

▲ calculators, 1 per pair of students

Time

▲ two class periods

Teaching Directions

1. On the board, draw the following:

#	?

172

Tell the students that they are going to play *Guess My Rule* and the T-chart will be used to keep track of information as they play the game. Explain the meaning of the symbol # at the top of the left column of the T-chart and why you used a question mark at the top of the right column of the T-chart.

2. Explain to the students that you'll write a number in the left-hand column of the T-chart and then use your rule to determine what number to write in the right-hand column. Tell the students their task is to use the pairs of numbers on the T-chart to figure out your rule.

3. To begin the game, call on a student to suggest a one-digit number. Write it in the left column of the T-chart. Without telling the students your rule, multiply the number in the left column by ten and record the product in the right column across from the suggested number.

4. Ask students to consider the pair of numbers to figure out what the rule could be. Remind them not to tell what they think the rule is. Tell students that they'll soon have the chance to predict what goes in the right-hand column.

5. Write another one-digit number in the left column. Ask for a volunteer to predict the number that should go in the right column. Remind students not to tell the rule. If the prediction is correct, record it in the right-hand column and draw a tally mark to indicate a correct prediction. If the prediction is incorrect, thank the student for the contribution and then write the correct number in the right-hand column. Explain that after students have made four correct predictions, someone will have the opportunity to guess the rule.

6. Repeat Step 5 for other numbers. If students are comfortable with single-digit numbers, consider using numbers such as eleven, twelve, and nineteen. Continue until there are four correct predictions.

7. Have students share with their partners their ideas about the rule you used. Then call on a volunteer to state the rule. When someone has correctly stated the rule, replace the question mark above the right-hand column with the rule.

8. Lead a discussion for the students to share patterns they notice in the numbers on the T-chart. Ask the students: "Do you think any whole number will have a zero in the ones place when multiplied by ten?"

Multiplication by Ten and One Hundred   173

9. Have students work in pairs to investigate the results of multiplying whole numbers by ten. Partners should each record on their own T-charts. Together they should select and record a number in the left column of the T-chart, predict the product when the selected number is multiplied by ten, record their prediction in the right column of the T-chart, and, finally, check their prediction using a calculator. Students should continue until they have at least five or six pairs of numbers on their T-charts. Also, write a question on the board for students to consider:

> *When multiplied by ten, will all whole numbers have a product with a zero in the ones place?*

10. Circulate through the class as students work, observing and noting the numbers students choose. When most students have at least five or six pairs of numbers on their T-charts, to help them to prepare for a class discussion, ask them to write one or two sentences about what they learned.

11. Lead a class discussion for students to share what they learned.

12. On another day, to reinforce multiplication by ten, play *Guess My Rule* again, using the same rule of multiplying by ten. After playing one or two games, change the rule to multiplying the number in the left column by one hundred to get the number in the right column. Discuss patterns the students notice.

13. Have students work in pairs or independently to investigate the results of multiplying whole numbers by one hundred as they did in the investigation described in Step 9.

14. Lead a class discussion for students to share what they discovered.

Teaching Notes

The game *Guess My Rule* provides a context for students to consider patterns that emerge when whole numbers are multiplied by ten and, later in the lesson, by one hundred. Using T-charts to keep track of pairs of numbers helps students more easily search for patterns that lead to discovering the rule. During the two investigations in this lesson, students cement their understanding about the results of multiplying whole numbers by ten and one hundred. They then draw on what they know about place value to describe what happens to numbers that are multiplied by ten and one hundred.

Understanding that multiplying a whole number by ten results in a zero in the ones place, and multiplying by one hundred results in zeros in the tens and ones places, provides an important foundation for multidigit multiplication. For example, to solve 12×23, a student might decompose 12 into $10 + 2$ and then multiply $10 \times 23 = 230$ and $2 \times 23 = 46$. Finally, the student would combine the two partial products, $230 + 46$, to get a final product of 276.

Prior to this lesson, the students in the following vignette had had a few experiences using T-charts and looking for patterns in the numbers on the charts. If your students have not had this experience, to familiarize them with T-charts, allow time to play a few extra games of *Guess My Rule* and to discuss how to find patterns in the numbers on the T-chart. Also, the students were familiar with beginning multiplication concepts; they understood that the times sign can mean groups of and that multiplication of whole numbers is about combining equal groups. The students were comfortable counting by tens and hundreds and had had many concrete experiences verifying the results of their counting using base ten blocks.

The Lesson

▲▲▲

DAY 1

To begin the lesson, I drew a T-chart on the board and labeled the columns.

I said to the students, "Today we are going to play *Guess My Rule*. We'll use a T-chart to help keep track of information as we play." I pointed to the label of the left column and continued, "I used this symbol because it means number. I'll write a number in the left column and then use my rule to find the number that belongs next to it in the right column. I used a question mark to label the right column because it will be your job to figure out the rule I'm using and then use the rule to figure out numbers for the right column. When you discover the rule, we'll replace the question mark with it." The students nodded, indicating their understanding.

I continued, "Jessie, please tell us a one-digit number." Other students who were eager to share waved their hands in the air as Jessie selected her number.

Jessie said, "I'll choose five."

I explained to the class, "I'll record Jessie's number in the left column on the T-chart. Then I'll use my rule and write the new number in the right column, under the question mark." I did so, writing *5* about halfway down the left column; then I used my rule of multiplying the number in the left column by ten and wrote *50* in the right column across from the 5. I wrote the pair of numbers about halfway down the chart to allow me to record information in numeric order. I did not tell the students my rule.

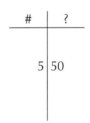

Then I said, "Your job is to think about the pair of numbers on the T-chart and how they are related. What rule did I use to change five to fifty? If you think you know my rule, keep it to yourself. This will give everyone a chance to think and discover the rule. In just a minute, you'll have the chance to test out your idea to see if it works."

I paused for a few moments to give the students time to think about the rule I used to change five to fifty. Hands started to go up. When about half the students had their hands up, I said, "Your raised hands tell me that you think you know my rule. Thank you

Multiplication by Ten and One Hundred   175

for not blurting out what you were thinking. Now you'll have the chance to see if your idea works. First, I'll choose a one-digit number for the left column. Then I'll ask someone who wants to test an idea about my rule to predict what the new number will be in the right column. Remember, don't tell what you think the rule is; tell only what you think the new number should be. After you make four correct guesses, we'll talk about what you think the rule is."

I recorded a *3* above the 5 on the left side of the T-chart and then called on Ana.

"Ten," Ana guessed. Several students put their thumbs down to show their disagreement. I said, "Thanks for your guess, Ana, but when I apply my rule to the number three, I get the number thirty. It's hard to guess a rule with hardly any information. See if this new information helps." I recorded *30* on the T-chart.

#	?
3	30
5	50

Next I wrote *7* in the left column and called on Tina. Tina said, "Seventy should go in the right column." I nodded my agreement, wrote *70* in the right column on the T-chart, and made a tally mark to show one correct guess.

Next I wrote *9* in the left column. Most students raised their hands. Christopher correctly guessed ninety. The others cheered. I recorded *90* on the chart and made the second tally mark.

Judging by the eagerness of the students, I was confident they had figured out my rule. To add a bit more challenge, I wrote *11* in the left column. Again, hands leaped into the air. Reggie guessed 101, a mistake that's common when children multiply numbers larger than ten by ten. I gently shook my head "no" and wrote *110* on the T-chart.

#	?	
3	30	ll
5	50	
7	70	
9	90	
11	110	

Reggie and a couple of others looked mildly confused. I said, "Look carefully at the numbers in the right column of the T-chart. What do you notice about the ones place? What do you notice about the rest of each number?" I paused to give students time to search the numbers for patterns. After a few moments, I added, "Finding patterns is a way for you to discover my rule."

I chose not to have a discussion about the patterns the students saw at this time, knowing that a discussion would follow at the end of the game. I next wrote *12* under the 11 in the left column and called on Ben, who correctly guessed 120. I drew a third tally mark for this correct guess and then wrote *120* in the right column.

Next I wrote *19* in the left column. All hands were up. I called on Keara, who correctly guessed 190. This was the fourth correct guess, and the students were eager to share their ideas about my rule. To allow more children the opportunity to be heard, I asked the students to turn to their partners and explain their ideas about my rule. The room erupted in excited conversations. I observed and listened as the children shared with each other. After a few minutes I asked the children to finish their conversations and be ready to share with the class.

A Class Discussion

I asked for the students' attention. When they were once again quiet, I asked, "Who would like to guess my rule?" I called on Kassidee.

Kassidee said, "I think you multiplied the number in the left column times ten to get the new number in the right column."

I recorded Kassidee's thinking on the board:

Kassidee   Multiply the number in the left column by 10 to get the number in the right column.

The others nodded their agreement. I asked, "Does someone have another way of saying Kassidee's idea?"

Sam volunteered, "Left number times ten equals right number." I recorded Sam's sentence on the board beneath Kassidee's.

Kassidee   Multiply the number in the left column by 10 to get the number in the right column.

Sam   Left number times 10 equals right number.

The students were quiet. I asked, "Does someone have a different idea?" No one did. I erased the question mark at the top of the right column and replaced it with my rule:

#	# × 10	
3	30	IIII
5	50	
7	70	
9	90	
11	110	
12	120	
19	190	

I asked, "What can you say about the ones place of all the numbers in the right column?"

Rachel said, "I see a pattern. The ones places always is zero when you times by ten."

I asked the class, "Do you think any whole number when multiplied by ten will have a zero in the ones place?"

Kito said, "I'm not sure about fractions and decimals."

I replied, "For now, let's think only about whole numbers. Do you think that any whole number multiplied by ten will have a zero in the ones place?" I gave the students a moment of think time and then asked them to show their agreement with

my question with a thumb up, disagreement with a thumb down, or uncertainty with a thumb sideways. Some students showed thumbs up, others showed thumbs down, and others showed thumbs sideways, indicating the class needed more experience with multiplying by ten. This didn't surprise me.

An Investigation

To strengthen the fragile understanding of some and give access to others, I wanted to provide an opportunity for students to further explore multiplication by ten. I said to the class, "Now I'd like you to work with a partner to investigate further whether any whole number when multiplied by ten results in a product with zero in the ones place. You'll need a sheet of paper for each person and one calculator to share. Draw a T-chart on your paper." I drew a T-chart on the board as I explained, "I'm labeling the left column with the number symbol and the right column with the number symbol times ten because we want to find out more about what happens when whole numbers are multiplied by ten."

"Together, pick a whole number and each of you record it on your T-chart. Then talk together and predict what you think the product will be when the number is multiplied by ten. Record your prediction in the right column. Finally, use the calculator to check your prediction. Then choose another number and multiply it by ten. Do this for at least five or six numbers to help you discover what happens when whole numbers are multiplied by ten."

Multiplication by Ten and One Hundred   177

"What if we predict wrong?" Halley asked.

"Correct your prediction and then use the correct answer, or product, to help you make a better prediction next time," I answered. Halley nodded.

To help the students stay focused on the purpose of the investigation, I wrote the following on the board:

When multiplied by ten, will all whole numbers have a product with a zero in the ones place?

I quickly assigned partners by asking each student to work with the person sitting beside him or her. Then I instructed the pairs to get their paper and a calculator. In just a few moments, the room buzzed with activity and conversation as the students settled around the room and began their investigations.

I circulated through the room, watching as the students worked and making mental notes about the types of numbers they were choosing to use. For example, Vinay and Christopher used larger numbers. Vinay was able to make quick, accurate predictions about the resulting products when the selected numbers were multiplied by ten. Initially Christopher wasn't as sure, but as they continued to check with the calculator, Christopher became more convinced and confident with his predictions. Vinay was pleased to share what he'd learned. I asked him to write about it. His writing was typical of many of the students. (See Figure 13–1.)

Besides noticing that a whole number multiplied by ten has a product with a zero in the ones place, Paul also noticed that the original number remained in the product. (See Figure 13–2.)

Sometimes when students multiply a number ending with zero by ten, for example $20 \times 10 = 200$, they become confused when the resulting product ends with two zeros rather than one. This was not an issue for this class. I was both

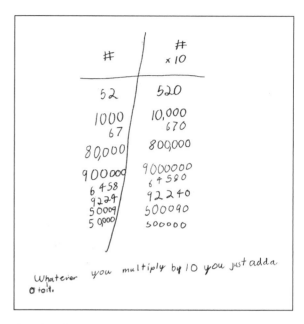

▲▲▲▲▲▲**Figure 13–1** *Vinay made the same observation as some of the other students.*

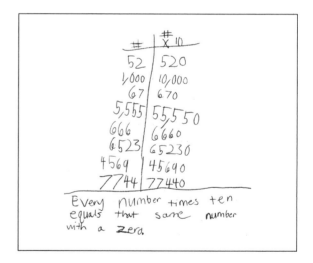

▲▲▲▲▲▲**Figure 13–2** *Paul's work.*

surprised and pleased about this. (See Figure 13–3.)

When most students had a list of five or six pairs of numbers, I gave a two-minute warning. At the end of two minutes, I called the class to attention. To help students focus their thoughts in preparation for a class discussion, I asked the students to write one or two sentences about what they had learned.

178   Lessons for Extending Place Value

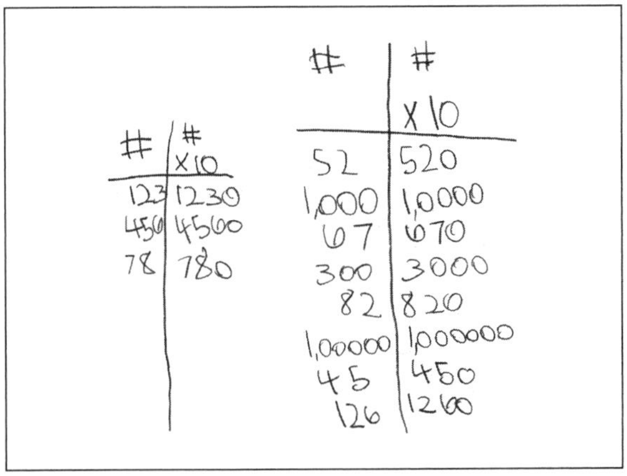

▲▲▲▲▲Figure 13–3 *Arin had no trouble multiplying numbers ending with zero by ten.*

A Discussion

"What did you find out?" I asked the students. Hands waved in the air. I called on Olina.

Olina said, "My partner and I did some smaller numbers and some bigger ones, too, but they always ended in zero when we multiplied them by ten. We think that no matter what, if you multiply a number by ten, it will have a zero at the end."

To push Olina to be more specific and use correct mathematical language, I said, "Which end do you mean?"

Olina responded, "The back end, the last number in the number."

I asked, "What place do you mean, the tens, the ones, the hundreds?"

Olina grinned and said, "Ohh! The ones place has a zero!" I nodded.

Tanya said, "Roberto and I think the same thing. The ones place turns to zero."

Connor added, "I think that's because when you count by tens, the numbers always end in zero."

James challenged Connor. "I agree if you count by tens beginning with ten or zero or any number that ends with zero . . . I mean has a zero in the ones place. But if you count by tens and start with a number like three, then your idea doesn't work."

Connor tested James's idea by quietly counting by tens starting with three. "Oh yeah!" he replied after thinking for a few moments.

Paul shared what he'd explained on his paper. He said, "The number you start out with is in the product. The number looks almost exactly the same, except there's a zero in the ones place and all the other numbers got bumped over one place. Like fifteen times ten equals one hundred fifty. The one and five in fifteen got bumped over a place and the ones place became a zero."

To push the students' thinking, I wrote *20* on the board and said, "Twenty already has a zero in the ones place. What happens when I multiply twenty times ten?" Hands went up quickly. I paused a moment to give those who hadn't raised their hands a bit more time to think. When most hands were up, I called on Adama.

Adama said, "Twenty times ten still ends with a zero in the ones place. The answer is two hundred. Like Paul said, the two and the original zero got moved over one place so there would be room for the new zero in the ones place. And you can check to make sure that twenty times ten is two hundred by counting by tens twenty times or counting by twenty ten times." Adama proved her point by quickly skip-counting by twenty ten times, using her fingers to help her keep track of how many twenties she'd counted.

The students were quiet. I asked for a volunteer to summarize what we had found out. Jillian volunteered.

Jillian said, "When you multiply any whole number by ten, the product has a zero at the end and the original number is still a part of the answer, just moved over." The students nodded their agreement. With Jillian's comment, I ended the lesson.

DAY 2

A few days later, I returned to our investigation. Once again I drew a T-chart on the board and explained to the students that

Multiplication by Ten and One Hundred   179

we were going to play *Guess My Rule.*

To reinforce what we'd discovered a few days earlier, I used the same rule: I multiplied the number in the left column by ten to produce the number in the right column. As I'd done before, I asked the students to make four correct guesses before giving someone a chance to state my rule.

When the first game was completed and the students had correctly guessed my rule, I said to the class as I drew a new T-chart beside the first, "I have a new rule. See if you can guess it. But remember, no one can state my rule until there have been four correct guesses. I'll give you a pair of numbers as a hint." I wrote *4* and *400* on the T-chart.

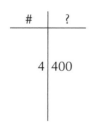

I paused to give students time to consider the pair of numbers; then I wrote *5* in the left column just below the *4*. I said, "Who would like to guess what goes in the right column?" I called on Jael.

Jael guessed, "Fifty."

I said, "Fifty is the answer I would have gotten with my old rule. I have a new rule and this is the answer I get when I use my new rule." I wrote *500* in the right column. Initially Jael looked confused, but she brightened up quickly as she seemed to get another idea.

Next I wrote a *7* in the left column. I called on Jessie to guess the new number. She correctly guessed seven hundred. I recorded *700* in the right column and made a tally mark to indicate one correct guess. I repeated this process a few more times—listing a number in the left column, calling on a student to guess the number, then recording the correct number in the right column, and finally making a tally mark for each correct guess. After the fourth correct guess, I called on Karlee to guess my rule.

Karlee said, "I think you take the first number and multiply it by one hundred. And that's how you get the second number." The other students indicated their agreement with thumbs up.

I said, "You have guessed my rule. Is there anything else you notice or would like to share about what happens when a whole number is multiplied by one hundred?"

Several students raised their hands. I called on Halley.

Halley shared, "When you multiplied by ten, the ones place was always a zero. When you multiplied by one hundred, the ones place and the tens place both turned to zero."

After allowing a moment of think time for the students to consider Halley's statement, I said, "Why do you think that happens?" Halley shrugged, but a few others had ideas.

Sam had an intense look on his face and was eager to share with the rest of the class. Sam explained, "Ten times ten is one hundred. So I think that multiplying a number by one hundred is like multiplying the number by ten and then by ten again." Sam paused and appeared to be thinking about his explanation. Then he continued, "If you wanted to multiply five times one hundred, you could first multiply five times ten. That's fifty. Then multiply fifty times ten, and that's five hundred, which is the answer to five times one hundred."

I recorded on the board:

Sam $100 = 10 \times 10$
$5 \times 100 = 5 \times 10 \times 10$
$5 \times 10 = 50$
$50 \times 10 = 500$
$5 \times 100 = 500$

Connor said, "I agree with Sam, but I think an easier way is to just think of five groups of one hundred, and that's five hundred."

Tina observed, "Multiplying by ten and by one hundred reminds me of multiplying by one. You multiply whatever number you have by one and then put one zero in the ones place if you're multiplying by ten or a zero in the ones place and a zero in the tens place if you're multiplying by one hundred."

I asked the class, "Do you think all whole numbers multiplied by one hundred will have a zero in both the ones place and the tens place?" Most students nodded.

The students had enjoyed using calculators to explore multiplying whole numbers by ten. The calculator provided a quick way for them to check predictions. I decided to have students again investigate

as they had before so they could verify for themselves the results of multiplying whole numbers by one hundred. This time, I gave the students the choice of working in pairs or independently. Most chose to work alone, although there was some discussion among table group members.

As the students worked, I answered questions for some students and posed questions to others. The students were quick to verify that multiplying by one hundred results in a product with zeros in the ones and tens places. Kassidee's and Paul's work was typical of the class. (See Figure 13–4 and 13–5.)

I led a short class discussion for the students to summarize what they'd discovered and then ended class for the day.

EXTENSIONS

As your students gain confidence, repeat *Guess My Rule* and the investigation to explore multiplying whole numbers by multiples of ten and one hundred—twenty, two hundred, and so on. (See Figures 13–6 through 13–10 on the following pages.)

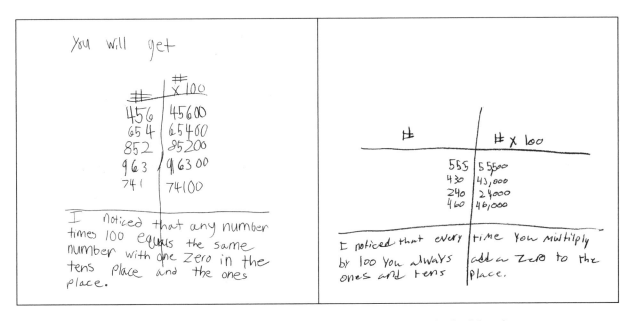

▲▲▲▲▲▲Figures 13–4 and 13–5   *Kassidee's and Paul's work was typical of the class.*

Multiplication by Ten and One Hundred   181

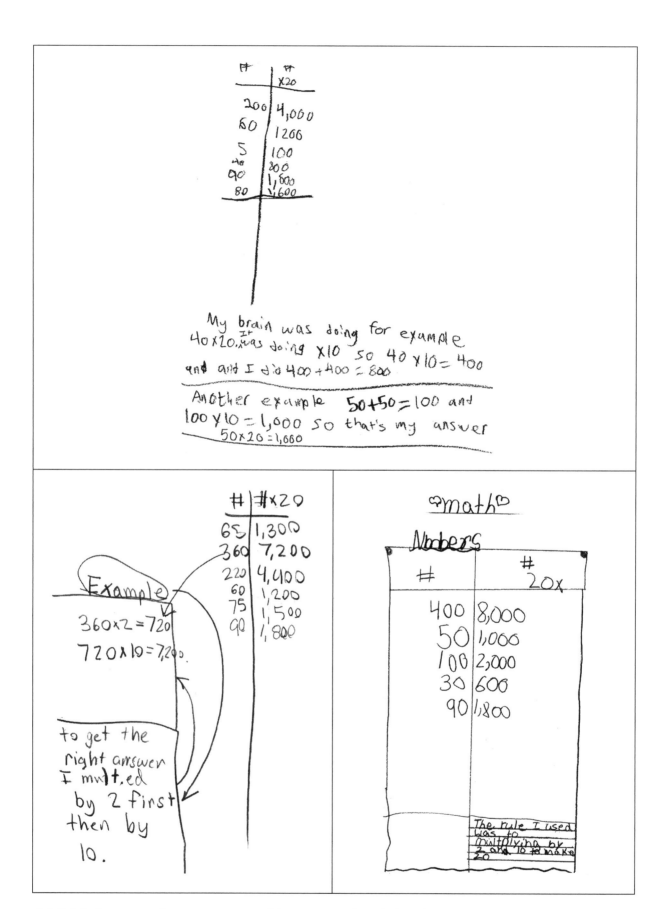

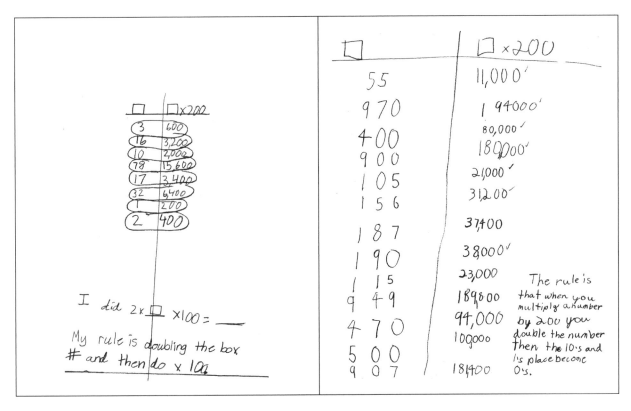

▲▲▲▲▲▲Figures 13–9 and 13–10 *Jessie and Vinay investigated multiplying numbers by two hundred.*

Questions and Discussion

▲▲

▲ *I have special-needs students. What can I do to make this lesson more accessible to them?*

Base ten blocks can be a useful tool for giving students greater access. One way to use base ten blocks is to bring them out after the class has finished playing *Guess My Rule*. Use base ten longs to verify that the numbers in the left column were multiplied by ten to get the numbers in the right-hand column. Take a pair of numbers from the T-chart, for example 5 and 50. Remind the students that another way to think of $5 \times 10 = 50$ is five groups of ten equal fifty. Five groups of ten can be shown using five base ten longs. Students can count the longs by ten to verify that fifty is the correct answer.

During the investigation, limit the size of numbers students use. Keep them small enough so that students can use base ten longs in addition to a calculator to verify what number goes in the right-hand column.

Later in the lesson, when students multiply the number in the left column by one hundred to get the number in the right column, use base ten flats to support their thinking and understanding.

Multiplication by Ten and One Hundred   183

CHAPTER FOURTEEN
LINKING PLACE VALUE TO MULTIPLICATION AND DIVISION

Overview

This lesson builds on an idea found in the book *Good Questions for Math Teaching: Why Ask Them and What to Ask, K–6,* by Peter Sullivan and Pat Lilburn (Sausalito, CA: Math Solutions Publications, 2002). The lesson begins by asking the students: How many numbers can you write with an eight in the hundreds place? In a class discussion, students realize that there are an infinite number of numbers with an eight in the hundreds place. Then students figure the number of tens in 800, representing their thinking with multiplication and division. After investigating the number of tens in several other numbers—70, 810, and 841—students choose their own numbers and use multiplication or division to determine how many tens are in them.

Materials

▲ base ten blocks, at least 8 flats, 90 longs, and 15 units

Time

▲ two class periods

Teaching Directions

1. Write on the board:

How many numbers can you write with an 8 in the hundreds place? Show your thinking.

2. Discuss and then have students work independently on the task.

3. As students work, circulate and observe. Notice who is unable to write a number with an eight in the hundreds place, who writes only three-digit numbers with an eight in the hundreds place, and who also writes numbers larger than three-digit numbers. Occasionally ask a student to read his or her list of numbers aloud to you.

4. Lead a class discussion and ask students to report numbers from their lists. As each student shares a number, record it on the board.

5. After listing at least eight numbers, ask students: "Do we have all the numbers with an eight in the hundreds place?" Through discussion, students should come to the understanding that the list is infinite.

6. On Day 2, write *800* on the board and use base ten flats to verify for students that there are eight hundreds in eight hundred. Ask students how to show this using a multiplication sentence. ($8 \times 100 = 800$)

7. Ask students: "How many tens are in eight hundred?" Lead a discussion about their ideas. Guide students to understand that the number of tens in eight hundred can be figured with either multiplication ($\square \times 10 = 800$) or division ($800 \div 10 = \square$).

8. Repeat Step 7 for the number 70 and then for 810 and 841. For example, use base ten longs to verify that 841 has 84 tens and a remainder of 1. Then guide the students to understand that 841 can be shown as $841 = 84 \times 10 + 1$ or $841 \div 10 = 84$ R1.

9. Ask students to each choose a number and record it on their paper. Then ask them to show how many tens are in their number by writing a multiplication or division sentence. Circulate and observe as the children work, helping when appropriate.

Teaching Notes

This lesson provides students with a numerical context to consider hundreds and tens. Because of the abstract nature of this numerical context, base ten blocks are useful to help individual students gain understanding and to verify ideas raised in class discussions. For this reason, we recommend that you have base ten blocks accessible for use as needed.

Students connect several important ideas in this lesson: place value, multiplication, and division. During the lesson, children demonstrate their knowledge of where the hundreds place is by generating only numbers with an eight in the hundreds place when asked, "How many numbers can you write with an eight in the hundreds place?" Some children will think only of three-digit numbers beginning with eight while others will go beyond and include larger numbers with an eight in the hundreds place. In the following vignette, the students discovered that there are infinite number of numbers with an eight in the hundreds place.

Linking Place Value to Multiplication and Division **185**

Children are also asked in the lesson to figure out both the number of hundreds and the number of tens in a given number. When the students are asked to figure the number of tens, some solve the problem with multiplication, for example, $\square \times 10 = 450$ while others may find the number of tens using division ($450 \div 10 = \square$).

Prior to this lesson, the students in the following vignette had had experience with base ten blocks, beginning multiplication and division concepts, and thinking about how multiplication and division relate to each other.

The Lesson

▲▲▲

DAY 1

Before the students arrived, I put a sheet of paper on each desk and wrote on the board:

How many numbers can you write with an 8 in the hundreds place? Show your thinking.

As the students settled, many read and began to discuss among themselves what I'd written on the board. I called them to attention and asked for a volunteer to read aloud. I called on Keara.

After Keara read, I asked the students, "What strategy could you use to find out how many numbers have an eight in the hundreds place?" Hands shot up quickly. I called on Kassidee.

Kassidee suggested, "List all the numbers you can think of that have eight in the hundreds place."

Jessie added, "I think it would help if you listed the numbers in order, like the smallest number to the largest number. That way you won't skip any."

"This is going to be easy!" Vinay said, eager to get started.

Olina asked, "Is it OK to use numbers bigger than eight hundred?"

I replied, "Give me an example."

"Like eight hundred eight," Olina said.

I wrote on the board *808* and then asked, "In eight hundred eight, is there an eight in the hundreds place?" Olina nodded and I continued, "I agree that there is an eight in the hundreds place. You may use any number you like as long as there is an eight in the hundreds place." There were no other questions or comments, so I said, "Show your thinking on the paper on your desk."

Students chatted quietly as they began their work. I circulated through the class, looking over the students' shoulders at their papers. I stopped occasionally to ask students to read aloud numbers they'd written as a way for me to check that they could accurately read larger numbers. I noted to myself when a student showed understanding of where the hundreds place was, based on the location of the eight in the numbers he or she had written, and when a student used numbers larger than the eight hundreds, for example, eighteen hundred. Most students were able to accurately write and read numbers in the eight hundreds.

A few students showed on their written work little understanding of where the eight should go. One such student, Arin, had written nine numbers, all with an eight in the ones place. Only the last number also had an eight in the hundreds place. (See Figure 14–1.) I wasn't sure if Arin lacked understanding of the task or of place value. To help me gain insight about Arin's understanding, I asked her to read her numbers aloud. When she finished I said, "All of your numbers have at least one eight in them. What does the eight mean in three hundred eight?"

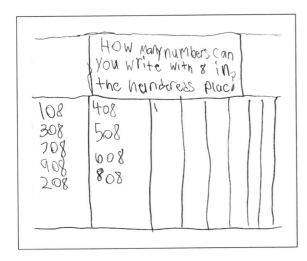

▲▲▲▲▲▲Figure 14–1 *Arin wrote numbers with an eight in the ones place instead of the hundreds place.*

Arin explained, "The eight stands for eight ones."

I nodded my agreement and asked Arin to read the instructions aloud. She did so. Pointing to the 308 on her paper, I asked, "In this number, which digit is in the hundreds place?" Arin looked uncertain and then shrugged. I asked her to go get from the shelf a basket of base ten blocks containing ones cubes, longs, and flats. I said, "Please use the fewest blocks possible to build three hundred eight."

Arin quickly built 308 using three flats and eight ones cubes. "Oh! I see now. I should have eight flats to have eight in the hundreds place. Oops!" She reached for another sheet of paper and started again, this time writing numbers with an eight in the hundreds place.

A few tables away, I noticed Karena had made similar errors. Confident that Arin understood, I asked her to share with Karena what she had learned. Arin grabbed her paper and the basket of base ten blocks and sat down beside Karena. I listened for a few moments to be sure Arin was on the right track and then moved on to check on other students.

At just about that time, Paul and Halley announced that they were finished. I checked their work and found that both had written only the number *800* on their papers, but their explanations differed. Halley wrote: *The 8 in the hundred's place keep's going so my best guess is probably 800 numbers!* She explained verbally, "There are too many numbers to write down. I think eight hundred is probably the smallest number, but all the eight hundreds have an eight in the hundreds place and then bigger numbers can, too, like one thousand eight hundred eighty-eight!" I suggested that Halley add her verbal explanation to what she'd already written.

Paul wrote, *I think there is just 800. That's one number.* I gave Paul a counterexample. I wrote *825* on a sheet of scratch paper and asked what number was in the hundreds place. Paul smiled and said, "The eight. I didn't think about the other places. I just thought they'd have zero." He began writing more numbers on his list as I moved on to observe others.

Many students created an organized list of numbers beginning with eight hundred. (See Figure 14–2.) Others wrote numbers in the eight hundreds but did not organize them in any particular fashion. (See Figure 14–3.) Rachel used an organized list and made the observation that the numbers with an eight in the hundreds place would go on and on. (See Figure 14–4.)

Several students included numbers beyond the 800s. Initially, Kassidee indicated that only three possible numbers could be written. But as she continued to consider the task, she discovered other three-digit numbers and then moved on to numbers larger than 899 but still with an eight in the hundreds place. (See Figure 14–5.)

Vinay organized his thinking in a unique manner. He recorded spans of one hundred numbers with eight in the hundreds place. (See Figure 14–6.)

Linking Place Value to Multiplication and Division   187

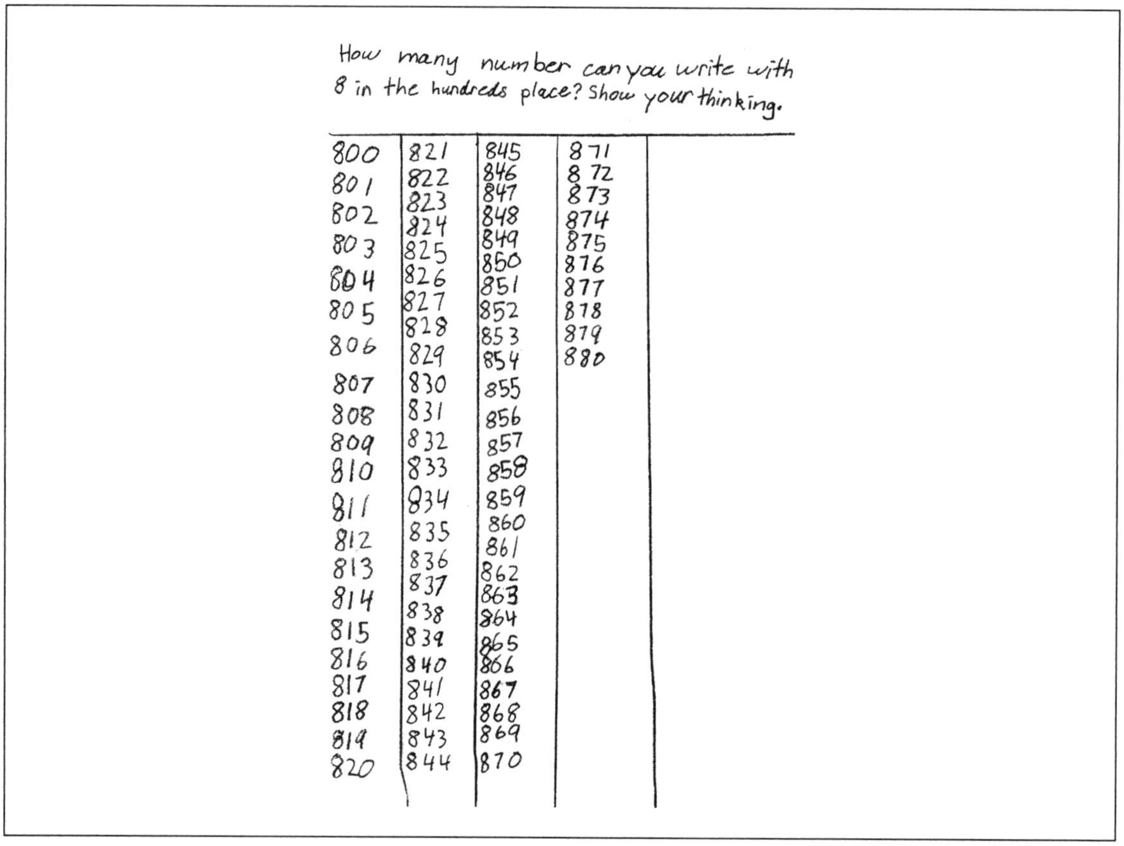

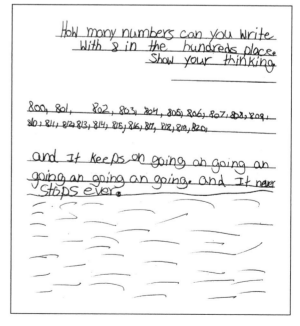

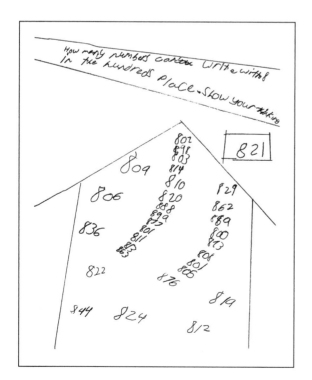

▲▲▲▲▲▲Figure 14–2   *Jessie organized her list in numerical order. Her list included only numbers in the eight hundreds.*

▲▲▲▲▲▲Figure 14–3   *Karlee listed numbers in the eight hundreds in no particular order.*

▲▲▲▲▲▲Figure 14–4   *Rachel stated that numbers with an eight in the hundreds place go on forever.*

188   Lessons for Extending Place Value

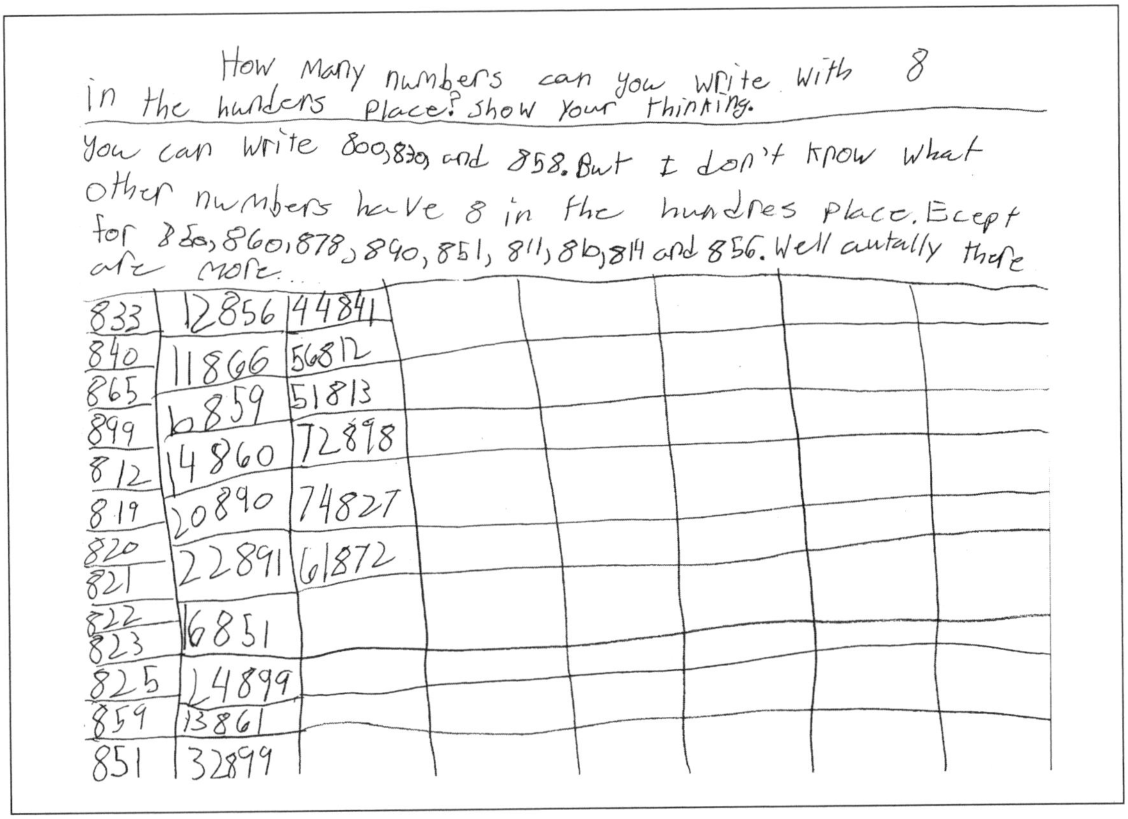

▲▲▲▲▲▲Figure 14–5   *Kassidee's completed list.*

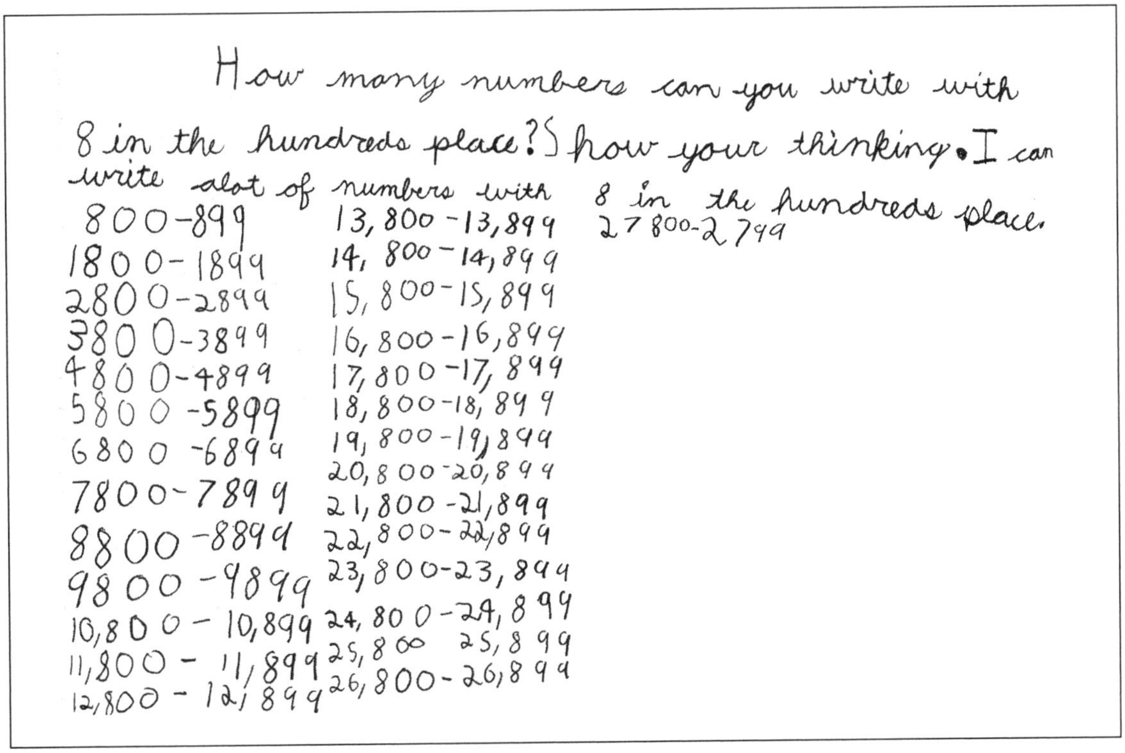

▲▲▲▲▲▲Figure 14–6   *Vinay used spans of numbers to list numbers with an eight in the hundreds place.*

Linking Place Value to Multiplication and Division   **189**

A Class Discussion

After ten minutes, I called the class to attention. I said, "Raise your hand if you'd like to report one number that has an eight in the hundreds place." As each student made a suggestion, I wrote the number on the board and asked the others to indicate their agreement with thumbs up, down, or sideways. When we verified that a number had an eight in the hundreds place, I added it to our list on the board.

Vinay shared first. With a twinkle in his eye, he said, "Two hundred thousand eight hundred."

I asked Vinay, "How should I write your number on the board?"

Vinay replied, "First write a two, then two zeros, a comma, and then an eight and two more zeros."

Following Vinay's instructions, I wrote on the board *200,800*. I said to the class, "If you agree that Vinay's number has an eight in the hundreds place, put your thumb up; if you disagree, put your thumb down; and if you're not sure, put your thumb sideways." Most students put their thumbs up to show their agreement.

Pointing to the 8 in Vinay's number, I said, "Vinay's number has an eight in the hundreds place. Who would like to suggest another number?"

Olina suggested the number eight hundred. The others showed their approval with thumbs up. I wrote Olina's number on the board below Vinay's number.

Jenae raised her hand and suggested that 108 be added to the list. I wrote *108* on the board and the other students put their thumbs down, indicating they disagreed with Jenae's idea.

I asked the students, "Since many of you disagree that one hundred eight has an eight in the hundreds place, how can it be changed so that the eight is in the hundreds place?"

Adama explained, "One hundred eight has an eight. It's just in the wrong place.

You have to switch it with the one. Then the eight would be in the hundreds place and the one in the ones place. The new number would be eight hundred one." The students gave Adama's suggestion thumbs up.

Jenae raised her hand. She said, "Or you could make one hundred eight into eight hundred ten. Put an eight, then a one, then the zero." I recorded this number on the board and the others indicated their agreement.

After eight students had shared, the list on the board looked as follows:

Vinay:	*200,800*
Olina:	*800*
Adama:	*801*
Jenae:	*810*
James:	*5,800*
Esperanza:	*802*
Abel:	*1,829*
Tanya:	*32,819*

I gave the students a moment to study the list. Then I asked, "Do we have all the numbers with an eight in the hundreds place?"

Sam said, "I don't think there is an actual amount of numbers with an eight in the hundreds place."

I said to the rest of the class, "Who can state Sam's idea in another way?"

Tina said, "I agree with what Sam said because I think he means that the number of numbers with eight in the hundreds place can go on and on because numbers go on and on." Several students nodded their agreement.

I said, "Mathematicians would say there are an infinite number of numbers with an eight in the hundreds place. How many of you had this same idea about the numbers going on and on, as Sam and Tina had?" Several raised their hands. Then Kito raised his hand. He shared, "I really thought before our discussion that there were one hundred numbers with eight in the hundreds place, the eight hundreds. I never thought about bigger numbers, like Vinay,

Tanya, Abel, and James. I have to remember to think bigger!"

Jillian shared, "I've been thinking about the idea of infinity. When I think about it really hard, I feel small because it goes on and on to places my brain can't go. It's amazing!"

DAY 2

Figuring How Many Tens

I waited for the students to settle. When they were quiet, I said to the class, "Yesterday, we thought about numbers with an eight in the hundreds place. One of the numbers you shared was eight hundred. We know there are eight hundreds in eight hundred. We can show this with eight flats." I laid out eight base ten flats to make my point and then continued. "How could we show there are eight hundreds using a multiplication sentence?" Everyone raised a hand immediately.

I called on Esperanza. She said, "You write an eight, then the times sign, then one hundred, then equals, and then eight hundred." I followed Esperanza's instructions and wrote on the board $8 \times 100 = 800$.

I then asked, "How many tens are there in eight hundred?"

The students began talking among themselves. I paused for a few moments to give them time to think and share their ideas. As the students talked, I listened. Most thought there were eighty tens in eight hundred. As the students began to quiet, I asked for their attention. More than half the students had their hands in the air. I called on Tanya.

Tanya said, "There are eighty tens in eight hundred."

I said to the other students, "Show me if you agree with Tanya's idea by putting a thumb up. If you disagree, put a thumb down, and if you're not sure, put a thumb sideways." Most students held their thumbs up. I asked Tanya, "How did you figure there are eighty tens in eight hundred?"

Tanya responded confidently, "Eighty times ten is eight hundred."

Connor said, "I thought this was a division question. But Tanya's right . . . maybe. I think I'm confused." Several others looked confused along with Connor. The students were just forming their understanding about the relationship between multiplication and division.

I said to Connor and the others, "You can figure out how many tens are in eight hundred by thinking about either multiplication or division. Tanya's idea could be shown like this." I wrote on the board:

$$\square \times 10 = 800$$

I continued while I pointed to what I'd written, "The box means we have to figure out what number to put in it to make the sentence true. What number times ten equals eight hundred, or how many groups of ten equal eight hundred? Tanya said she thought it would take eighty groups of ten to equal eight hundred. We can replace the box with eighty to make the number sentence true." I wrote 80 in the box.

I continued, "Connor thought it was a division problem. His idea can be written as a number sentence like this." I wrote the following on the board under the multiplication sentence:

$$800 \div 10 = \square$$

"In this case, the question is How many groups of ten are in eight hundred? There are eighty." I filled in the box with 80. "Both multiplication and division can help us figure the number of tens in eight hundred. Let's try another, smaller problem to verify this works. How many tens are in seventy?"

"That's easy!" chorused many of the students.

I said, "Tell me in a whisper voice."

"Seven," the students replied.

"Who would like to tell me how to find the number of tens in seventy using multiplication?" Most students waved their hands eagerly.

Linking Place Value to Multiplication and Division   **191**

James said, "Seven times ten equals seventy. I can prove it with the base ten blocks, too. Just take seven longs and it's seventy, and the longs are tens and you need seven, so it's seven tens make seventy."

I wrote on the board $7 \times 10 = 70$. I said to the class, "Who would like to tell a division sentence that could be used to find the number of tens in seventy?"

Tina said, "Seventy divided by ten equals box. You can write a seven in the box. There are seven tens in seventy."

I recorded on the board:

$70 \div 10 = \square$
$70 \div 10 = 7$

To push the students' thinking a little more, I posed another question. I said, "Eight hundred ten is another number from the list we made yesterday." I wrote 810 on the board and continued, "There are eight hundreds in eight hundred ten, but how many tens are there altogether in eight hundred ten?" After a moment I said, "Talk with your neighbor about how many tens you think are in eight hundred ten." The room came alive with animated conversations. After a few moments I asked for the students' attention. The students were eager to share their ideas. I called on Roberto.

Roberto said, "There are eighty-one tens."

The students indicated their agreement with Roberto with thumbs up.

"Why do you think there are eighty-one tens?" I asked.

Halley explained, "I know that any number times ten is the same number only with a zero in the ones place. Eighty-one times ten is eight hundred ten."

Adama shared, "I just used my brain. Eight hundred ten is one ten more than eight hundred. We already figured out there were eighty tens in eight hundred, so that means there are eighty-one tens in eight hundred ten. It's easy."

Sam said, "When you divide by ten, if the ones place is zero, you can just cover

up the zero and that will tell you how many tens. With eight hundred ten, just cover up the zero in the ones place, and that leaves eighty-one, which is how many tens are in eight hundred ten. A division sentence would be eight hundred ten divided by ten equals eighty-one." The students sat quietly.

I then said, "What about eight hundred forty-one? How many tens are in eight hundred forty-one?" I wrote 841 on the board. Hands shot into the air.

"Use your whisper voice to tell me," I said.

"Eighty-four!" the class whispered.

Vinay waved his hand to get my attention. He said, "There's a leftover. It's really eighty-four tens and one leftover." I nodded my agreement with Vinay.

I asked the students, "What is a division sentence that could represent Vinay's idea?"

Ben volunteered, "Eight hundred forty-one divided by ten equals eighty-four with a remainder of one."

I wrote on the board:

$841 \div 10 = 84 \ R1$

I asked the class, "Can we show how many tens in eight hundred forty-one using multiplication?"

Jillian said, "I'm not really sure, but I think it's box times ten equals eight hundred forty-one. But that's where I get confused because eighty-four times ten is only eight hundred forty and it's supposed to be eight hundred forty-one."

I wrote on the board:

$\square \times 10 = 841$

I said to the students, "What do you think about Jillian's dilemma? Talk with your partner. First one of you talks for thirty seconds while the other listens. At the end of thirty seconds, I'll give a signal and you'll switch roles so that the first talker listens and the first listener talks." I told the students to begin. At the end of thirty seconds I gave a signal to switch roles, and at the end of the second thirty seconds I asked for the students' attention.

James shared, "I think Jillian's idea works, except that you have to add one to the multiplication part because that is the leftover. You'd write box times ten plus one equals eight hundred forty-one. The box is eighty-four."

I wrote on the board:

$$\square \times 10 + 1 = 841$$

Jessie stated James's idea slightly differently. "You just add the leftovers to what you multiply."

I said to Jillian, "What do you think about James's and Jessie's ideas?"

Jillian replied, "I think their ideas would work."

To verify for Jillian and the others that Jessie and James were correct, I asked Jillian, James, Jessie, Jenae, Abel, Esperanza, Karlee, and Ana to each count out ten longs and place them in piles of ten on the chalkboard tray so everyone could see them. This took a couple of minutes. While the students were getting the longs, I said to the rest of the class, "There are eight students each getting ten longs. When they put their piles of ten longs on the board, how many longs will there be?"

"Eighty," chorused the students.

I asked, "If there are eighty longs, how many tens is that?"

"Eighty," they immediately responded together.

"How many hundreds in eighty tens?" I asked.

"Eight," they quickly replied. By this time the eight students had each gathered ten longs and placed them in piles of ten on the chalkboard tray.

Connor had his hand up. "That's only eight hundred. We were talking about eight hundred forty-one. You need four more tens and one ones cube." The others indicated their agreement with Connor. I sent

Connor to get the remaining blocks. He placed them on the chalkboard tray beside the other piles.

Pointing to the piles of tens, I said, "We can verify Jessie's and James's ideas by figuring out the value of the base ten blocks. The longs, or tens, are in piles of ten. Let's count together." We counted together the piles of ten for a total of eighty tens. I said, "Then there are the four tens that Connor added. That's eighty-four tens. If we add one to the eighty-four groups of ten, then we have a total of eight hundred forty-one. We can write both a multiplication and a division sentence to show this." I wrote on the board:

$$841 = 84 \times 10 + 1$$
$$841 \div 10 = 84 \, R1$$

"Just like Jessie and James said," Jillian commented.

Checking for Understanding

To check for understanding, I said to the students, "In a moment, I'll give you a sheet of paper. I'd like you to work by yourself so I can get an idea of what each of you knows. First, choose a number and write it on your paper. Your task is to tell how many tens are in your number. Write a multiplication or division sentence that tells the number of tens in the number you chose."

Abel had his hand up. "Can I choose a really easy number?"

I replied, "Choose a number that's not too easy or too hard. The number you choose can tell me about your number sense. If you choose a number that's easy for you, and I don't know it's easy for you, then I might think you don't know as much as you actually do."

Adama asked, "Can we do an easy number, a medium number, and a hard number?"

"If you wish," I replied. There were no more questions, so I handed each child a sheet of paper and the students got to work.

I observed the children as they worked. Most chose three-digit numbers although Arin choose thirty. (See Figure 14–7.) At the

Linking Place Value to Multiplication and Division 193

other extreme was Vinay. When I looked at his paper, I noticed that he had made an error in division. He'd left out a section of his large number. I asked him to explain his strategy to me and as he did so, he caught his error. When I checked back with him a little later, I noticed that he had made an error in his multiplication sentence. I knew Vinay knew that numbers multiplied by ten end with a zero. I said to him as I pointed to his paper, "I notice that

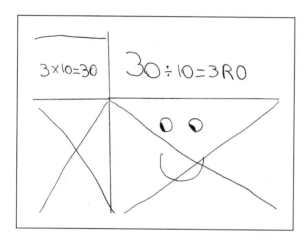

▲▲▲▲▲▲Figure 14–7 *Arin chose a smaller number than most.*

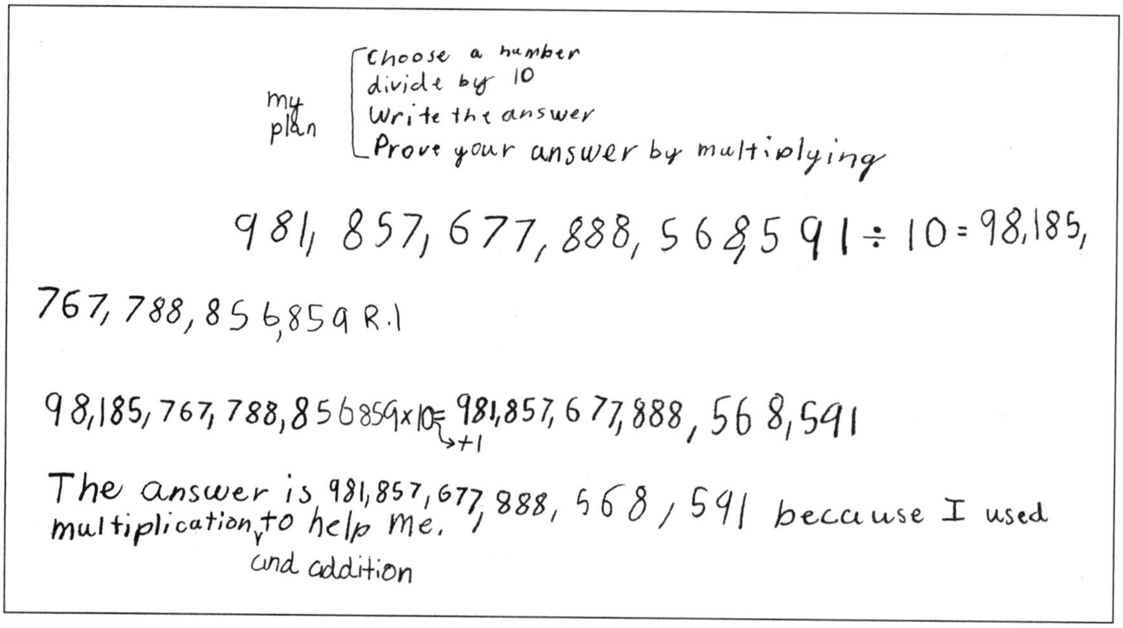

you multiplied this large number by ten. How do numbers multiplied by ten end?"

Vinay got a puzzled look on his face and replied, "They end with zero . . ." He paused and then brightened up and said, "Oh yeah! It's like what we talked about before. There's a leftover, so I have to add the leftover part to what I multiplied." Vinay made the correction to his paper. (See Figure 14–8.)

Jael made a big breakthrough and choose three numbers. She pointed to her paper and explained, "I chose three numbers. I used division to find out how many tens there are. I did an easy number, a medium number, and a hard number. One thousand was the easy number, two hundred thirteen was the medium one, and I think three thousand four hundred fifty is the hardest."

"Why do you think that?" I asked, curious to know what made numbers seem hard to Jael.

Jael said, "We did a lot with one thousand with the blocks and stuff. I can picture it in my head and count in my head all the tens. One thousand is ten flats stacked up and there are ten tens in a flat, so count

▲▲▲▲▲▲Figure 14–8 *Vinay wanted to challenge himself and chose large numbers.*

194   Lessons for Extending Place Value

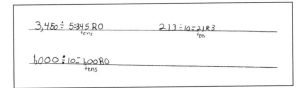

$$3,450 \div 5 = 345\ R0 \quad\text{tens} \qquad 213 \div 10 = 21\ R3\ \text{tens}$$

$$6000 \div 10 = 600\ R0\ \text{tens}$$

▲▲▲▲▲Figure 14–9 *Jael chose three numbers, one easy (1,000), one medium (213), and one hard number (3,450).*

by ten, ten times. That's a hundred tens in one thousand. Two hundred thirteen isn't as big as one thousand, but it has numbers that aren't zero in the ones and tens and that makes it harder. And three thousand four hundred fifty is big and has lots of numbers." (See Figure 14–9.)

Paul's paper was typical of many of the children's work. He chose five hundred and wrote both a division and a multiplication sentence to show the number of tens in five hundred. He also showed the number of one hundreds in five hundred. (See Figure 14–10.)

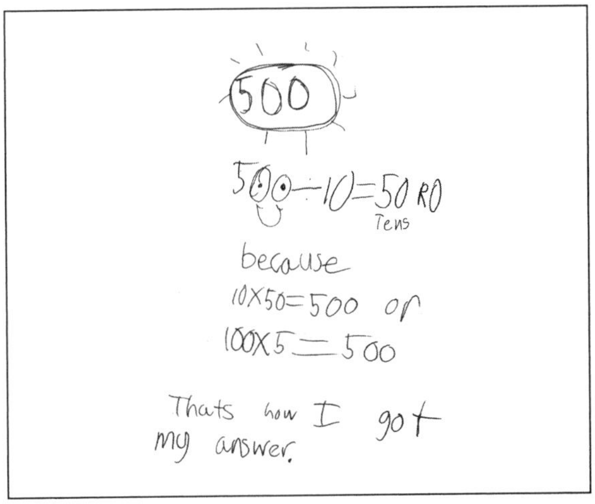

$$500$$
$$500 \div 10 = 50\ R0\ \text{Tens}$$
because
$$10 \times 50 = 500\ \text{or}$$
$$100 \times 5 = 500$$
Thats how I got my answer.

▲▲▲▲▲Figure 14–10 *Paul's paper was typical.*

As the students finished, I checked their papers and asked questions as appropriate. When most students were finished, I gave a two-minute warning. After two minutes, I collected the papers and ended class for the day.

Questions and Discussion

▲▲

▲ *My students don't have much experience yet with multiplication and division. What do you suggest?*

If your students aren't yet experienced with multiplication and division, there are several choices. One choice is to wait until your students have experience with multiplication and division and then teach this lesson. Another option is to stop at the end of Day 1 and return to do Day 2 when your students have experience with multiplication and division. Or, if you feel your students are ready and they understand that multiplication is about equal groups, this lesson can provide a context for further developing their understanding about multiplication. If you decide to use this lesson even though your students are not familiar with multiplication and division, I suggest you add some steps that weren't included in the vignette. For example, start with a number such as fifty. Using base ten blocks, show that fifty can be made with five tens. This can be shown as a multiplication sentence: $50 = 5 \times 10$. Explain that the times sign, $\times$, can be read as "groups of." When students have made this connection, move to a slightly more complicated number, such as sixty-eight, which can be written as $68 = (6 \times 10) + (8 \times 1)$.

Linking Place Value to Multiplication and Division 195

ASSESSMENTS

Overview

This section suggests eight assessments, each intended to take students a short time, generally fifteen minutes or so, to complete. You can write the directions for the assessments on the board or on a transparency to be projected so that students can copy them. Or, make a blackline master and duplicate it for the students if that works better for you and them.

Ways to Make 327, How Are They Related? and *Ways to Make Ten Thousand* relate to the structure of our base ten number system. *The Coral Reef* involves both addition and subtraction while *The Aquarium Problem* involves subtraction for comparing two quantities. The numbers used in *The Aquarium Problem* can be changed to increase or decrease the difficulty of the problem to better meet the variety of levels of your students and challenge them as their skills increase. *Are They the Same? Comparing Addition and Multiplication, What's My Rule?* and *How Many Groups of One Hundred?* can help you better understand your students' skill at applying place value ideas to solve problems involving multiplication and division. All assessments relate directly to lessons in this book.

Teaching Notes

Assessing student understanding through writing gives teachers insights into what students have and have not learned. For students, writing assignments provide opportunities to reflect on their learning, solidify their thinking, raise questions, reinforce new ideas, review older ideas, and apply both to a new situation. We typically give students writing assignments at least once per week.

Class discussions are important to the writing process. A discussion before writing provides students ideas to consider and include in their writing. This can be especially helpful when children's learning is new and fragile. Leading a discussion after students write gives them the chance to share their own thinking while considering the ideas of others. These discussions help students become flexible thinkers.

When students are working on writing assignments, I circulate throughout the class, offering assistance. When students need help, I begin either by asking them to

197

explain their ideas to me or asking them questions to spark their thinking. Examples of questions I use include the following: What do you think the problem is about? What can you do to solve it? Can you draw a picture of the information in the problem? Do you understand all the words in the problem? Where can you start? The students' responses to these questions guide the help I give them or get them started on an independent solution. After I listen to students' explanations, I suggest that they begin by writing down the exact words they just spoke. I sometimes tell students to make their thoughts go from their brains, past their mouths, down their arms, and out their pencils onto the paper.

Ways to Make 327

PROMPT

Using base ten blocks, show at least three ways to build 327. Use numbers, words, and pictures to explain why what you did makes sense.

This assessment can be used after students have had experience with Chapter 3, "Exploring Ones, Tens, and Hundreds with Base Ten Blocks," and have had experience with the base ten blocks and thinking about how they are related to one another. Students describe how they use the base ten blocks to build the number 327 in at least three different ways.

The purpose of this assessment is to give you insight into how flexibly your students are thinking about numbers. It is important for students to realize that in 327, the three can be represented by using three hundreds flats, the two can be represented using two longs, and the seven can be represented by using seven units. In addition, students need to understand and show that 327 can also be represented in many other ways—for example, two hundreds flats, twelve longs, and seven units

or thirty-two tens and seven units, to name a few. It is this understanding and flexibility that supports regrouping.

To introduce this assessment, I wrote the prompt on the board. Then I explained to the children, "I am interested to see the different ways you can make the number three hundred twenty-seven using your base ten blocks. When you make one way, record it carefully on your paper to show what you did. Please label your work so I can understand your drawing as clearly as possible. Even though you should work carefully, don't take too long to record one way. I am interested in seeing the different ways you make three hundred twenty-seven."

As the children work, observe their approaches. Do they use a systematic method of finding different ways to make 327, or are they approaching the task randomly? As the children work with the materials, can you see them easily and accurately exchanging blocks—for example, to exchange a hundred flat for longs, does the student count out ten longs or does the student have to rely on a method such as laying out ten longs on top of the flat to verify they are equivalent? (See Figures 1 through 3.)

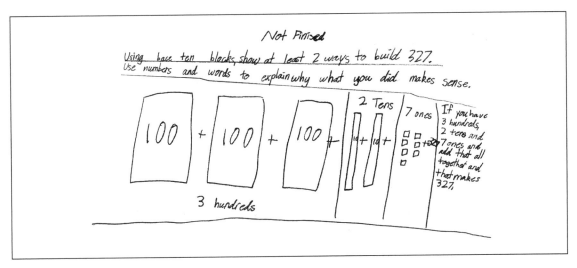

▲▲▲▲▲Figure 1 *Jessie showed only one way to make 327, but her work indicated she had made a connection among materials, words, and numbers.*

▲▲▲▲▲▲Figure 2   *Sam showed four ways to make 327 using base ten blocks.*

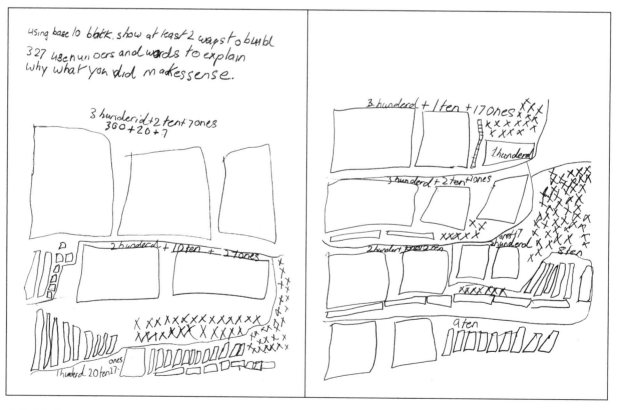

▲▲▲▲▲▲Figure 3   *Ben was systematic in his approach although his last two drawings had errors.*

200   Assessments

How Are They Related?

PROMPT

Use words, pictures, and numbers to explain what you've learned about base ten blocks. How do they relate to each other? What patterns do you notice?

This assessment is appropriate after Chapter 4, "Thousands and Beyond: Exploring Larger Numbers." Students are asked to demonstrate their understanding of the relationships among the following base ten blocks: units, longs, hundreds flats, and thousands cubes. Students should indicate an understanding that consecutively larger blocks will be ten times bigger than the previous block. For example, the long is equal to ten units and is ten times larger than the unit block. The hundreds flat is equal to ten longs and is ten times bigger than the long block.

Students should also show understanding of other relationships among the blocks. For example, the hundreds flat is equal to ten longs and is also equal to one hundred units. The thousands cube is equal to ten hundreds flats, one hundred longs, or one thousand units. A student might also say that a hundreds flat could be made with a combination of blocks, such as nine longs and ten units.

Based on the work they did in the *Thousands and Beyond* lesson, some students may notice a pattern to extending the shapes of the blocks for larger numbers: cube, long, flat, cube, long, flat, and so on. (For example, the next block after the one-thousand cube would be made of ten one-thousand cubes arranged in the shape of a long and the block after that would be a hundred-thousand flat made of ten ten-thousand longs.) Students may even recognize that the next cube would be a one-million cube, made of ten hundred-thousand flats! While this kind of thinking and predicting is wonderful, the most important aspect of this assessment is that students indicate an understanding of the relationships among the units, longs, hundreds flats, and thousands cubes. (See Figures 4 through 7.)

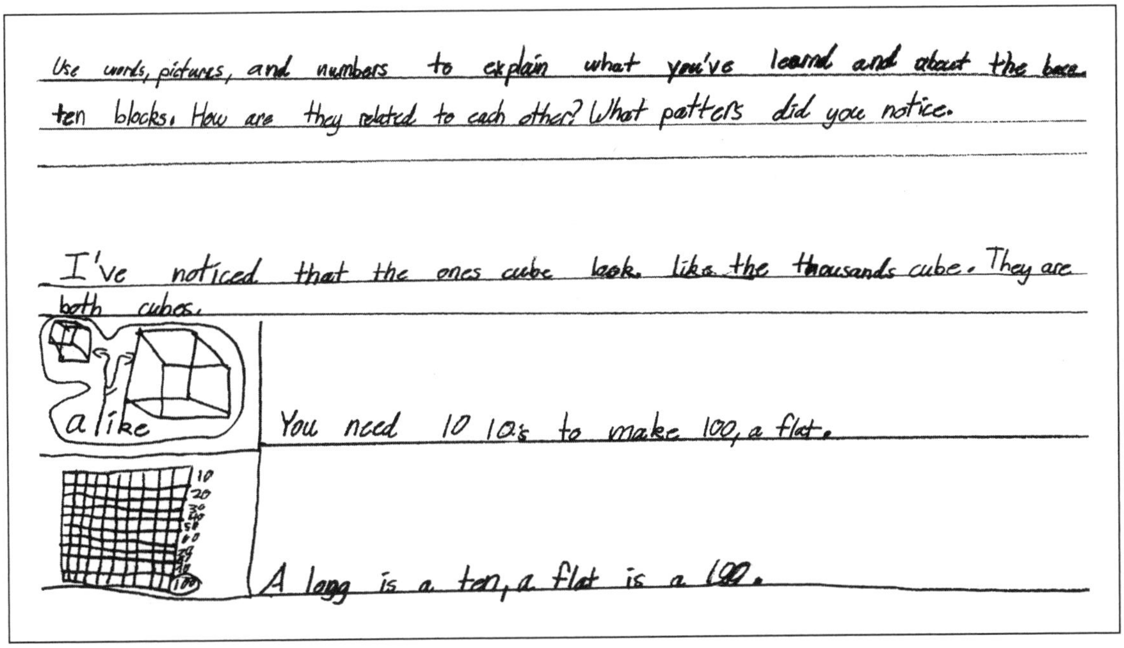
Use words, pictures, and numbers to explain what you've learnd and about the base ten blocks. How are they related to each other? What patters did you notice.

I've noticed that the ones cube look like the thousands cube. They are both cubes.

alike

You need 10 10's to make 100, a flat.

10 20 30 40 50 60 70 80 90 100

A long is a ten, a flat is a 100.

Figure 4 *Jessie made a connection between the shape of the ones unit and the shape of the thousand cube.*

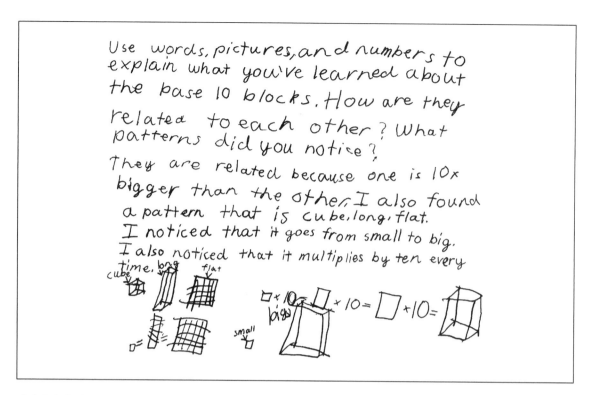

▲▲▲▲▲▲Figure 5 *Vinay recognized how consecutive base ten blocks grow.*

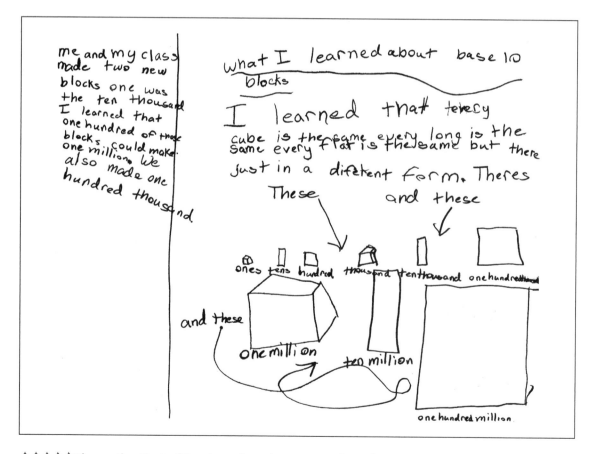

▲▲▲▲▲▲Figure 6 *Part of Sam's explanation was unclear; however, he did try to show how the base ten blocks grow. He extended what he learned and drew a one-hundred-million flat.*

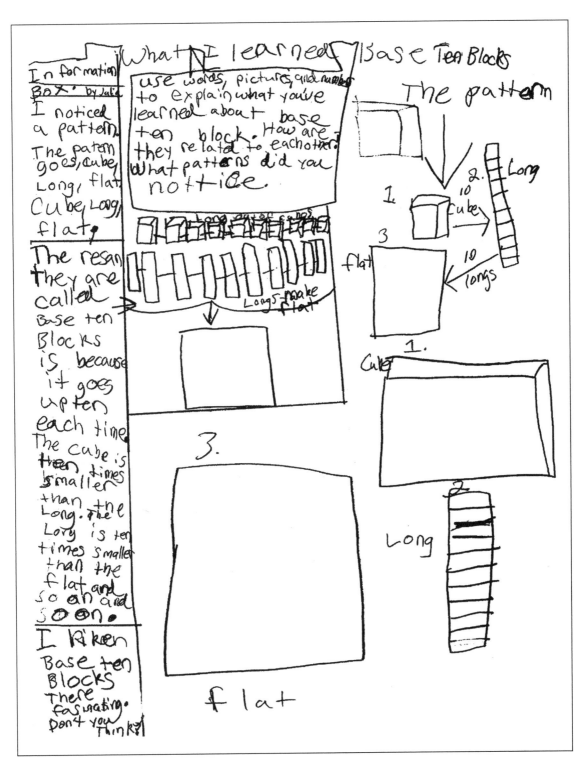

Ways to Make Ten Thousand

PROMPT

Ways to Make Ten Thousand

1	*10,000*
10	*1,000*
100	*100*
1,000	*10*
10,000	*1*

What patterns do you notice?

This assessment is appropriate after students have experienced Chapter 5, "Counting to Ten Thousand." Students are asked to look for patterns in the ways to make ten thousand using ones, tens, hundreds, thousands, and ten thousands.

Most students will notice that going down the left column consecutively, the number of zeros in each number increases by one. The reverse is true in the right column. Some students may recognize that the result of adding a zero to the ones place of a number increases the value of that number ten times while decreasing the number by one zero is like dividing it by ten. Students should recognize relationships between the number on the left and the number on the right. For example, there is one group of ten thousand in ten thousand and ten groups of one thousand in ten thousand and so on. (See Figures 8 through 11.)

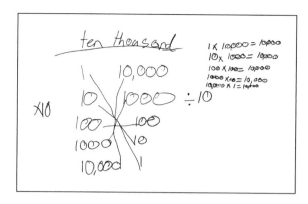

▲▲▲▲▲▲Figure 8   *Ben was able to use only numbers to show patterns he saw.*

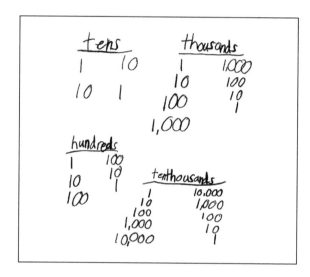

▲▲▲▲▲▲Figure 9   *Connor had a different way of thinking about the patterns. He showed the different ways to make tens, hundreds, thousands, and ten thousands.*

204   Assessments

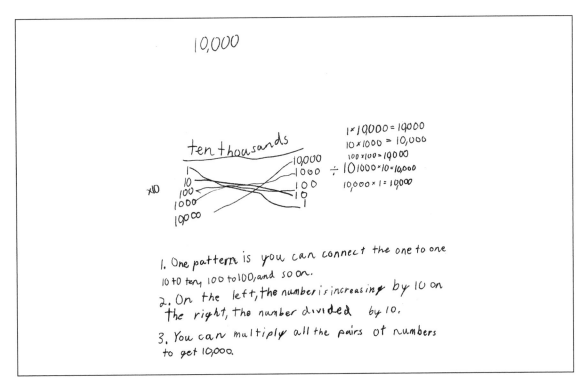

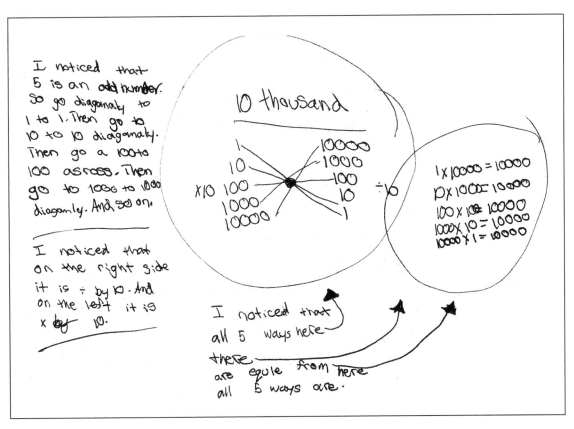

Figure 10   *Vinay wrote about three patterns he noticed.*

Figure 11   *Tina also saw three patterns and was able to write about them clearly.*

The Coral Reef

PROMPT

How many things to spot are there in the scene "Coral reef"? How many more things to spot would need to be added to make 100? Show how you know.

This assessment is appropriate after students have experienced Days 1–3 of Chapter 6, "1,001 Things to Spot." It is based on the scene "Coral reef" from the book *1001 Things to Spot in the Sea,* by Katie Daynes. Students use their addition skills to compute the total things to find in the scene "Coral reef," and then they use their knowledge of subtraction to figure how many more things would have to be added to the scene to make one hundred. Students approach the problem using a variety of addition skills, including using friendly numbers, combining numbers to make groups of ten, adding doubles, and using the standard algorithm. To figure the difference between the total things to spot and hundred, students typically use strategies such as the standard algorithm, counting on by groups of tens and ones, and counting back by groups of tens and ones.

Before class, prepare a chart for the scene "Coral reef" by listing the things to spot and how many of each.

10 anemone fish
7 feather stars
4 brain corals
5 groupers
6 porcupine fish
9 dart fish
8 sea slugs
10 angel fish
5 giant clams
9 trigger fish

Begin the assessment by posting the chart and writing the prompt on the board. Make available for students' use cubes and base ten blocks. Allow students time to copy the prompt and ask questions to clarify their understanding of the task.

As the students work, circulate through the class, checking for an accurate sum of the total things to spot in the scene. If students make errors, ask them to check their work or refigure the sum using a different strategy. As you check for accuracy, note the strategies students used. If necessary, ask them to explain their thinking and why it makes sense to them.

My experience has been that many students use efficient, accurate means to find the sum. They are more likely to make errors when figuring the difference between their sum and hundred. The most common mistake is misapplying the standard algorithm. Students who use other strategies, such as counting up from the smaller number to the larger number using groups of tens and ones, make fewer mistakes. When they do make errors, their answers generally are more reasonable. (See Figures 12 through 14.)

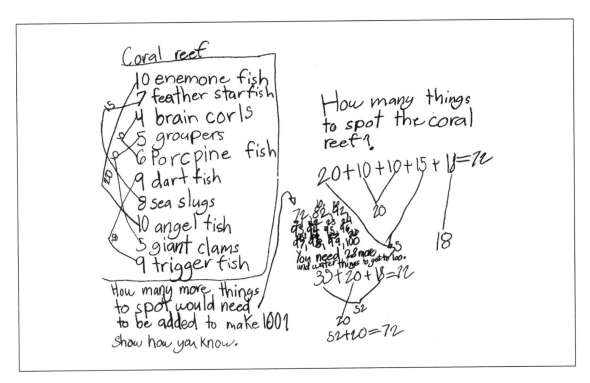

▲▲▲▲▲▲Figure 12   *Although Becky's answer was incorrect, it was reasonable. She made an error in addition but counted on correctly to find the difference between one hundred and seventy-two.*

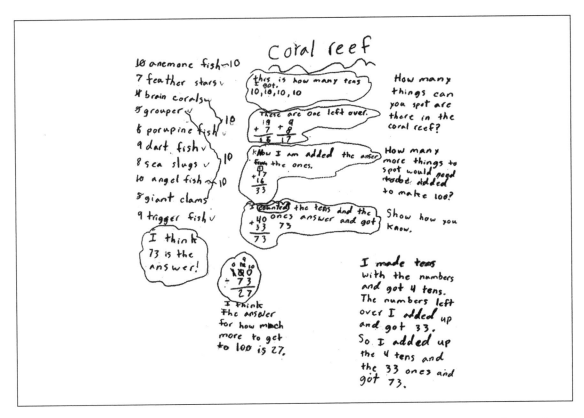

▲▲▲▲▲▲Figure 13   *Natalia used a combination of strategies to figure the sum. She made groups of ten and used the standard algorithm. She correctly used the standard algorithm to find the difference between her sum of seventy-three and one hundred.*

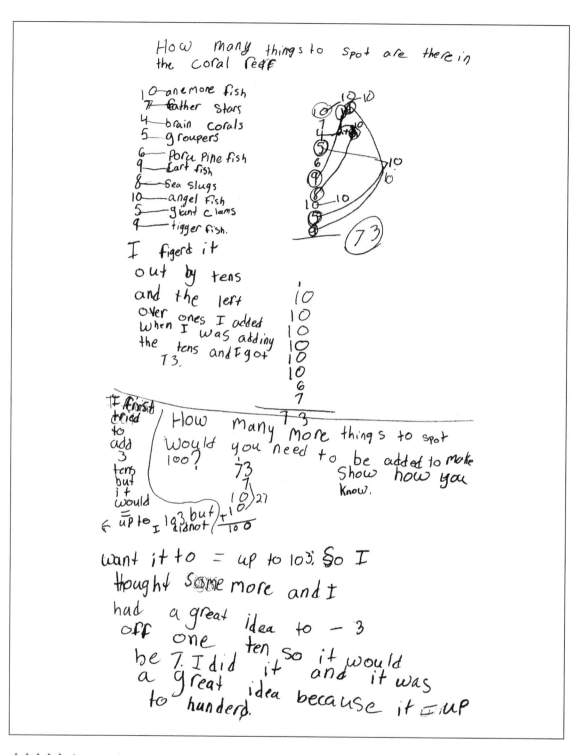

The Aquarium Problem

PROMPT

Sam's aquarium holds 218 gallons of water. John's aquarium holds 79 gallons of water. How many more gallons does Sam's aquarium hold?

In Chapters 8 and 9, "Finding Differences" and "Balancing Number Puzzles," students have many opportunities to practice computation by subtracting with larger numbers. This assessment can be given at any time while the students are working with the lessons in these chapters. Also, change the numbers in the problem to monitor student progress over time, using smaller, more friendly numbers for an easier problem or larger, less friendly numbers to increase the difficulty.

As students' understanding of subtraction increases, their work should reflect more efficient, accurate ways of finding differences while still indicating understanding of why the solution works.

Solution strategies you will likely see from your students include, but are not limited to, the following: adding on, starting with the smaller number and adding on, for example, groups of ten, one hundred, or one until the larger number is reached; adding or subtracting from one of the numbers to make it a more friendly number and then doing the same to the other and finally finding the difference between the two; using the standard subtraction algorithm accurately; using the standard subtraction algorithm inaccurately; and starting with the larger number and repeatedly counting backward by ones, tens, or hundreds until the smaller number is reached. It's important that your students use a method that is accurate and efficient and that they understand what they're doing. (See Figures 15 through 18.)

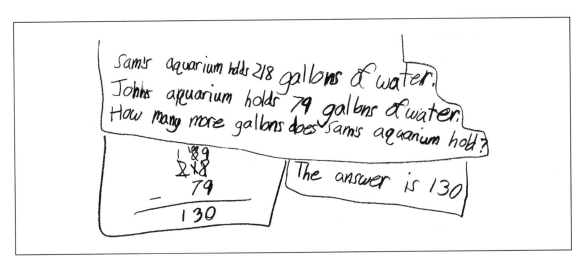

▲▲▲▲▲▲Figure 15   *Connor lacked understanding of the algorithm and was unable to get a correct answer.*

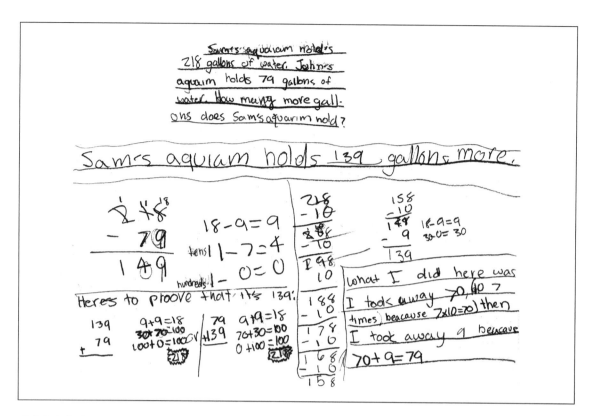

Figure 16   *Olina missed the standard algorithm, but she showed clear understanding of place value in her other solutions.*

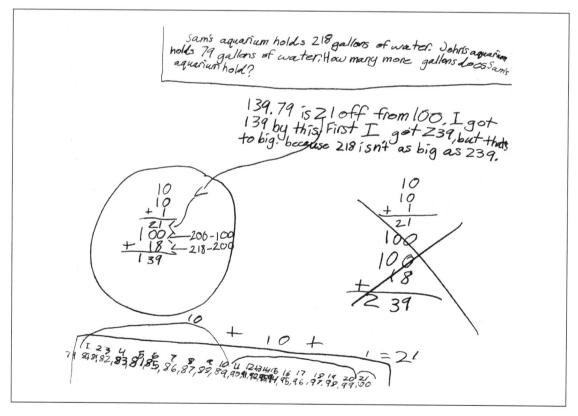

Figure 17   *Jessie used her number sense to realize her first answer was correct.*

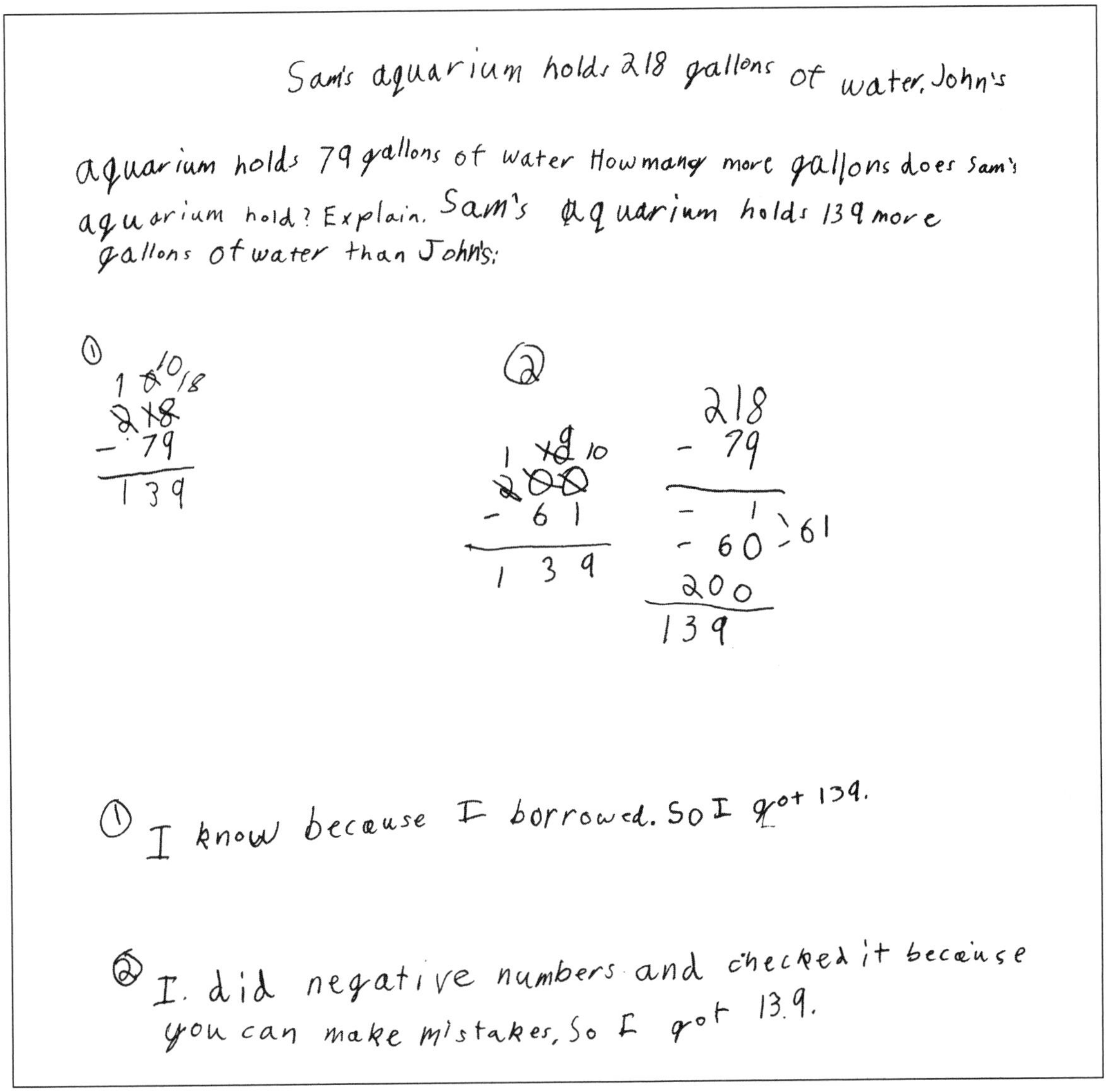
Sam's aquarium holds 218 gallons of water. John's aquarium holds 79 gallons of water How many more gallons does Sam's aquarium hold? Explain. Sam's aquarium holds 139 more gallons of water than John's.

① 218 − 79 = 139

② 200 − 61 = 139

218 − 79: −1, −60 → −61; 200; 139

① I know because I borrowed. So I got 139.

② I. did negative numbers and checked it because you can make mistakes, So I got 13.9.

▲▲▲▲▲Figure 18 *Vinay showed two ways to find the answer.*

Are They the Same? Comparing Addition and Multiplication

PROMPT

6 + 10 =

6 × 10 =

Draw base ten blocks and use words to help you explain how to solve these two problems.

This assessment is a good follow-up to Chapter 12, "Ten Times Better." To begin, I wrote the prompt on the board and asked the students to copy it onto their papers. I made base ten blocks available to the students. I wanted to be certain that students were moving beyond additive thinking (combining two groups, a group of six and a group of ten) and moving toward devel-

oping multiplicative understanding (combining equal groups, in this case, six groups of ten). The numbers are the same in both problems, but the outcomes are quite different. This may not be obvious to children, particularly those who lack understanding of the difference between additive and multiplicative thinking.

Most students had little trouble with the task. About half used the blocks to support their thinking while about half chose not to do so. Allowing the use of base ten blocks supported concrete thinking and clear explanations from those students who still needed concrete materials. Whether or not they used base ten blocks, most students' pictures and explanations indicated that they were developing a clear understanding that multiplication involves equal groups of something, in this case, six groups of ten, or six longs. (See Figures 19 through 21.)

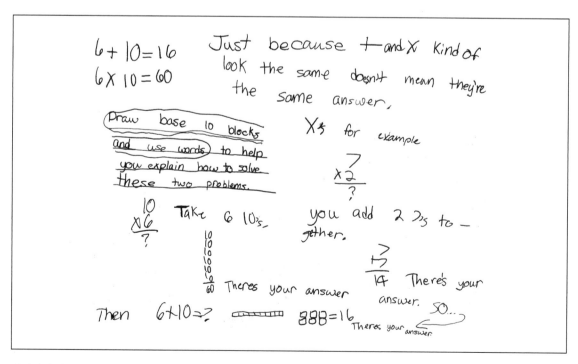

▲▲▲▲▲▲Figure 19   *Olina understood the meaning of the multiplication sign. She did not indicate understanding of the addition sign.*

212   Assessments

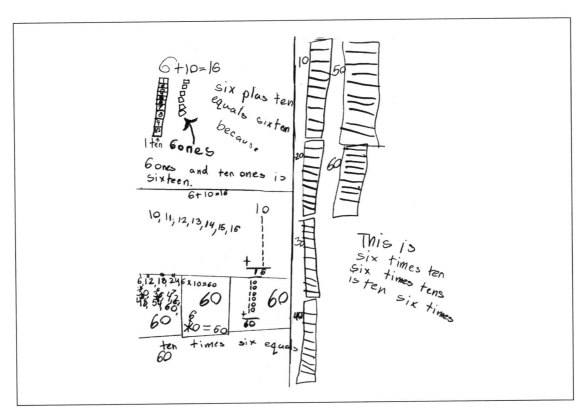

▲▲▲▲▲▲Figure 20   *Sam showed clear understanding of the difference between the addition and multiplication signs.*

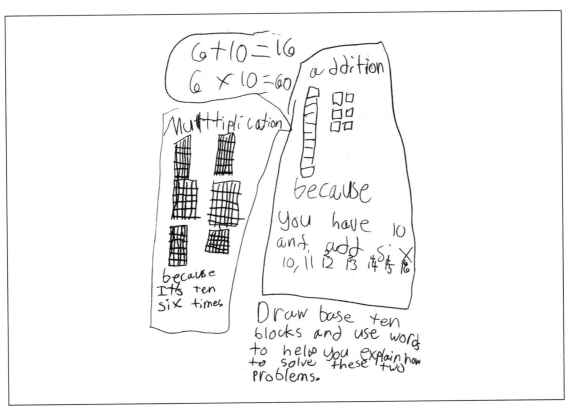

▲▲▲▲▲▲Figure 21   *Paul tried to draw pictures of base ten blocks to show his understanding.*

What's My Rule?

PROMPT

#	?
0	0
3	30
7	70
11	110
23	230
56	560
72	☐
☐	850

What's my rule? Explain how you know. What patterns do you see?

After students have experienced Chapter 13, "Multiplication by Ten and One Hundred," this assessment will allow you to see if students can apply what they learned about multiplication by ten to complete the above T-chart correctly.

This assessment was enjoyable for the students to do as it closely resembles the game played in Chapter 13. Most students were able to correctly multiply 72 by 10 to figure the first missing number on the chart. The second missing number was more challenging, as students had to think about what number times 10 equals 850 or divide by 10 to figure the missing number. Even so, most students persevered and were able to accurately accomplish the task.

It is possible that a student may state the rule for the right column as adding a zero rather than multiplying by ten. This is unlikely because of the modeling while playing *Guess My Rule* (see Chapter 13). Should this occur, help the student make the connection that the "extra" zero is the result of multiplying a number by ten. Play a game of *Guess My Rule* using small numbers. Verify what goes in the right column by modeling with base ten blocks. (See Figures 22 through 25.)

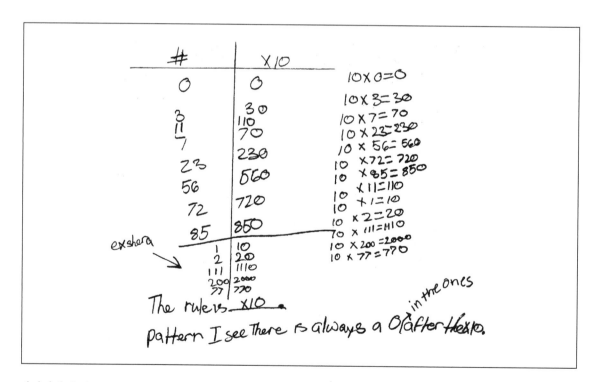

▲▲▲▲▲▲Figure 22   *Ben completed the chart correctly and extended it based on his understanding. He also wrote out a number sentence to show how he got each of the numbers in the right-hand column.*

214   Assessments

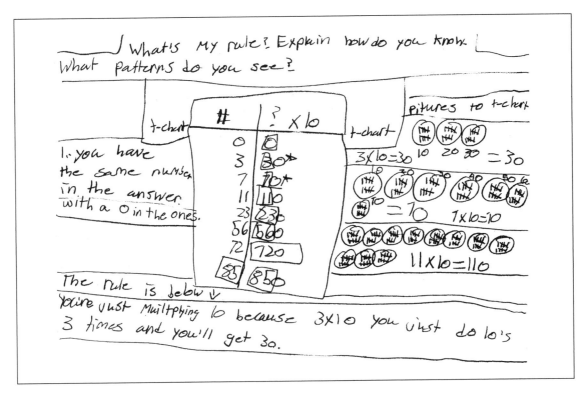

▲▲▲▲▲Figure 23　*Kassidee used pictures to demonstrate her idea.*

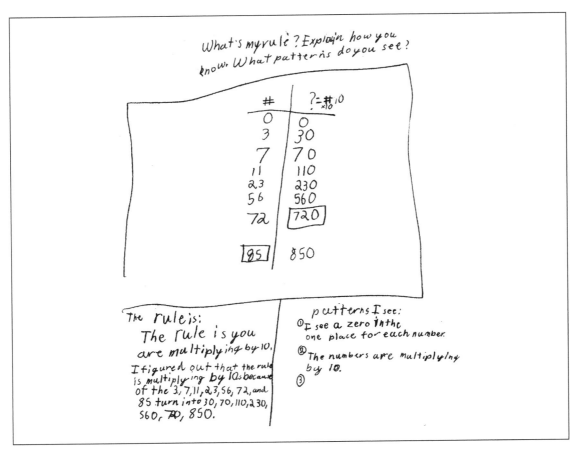

▲▲▲▲▲Figure 24　*Vinay wrote about the rule clearly.*

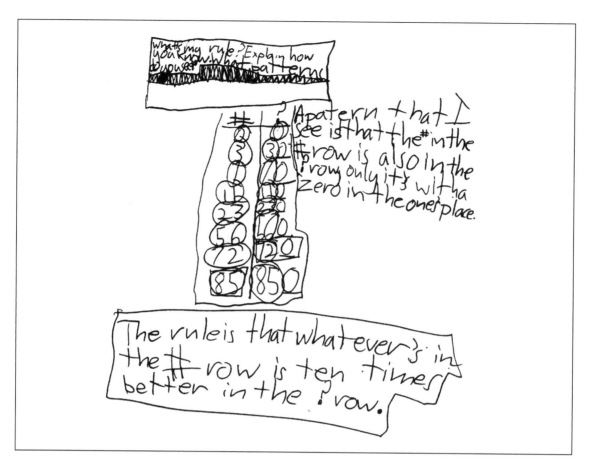

▲▲▲▲▲▲Figure 25   *James correctly completed the table and explained his thinking.*

How Many Groups of One Hundred?

PROMPT

Larry, the Lego master, has 8,100 Legos. He must put them into groups of 100. How many groups of 100 are in 8,100 Legos? Show your work and explain how you know.

Begin by writing the prompt on the board and allowing students time to copy it onto their papers. Allow students the opportunity to ask questions to clarify the task.

Because this task requires students to use knowledge they have developed as a result of the experiences in both Chapters 13 and 14—specifically multiplication by one hundred in Chapter 13 and linking place value to multiplication and division in Chapter 14—this assessment should follow the lessons from those chapters. The large numbers make drawing pictures less practical and serve as encouragement for students to rely more on their understanding of how to apply place value.

The strategies the students used included thinking about what times one hundred equals eighty-one hundred, dividing, and counting by hundreds. While some of the strategies were more efficient than others, most students were able to solve the problem correctly. (See Figures 26 through 29.)

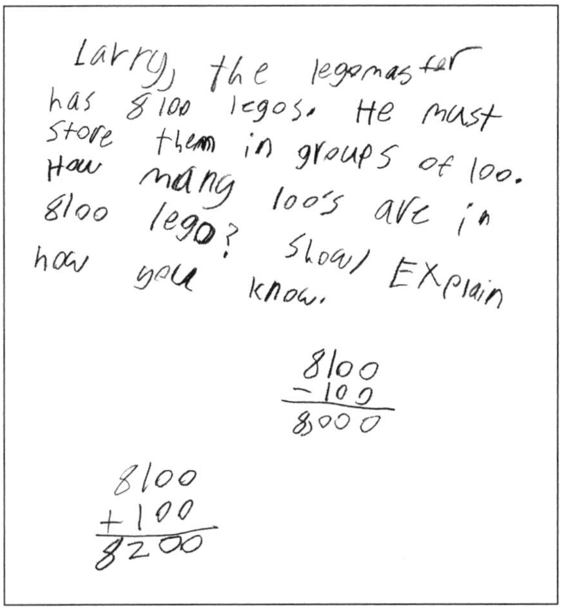

Larry, the legomaster has 8100 legos. He must store them in groups of 100. How many 100's are in 8100 lego? Show/ Explain how you know.

8100 − 100 = 8000

8100 + 100 = 8200

Figure 26 ***Abel's paper showed little understanding. He needed additional experiences to help him better understand.***

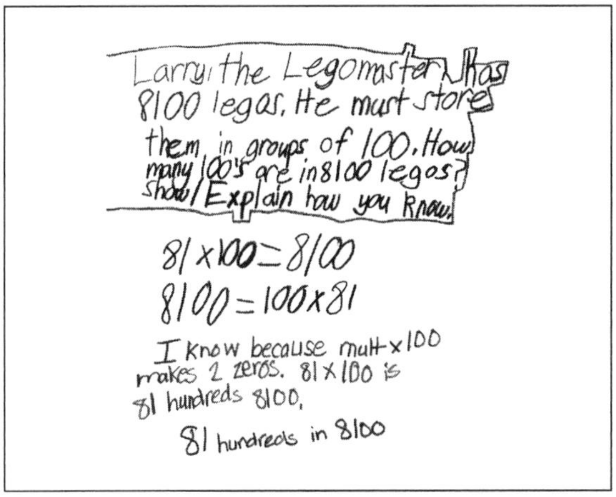

Larry, the Legomaster has 8100 legos. He must store them in groups of 100. How many 100's are in 8100 legos? Show/Explain how you know.

81 x 100 = 8100
8100 = 100 x 81

I know because mult x 100 makes 2 zeros. 81 x 100 is 81 hundreds 8100.
81 hundreds in 8100

Figure 27 ***Connor used multiplication by one hundred to solve the problem.***

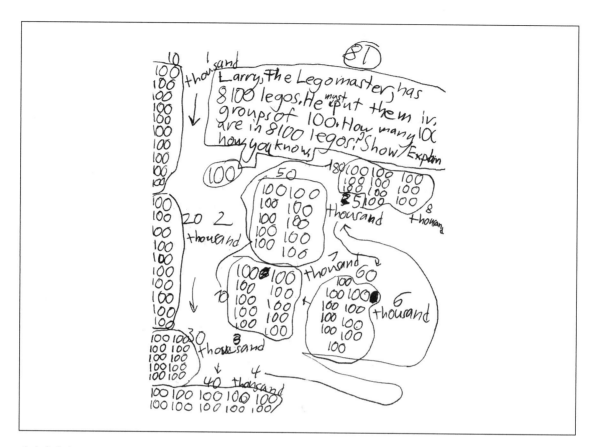

Figure 28 *James wrote out hundreds until he correctly figured the answer.*

Larry, the Legomaster, has 8100 legos. He must store them in groups of 100. How many 100's are in 8100 legos? Show/Explain how you know

There are 81 100's in 8100.

I got the answer by dividing 8100 by 100 and got 81. I also checked by multiplying 81 and 100 and I got 8100. So the answer is 81

8100÷100=81 100×81=8100
8100/100 = 81 100·81=8100
(100)(81)=8100
100)8100 = 81

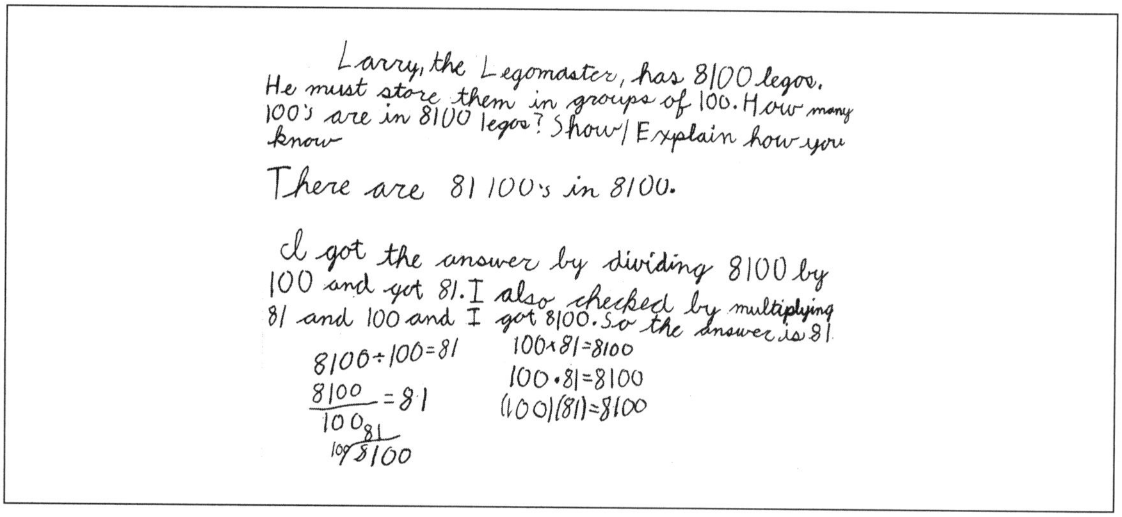

Figure 29 *Vinay accurately solved the problem using division and checked his answer with multiplication.*

BLACKLINE MASTERS

10-by-10 Grids

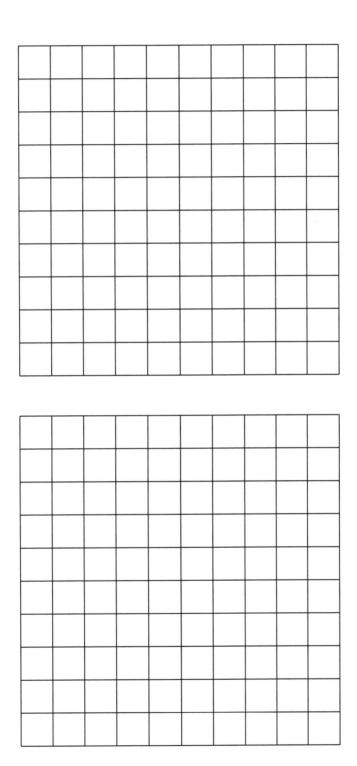

1–100 Chart

1	2	3	4	5	6	7	8	9	10
11	12	13	14	15	16	17	18	19	20
21	22	23	24	25	26	27	28	29	30
31	32	33	34	35	36	37	38	39	40
41	42	43	44	45	46	47	48	49	50
51	52	53	54	55	56	57	58	59	60
61	62	63	64	65	66	67	68	69	70
71	72	73	74	75	76	77	78	79	80
81	82	83	84	85	86	87	88	89	90
91	92	93	94	95	96	97	98	99	100

Base Ten Blocks

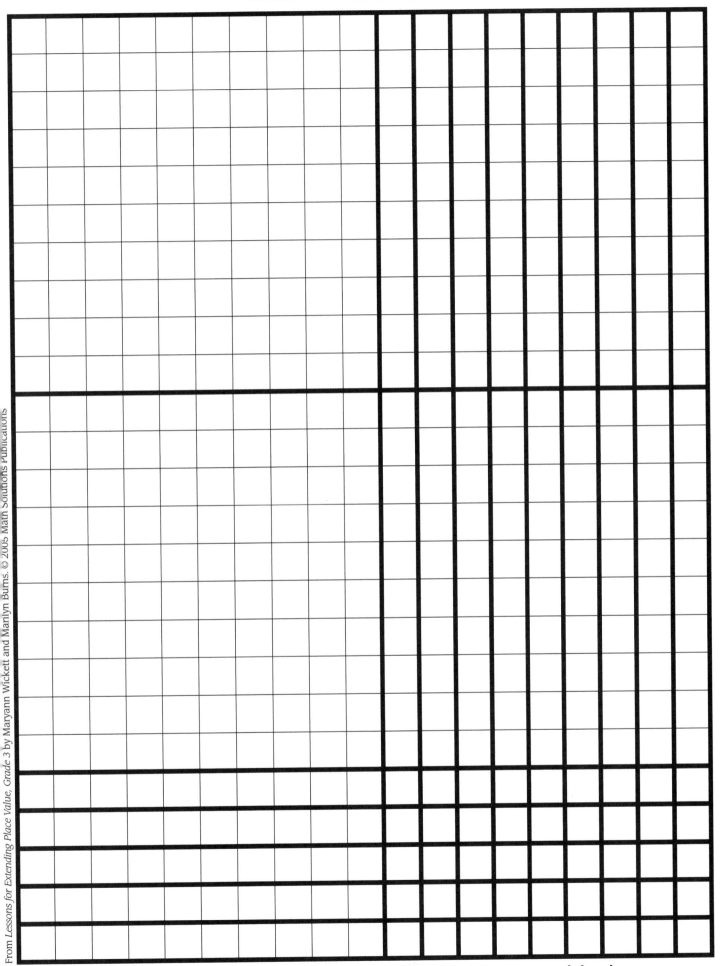

Cut along bold lines to make one set of base ten blocks.

Finding Differences Recording Sheet

Tens   Ones

Total

Tens   Ones

Total

Round 1

_____ had _____.
_____ had _____.
____ is ____ larger than _____.
____ − ____ = _____

Round 2

_____ had _____.
_____ had _____.
____ is ____ larger than _____.
____ − ____ = _____

Round 3

_____ had _____.
_____ had _____.
____ is ____ larger than _____.
____ − ____ = _____

Total

_____ had _____.
_____ had _____.
____ is ____ larger than _____.
____ − ____ = _____

Round 1

_____ had _____.
_____ had _____.
____ is ____ larger than _____.
____ − ____ = _____

Round 2

_____ had _____.
_____ had _____.
____ is ____ larger than _____.
____ − ____ = _____

Round 3

_____ had _____.
_____ had _____.
____ is ____ larger than _____.
____ − ____ = _____

Total

_____ had _____.
_____ had _____.
____ is ____ larger than _____.
____ − ____ = _____

Finding Differences

You need:

    a partner
    2 dice, each a different color
    a recording sheet

Rules

1. Before you begin to play, decide with your partner which color die will tell how many tens and which will tell how many ones.

2. Player 1 rolls both dice, figures out what number the dice show, and then records the number on the recording sheet. For example:

Tens	Ones	
6	4	

3. Player 2 repeats Step 2.

4. Players work together to figure the difference between their numbers and record next to the chart on their recording sheets. For example:

    Jillian had 36.
    Mrs. Wickett had 64.
    64 is 28 larger than 36.
    64 − 36 = 28

5. Players repeat Steps 2, 3, and 4 two more times for a total of three rounds of play.

6. Each player finds the total number of tens and ones he or she rolled and records on the bottom row of the chart. Then each player combines the total tens and the total ones to figure their total for the game. For example:

	Tens	Ones	
	6	4	
	4	4	
	5	5	
Total	15	13	163

7. Players work together to figure the difference between their totals and record on their recording sheets. For example:

    Jillian had 117.
    Mrs. Wickett had 163.
    163 is 46 larger than 117.
    163 − 117 = 46

From *Lessons for Extending Place Value, Grade 3* by Maryann Wickett and Marilyn Burns. © 2005 Math Solutions Publications **225**

Race to 200

Object: Be the player with the score closer to 200.

Rules

1. Each player must take six turns.

2. On your turn, roll the die. You may take ones or tens. The die tells you how many.

3. Both players record the turn. Add the total for each turn to the previous score. For example:

Race to 200	
Mrs. Wickett	Jillian
$6 \times 10 = 60$	$3 \times 10 = 30$
$6 \times 10 = \underline{60}$	
120	

4. After each player has taken six turns, compare scores to see whose score is closer to 200 and record underneath the chart. (It's OK to go over 200.)

_____ has _____ points.

_____ is _____ points from 200.

_____ has _____ points.

_____ is _____ points from 200.

_____ wins.

INDEX